Medieval Church Councils in Scotland

Medieval Church Councils in Scotland

D. E. R. WATT

T&T CLARK
EDINBURGH

T&T CLARK LTD
59 GEORGE STREET
EDINBURGH EH2 2LQ
SCOTLAND

www.tandtclark.co.uk

First published 2000

ISBN 0 567 08731 X

British Library Cataloguing-in-Publication Data
A catalogue record for this book is available from the British Library

Typeset by Waverley Typesetters, Galashiels
Printed and bound in Great Britain by MPG Books, Bodmin

Contents

Preface

This book was commissioned some twenty years ago by Professor Walter Brandmüller (then of the University of Augsburg in Bavaria) as a contribution to the massive *Konziliengeschichte* series, of which he is the general editor. More than fifty authors have been contracted to produce volumes covering the history of councils at various levels of the organised Christian church from the beginning to the early twentieth century. Since 1980 a flow of twenty-six volumes has been published in the German language, covering both general councils drawing members from many provinces of the church, and also a wide variety of more local councils confined to one country or part of a country. Valuable comparative studies are now becoming practicable.

This volume is devoted to church councils in the small independent country of Scotland in the later Middle Ages. It possessed a unique ecclesiastical organisation from the time when political unity was achieved in the early eleventh century to the year 1472, for though it conformed to the pattern of the Western church under Rome with a system of bishops and dioceses, it was only in the changing circumstances of 1472 that one bishopric (St. Andrews) was elevated above the rest with a metropolitan archbishop for the whole Scottish church. Some two-and-a-half centuries earlier in 1225 the Scottish bishops as a group had sought papal authorisation under the universal canon law to act in council so as to tackle common problems; and it was with papal encouragement that the Scottish provincial council was then established, and was instrumental thenceforward in helping the Scottish bishops to keep abreast with each other's problems, and with developments in the church as a whole.

Study of the sources for the history of this council, of its organisation and achievements, was given a fundamental boost as long ago as 1866 when Joseph Robertson published in Edinburgh two seminal volumes of *Concilia Scotiae* in the Bannatyne Club series. His work reached a wider readership in 1907 when David Patrick published English translations of Robertson's Latin texts. But since then, scholarly interest in an institution which held the Scottish church together for centuries (as its Protestant successor the General Assembly of the Church of Scotland has done since 1560) has lapsed. It has needed Professor Brandmüller's initiative to make possible this study of how the church in one small country on the periphery of medieval Western Christendom managed its affairs. It is being published at Paderborn in Germany as nearly as possible simultaneously in the German language as part of the *Konziliengeschichte* series as *Die Konzilien in Schottland bis zur Reformation.* This English-language text is the one from which the German translation has been made.

DONALD WATT
St. Andrews, Scotland
February 2000

Abbreviations

Aberdeen Registrum	*Registrum Episcopatus Aberdonensis* (Spalding and Maitland Clubs, 1845).
ALKG	*Archiv für Literatur- und Kirchen-Geschichte des Mittelalters.*
AMW	*Annals of the Reigns of Malcolm and William, Kings of Scotland*, ed. A. C. Lawrie (Glasgow, 1910).
AN	Paris, Archives Nationales
Anderson, 'Beginnings'	J. Maitland Anderson, 'The beginnings of St. Andrews University 1410–1418', *SHR*, viii (1911), 225–48, 333–60.
APS	*The Acts of the Parliaments of Scotland* (Edinburgh, 1814–75).
Arbroath Liber	*Liber S. Thome de Aberbrothoc* (Bannatyne Club, 1848–56).
AUP	*Auctarium Chartularii Universitatis Parisiensis*, ed. H. Denifle and E. Chatelain and others (Paris, 1894–1964).
Bagliani, *Cardinali*	A. P. Bagliani, *Cardinali di Curia*, vols. 1–2 (Padua, 1972).
Balfour-Melville, *James I*	E. W. M. Balfour-Melville, *James I, King of Scots* (London, 1936).
Barrow, *Bruce*	G. W. S. Barrow, *Robert Bruce and the Community of the Realm*, 3rd edition (Edinburgh, 1988).

Barrow, *Kingdom*	G. W. S. Barrow, *The Kingdom of the Scots* (London, 1973).
Bede, *History*	*Bede's Ecclesiastical History of the English People*, ed. B. Colgrave and R. A. B. Mynors (Oxford, 1969).
Bellenden, *Chronicles*	*Chronicles of Scotland compiled by Hector Boece*, translated into Scots by John Bellenden 1531 (Scottish Text Society, 1938–41).
Boethius, *Historiae*	Hector Boethius, *Scotorum Historiae*, 2nd edition (Paris, 1574).
Brandmüller, *Pavia-Siena*	W. Brandmüller, *Das Konzil von Pavia-Siena 1423–1424* (Münster, 1968–74).
Brechin Registrum	*Registrum Episcopatus Brechinensis* (Bannatyne Club, 1856).
Brett, *Henry I*	M. Brett, *The English Church under Henry I* (Oxford, 1975).
Burns, *Basle*	J. H. Burns, *Scottish Churchmen and the Council of Basle* (Glasgow, 1962).
C&S	*Councils and Synods*, I, parts i and ii, ed. D. Whitelock and others; II, parts i and ii, ed. F. M. Powicke and C. R. Cheney (Oxford, 1981, 1964).
CDS	*Calendar of Documents relating to Scotland*, ed. J. Bain and others (Edinburgh, 1881–1986).
Cheney, *Synodalia*	C. R. Cheney, *English Synodalia in the Thirteenth Century* (Oxford, 1941/1968).
Cheney, *Texts*	C. R. Cheney, *Medieval Texts and Studies* (Oxford, 1973).
Chron. Bower	*Scotichronicon by Walter Bower in Latin and English*, ed. D. E. R. Watt (Aberdeen, 1987–98).

Chron. Fordun	*Johannis de Fordun Chronica Gentis Scotorum*, ed. W. F. Skene (Edinburgh, 1871–2).
Chron. Holyrood	*A Scottish Chronicle known as the Chronicle of Holyrood*, ed. M. O. Anderson (SHS, 1938).
Chron. Lanercost	*Chronicon de Lanercost* (Maitland Club, 1839).
Chron. Melrose	*The Chronicle of Melrose*, ed. A. O. Anderson and others (London, 1936).
Chron. Pluscarden	*Liber Pluscardensis*, ed. F. J. H. Skene (Edinburgh, 1877–80).
Chron. Wyntoun	*The Original Chronicle of Andrew of Wyntoun*, ed. F. J. Amours (Scottish Text Society, 1903–14).
CIC	*Corpus Iuris Canonici*, ed. E. Friedberg (Leipzig, 1879–81).
Coupar Angus Chrs.	*Charters of the Abbey of Coupar Angus*, ed. D. E. Easson (SHS, 1947).
CPL	*Calendar of Entries in the Papal Registers relating to Great Britain and Ireland: Papal Letters*, ed. W. H. Bliss and others (London, 1893–).
CPL Benedict XIII	*Calendar of Papal Letters to Scotland of Benedict XIII of Avignon 1394–1419*, ed. F. McGurk (SHS, 1976).
CPL Clement VII	*Calendar of Papal Letters to Scotland of Clement VII of Avignon*, ed. C. Burns (SHS, 1976).
CUP	*Chartularium Universitatis Parisiensis*, ed. H. Denifle and E. Chatelain (Paris, 1889–97).
DDC	*Dictionnaire de Droit Canonique*
Delaruelle, *L'église*	E. Delaruelle and others, *L'église au temps du Grand Schisme et de la crise conciliaire 1378–1449* (Paris, 1962–4).

Donaldson, *Church History*	G. Donaldson, *Scottish Church History* (Edinburgh, 1985).
Dowden, *Bishops*	J. Dowden, *The Bishops of Scotland* (Glasgow, 1912).
Dumville, *Councils*	D. N. Dumville, *Councils and Synods of the Gaelic Early and Central Middle Ages* (Cambridge, 1997).
Duncan, 'Early parliaments'	A. A. M. Duncan, 'The early parliaments of Scotland', *SHR*, xlv (1966), 36–58.
Duncan, *Scotland*	A. A. M. Duncan, *Scotland: The Making of the Kingdom* (Edinburgh, 1975).
Dunfermline Registrum	*Registrum de Dunfermelyn* (Bannatyne Club, 1842).
Dunlop, *Kennedy*	A. I. Dunlop, *The Life and Times of James Kennedy Bishop of St. Andrews* (Edinburgh and London, 1950).
EHR	*English Historical Review*
ER	*The Exchequer Rolls of Scotland*, ed. J. Stuart and others (Edinburgh, 1878–1908).
ES	*Early Sources of Scottish History 500 to 1286*, ed. A. O. Anderson (Edinburgh, 1922).
Eubel, *Hierarchia*	C. Eubel, *Hierarchia Catholica Medii Aevi,* 2nd edition (Münster, 1913–)
Ferguson, *Papal Representatives*	P. C. Ferguson, *Medieval Papal Representatives in Scotland: Legates, Nuncios and Judges-Delegate 1125–1286* (Stair Society, 1997).
Finke, *Acta*	*Acta Concilii Constanciensis*, ed. H. Finke (Münster, 1896–1928).
Foedera	*Foedera, Conventiones, Litterae et Cuiuscunque Generis Acta Publica*, ed. T. Rymer (Record Commission edition, London 1816–69).

Foreville, *Latran*	R. Foreville, *Latran I, II, III et Latran IV* (Paris, 1965).
Formulary E	*Formulary E: Scottish Letters and Brieves 1286–1424*, ed. A. A. M. Duncan (Glasgow, 1976).
Glasgow Registrum	*Registrum Episcopatus Glasguensis* (Bannatyne and Maitland Clubs, 1843).
Graham, 'Ottoboni letters'	R. Graham, 'Letters of Cardinal Ottoboni', *EHR*, xv (1900), 87–120.
H&S	A. W. Haddan and W. Stubbs, *Councils and Ecclesiastical Documents relating to Great Britain and Ireland* (Oxford, 1869–78).
Hannay, 'Letter to Scotland'	R. K. Hannay, 'A letter to Scotland from the Council of Basel', *SHR*, xx (1923), 49–57.
HBC	*Handbook of British Chronology*, 3rd edition, ed. E. B. Fryde and others (London, 1986).
Hefele-Leclercq, *Conciles*	C. J. Hefele and H. Leclercq, *Histoire des Conciles* (Paris, 1907–38).
Holstein, *Lyon II*	H. Wolter and H. Holstein, *Lyon I et Lyon II* (Paris, 1966).
Hugh the Chantor, *History*	Hugh the Chantor, *History of the Church of York*, ed. C. Johnson (Edinburgh, 1961).
John Le Neve, *Fasti*	John Le Neve, *Fasti Ecclesiae Anglicanae 1066–1300*, ii, *Monastic Cathedrals* (London, 1971).
Kelly, *Dictionary of Popes*	*The Oxford Dictionary of Popes*, ed. J. D. N. Kelly (Oxford, 1986).

Kelso Liber	*Liber S. Marie de Calchou* (Bannatyne Club, 1846).
Kemp, *Counsel and Consent*	E. W. Kemp, *Counsel and Consent* (London, 1961).
Lecler, *Vienne*	J. Lecler, *Vienne* (Paris, 1964).
Liber Censuum	*Le Liber Censuum de l'Église Romaine*, ed. L. Duchesne and others (Paris, 1889–1952).
Lunt, *Financial Relations*	W. E. Lunt, *Financial Relations of the Papacy with England to 1327: Studies in Anglo-Papal Relations during the Middle Ages*, i (Cambridge, Mass., 1939).
Macfarlane, 'Primacy'	L. J. Macfarlane, 'The primacy of the Scottish church 1472–1521', *Innes Review*, xx (1969), 111–29.
Moray Registrum	*Registrum Episcopatus Moraviensis* (Bannatyne Club, 1837).
MRHS	*Medieval Religious Houses Scotland*, 2nd edition, ed. I. B. Cowan and D. E. Easson (London, 1976).
Nicholson, *Later Middle Ages*	R. Nicholson, *Scotland: The Later Middle Ages* (Edinburgh, 1974).
Patrick, *Statutes*	*Statutes of the Scottish Church 1225–1559*, ed. D. Patrick (SHS, 1907).
Pontal, *Statuts*	O. Pontal, *Les Statuts Synodaux* (Turnhout, 1975).
Pontificia Hibernica	*Pontificia Hibernica*, ed. M. P. Sheehy (Dublin, 1962–5).
Registres de Grégoire X	*Les registres de Grégoire X et Jean XXI* (Paris, 1892–1960).

Regestum Clementis V	*Regestum Clementis V* (Rome 1885–92).
Rothwell, *Documents*	*English Historical Documents 1189–1216*, ed. H. Rothwell (London, 1975).
RMS	*Registrum Magni Sigilli Regum Scotorum*, ed. J. M. Thomson and others (Edinburgh, 1882–1914).
RRS	*Regesta Regum Scottorum*, ed. G. W. S. Barrow and others (Edinburgh, 1960–).
SAEC	*Scottish Annals from English Chroniclers 500 to 1286*, ed. A. O. Anderson (London, 1908).
St. Andrews Acta	*Acta Facultatis Artium Universitatis Sanctiandree 1413–1588*, ed. A. I. Dunlop (Edinburgh and London, 1964).
St. Andrews Copiale	*Copiale Prioratus Sanctiandree*, ed. J. H. Baxter (Oxford, 1930).
St. Andrews Formulare	*St. Andrews Formulare 1514–1546*, ed. G. Donaldson and C. Macrae (Stair Society, 1942–4).
St. Andrews Liber	*Liber Cartarum Prioratus Sancti Andree in Scotia* (Bannatyne Club, 1841).
Scone Liber	*Liber Ecclesie de Scon* (Bannatyne Club, 1843).
Scot. Pont.	R. Somerville, *Scotia Pontificia* (Oxford, 1982).
Series Episcoporum	*Series Episcoporum Ecclesiae Catholicae Occidentalis ab initio usque ad annum MCXCVIII*, VI, *Britannia, Scotia et Hibernia, Scandinavia*, i, *Ecclesia Scoticana*, ed. D. E. R. Watt (Stuttgart, 1991).
SES	*Concilia Scotiae: Ecclesiae Scoticanae Statuta tam Provincialia quam Synodalia quae Supersunt, 1225–1559; Statuta Ecclesiae Scoticanae*, ed. J. Robertson (Bannatyne Club, 1866).

SHR	*Scottish Historical Review*
SHS	Scottish History Society
Stones, *Documents*	*Anglo-Scottish Relations 1174–1328: Some Selected Documents*, ed. E. L. G. Stones (Edinburgh, 1965).
Tanner, *Decrees*	*Decrees of the Ecumenical Councils*, ed. N. P. Tanner (London and Washington DC, 1990).
Theiner, *Monumenta*	A. Theiner, *Vetera Monumenta Hibernorum et Scotorum Historiam Illustrantia* (Rome, 1864).
Trexler, *Synodal Law*	R. C. Trexler, *Synodal Law in Florence and Fiesole 1306–1518* (Studi et Testi, 268; Vatican, 1971).
Valois, *La France*	N. Valois, *La France et le Grand Schisme d'Occident* (Paris, 1896–1902).
Watt, *Dictionary*	D. E. R. Watt, *A Biographical Dictionary of Scottish Graduates to A. D. 1410* (Oxford, 1977).
Watt, *Fasti*	D. E. R. Watt, *Fasti Ecclesiae Scoticanae Medii Aevi ad annum 1638*, second draft (St. Andrews, 1969).
Watt, 'Minority'	D. E. R. Watt, 'The minority of Alexander III of Scotland', *Transactions of the Royal Historical Society*, 5th series, xxi (1971), 1–23.
Williamson, 'Legate Otto'	D. M. Williamson, 'The Legate Otto in Scotland and Ireland 1237–40', *SHR*, xxviii (1949), 12–30.
Williamson, 'Legation of Cardinal Otto'	D. M. Williamson, 'Some aspects of the legation of Cardinal Otto in England 1237–41', *EHR*, lxiv (1949), 145–73.

Winning, 'Church councils'	T. Winning, 'Church councils in sixteenth-century Scotland', *Innes Review*, x (1959), 311–37.
Wolter, *Lyon I*	H. Wolter and H. Holstein, *Lyon I et Lyon II* (Paris, 1966).

I

Early evidence of church councils in Scotland to *c.* 1100

ASSEMBLIES of bishops and other senior officers of the Christian church to regulate doctrine and discipline (usually called councils, but sometimes synods) can be traced from the earliest days of the church at Jerusalem soon after the death of Christ, and on a fully developed imperial, provincial or more local basis by the time of the conversion of the Emperor Constantine in the early fourth century.[1] But though various parts of the area which now comprises Scotland were evangelised from about a century after that time, little evidence survives to illustrate the activities of councils there until the late eleventh century[2] – a circumstance which means that the early history of councils in Scotland is necessarily very sketchy indeed compared with that of councils on the Continent,[3] in Anglo-Saxon England,[4] or even in Ireland[5] (which like Scotland received Christianity while politically outside the bounds of the Roman Empire). It was only by the early eleventh century that anything like a single royal administration for what is now mainland Scotland (leaving the Western

[1] *New Catholic Encyclopedia*, iv, 373–7.

[2] The comprehensive modern studies are: *Concilia Scotiae: Ecclesiae Scoticanae Statuta tam Provincialia quam Synodalia quae Supersunt, 1225–1559: Statuta Ecclesiae Scoticanae* [*SES*], 2 vols., ed. J. Robertson (Bannatyne Club, 1866); A. W. Haddan and W. Stubbs, *Councils and Ecclesiastical Documents relating to Great Britain and Ireland* [H&S], II, part i (Oxford, 1873); *Statutes of the Scottish Church 1225–1559*, ed. D. Patrick (SHS, 1907).

[3] C. J. Hefele and H. Leclercq, *Histoire des Conciles* (Paris, 1907–38).

[4] H&S, I and III; H. Vollrath, *Die Synoden Englands bis 1066* (Paderborn, 1985).

[5] D. N. Dumville, *Councils and Synods of the Gaelic Early and Central Middle Ages* (Cambridge, 1997).

and Northern Isles as part of the kingdom of Norway) was replacing the earlier petty kingdoms, each of which must have had its own way of harnessing the clergy to the service of the state.[6] Before then for centuries the four-fold division of authority north of the old Roman boundary of Hadrian's Wall between the Solway and the Tyne (among the Britons of Strathclyde/Cumbria, the Angles of Lothian/Northumbria, the Picts of Pictavia north of the Forth, and the Scots of Argyll) had kept political rivalries fresh and must have inhibited ecclesiastical inter-kingdom co-operation. There was apparently a system of episcopal oversight of a kind, even if the succession in specific sees was at best irregular;[7] but political disunity must have militated against conciliar co-operation among such few bishops as may have been contemporaneously in office.

This does not appear to have been the case in Ireland. There from the time of St. Patrick in the fifth century council meetings must have been held which approved successive collections of *acta* or canons which were confirmed and enlarged at subsequent meetings until finally *c.* 700 an edited *Collectio canonum Hibernensis* was put together.[8] It is true that for the next four hundred years evidence for council meetings in Ireland is as exiguous as in Scotland.[9] But the church in Ireland did have this lasting definition of its customs which gave it an individual character. Remembering how much the church in Scotland was the offspring of the mid-sixth-century mission of St. Columba from Ireland to Iona and beyond, we might expect to find mention of some of these Irish rules in their mission area in Scotland, and perhaps even evidence that they had been formally confirmed by councils there. But the most famous examples, the individual ways in which the Irish calculated the date of Easter and shaped their tonsures, attract attention mainly when the leaders of the Scottish

[6] For a general guide to political developments see A. A. M. Duncan, *Scotland: The Making of the Kingdom* (Edinburgh, 1975).

[7] Cf. G. Donaldson, *Scottish Church History* (Edinburgh, 1985), chapter 2, 'Bishops' sees before the reign of David I', for presentation of maximum evidence for episcopal continuity.

[8] Dumville, *Councils*, 2–3. Cf. *Life of St Columba* by Adomnán of Iona, ed. R. Sharpe (Harmondsworth, 1995), 346–7, n. 341 for a discussion of Irish synods.

[9] Dumville, *Councils*, 32–3, 53–4.

church gave in to Anglo-Saxon pressure and agreed to give them up in favour of the customs of the universal church at Whitby in Northumbria in 664[10] (with Iona following suit in 716[11]). Here the influence is from Scotland back to Ireland. Another illustration on a different theme occurred at a council of some kind held at Birr in Co. Offaly in 697, when Adomnan the abbot of Iona secured the acceptance of a law for the protection of non-combatants in time of war (Law of the Innocents), attached to which are the names of ninety-one guarantors including a bishop of Iona, a bishop of Rosemarkie, and a king of the Picts and a king of the Scots.[12] But these are exceptional events: the kings on the Scottish mainland – the area conveniently called 'Alba' until the mid-ninth century and then 'Scotia' or 'Scotland'[13] – appear to have ruled their ecclesiastical subjects with little evident regard for developments of church law and practice elsewhere.

If there is little evidence of Scottish clergy keeping contact with Irish councils, there is even less for their participation in any of the general councils of the church as a whole. The only possible example is a council held at Rome by Pope Gregory II in 721, when the sederunt included two bishops who are accorded titles that identify one as a Scot and the other as a Pict.[14] Just possibly their areas of episcopal authority were Strathclyde and Abernethy in Perthshire;[15] but alternatively it has been assumed that they both came from Ireland or at any rate Gaeldom.[16] No other general councils are known to have been attended by bishops from Scotland until the twelfth century. And contacts of any kind with Rome since the earliest missionary days were very few indeed – Cellach II bishop of St. Andrews is said to have exceptionally gone

[10] *Bede's Ecclesiastical History of the English People*, ed. B. Colgrave and R. A. B. Mynors (Oxford, 1969), 295–309, bk. iii, c. 25.

[11] Bede, *History*, 553–5, bk. v, c. 22.

[12] K. Meyer, *Cáin Adamnáin*, in *Anecdota Oxoniensia*, Mediaeval and Modern Series, part xii (Oxford, 1905); M. Ní Dhonnchadha, 'The guarantor list of *Cáin Adomnáin*, 697', *Peritia*, i (1982), 191, 214.

[13] Duncan, *Scotland*, 90.

[14] H&S, II, i, 7, 116; cf. Hefele-Leclercq, *Conciles*, III, i, 597–8.

[15] *Series Episcoporum Ecclesiae Catholicae Occidentalis ab initio usque ad annum MCXCVIII*, VI, *Britannia, Scotia et Hibernia, Scandinavia*, i, *Ecclesia Scoticana*, ed. D. E. R. Watt (Stuttgart, 1991), 39, 54; cf. Donaldson, *Church History*, 14, n. 27.

[16] Dumville, *Councils*, 25–6.

there for confirmation 966 x 971;[17] and King Macbeth is reported to have gone there in 1050.[18] Mentions of contacts with the Anglo-Saxon church after Whitby are similarly minimal: just once in 978 is an otherwise unidentified Beornelmus mentioned as a bishop from *Scotia* (which at that date must surely mean Scotland north of the River Forth) when attending with Dunstan archbishop of Canterbury a council at Calne in Wiltshire.[19]

Against this background of exiguous sources Thomas Innes in 1735 identified a list of seven early Scottish royal councils for insertion in David Wilkins' *Concilia* (London, 1737) on the strength of the possibility that they dealt with ecclesiastical as well as civil business.[20] Such omnicompetence under royal presidency would echo contemporary practice in Gaelic Ireland,[21] and also in Anglo-Saxon England, where it was not the custom to make a demarcation between the religious and secular spheres: 'The relationship of church and state was a working partnership and one as yet not theorised over: it was undefined, unsuspicious, friendly.'[22] It follows that there is little to illumine the history of church councils *per se* to be found in the scrappy evidence for general law-making to which Innes drew attention. The collections of laws associated by Hector Boece in the early sixteenth century with King Kenneth mac Alpin in the mid-ninth century and with King Macbeth in the mid-eleventh century[23] do deal with some ecclesiastical topics; but though Boece here may have been

[17] *Series Episcoporum*, VI, i, 78–9.

[18] *Early Sources of Scottish History 500 to 1286* [*ES*], ed. A. O. Anderson (Edinburgh, 1922), i, 588.

[19] *Series Episcoporum*, VI, i, 79, n. 35.

[20] This list with Innes' comments is more conveniently to be found as reprinted in T. Innes, *The Civil and Ecclesiastical History of Scotland* (Spalding Club, Aberdeen, 1853), pp. xxxix–lii, especially pp. xl–xli. A shorter list is to be found in T. Innes, *A Critical Essay on the Ancient Inhabitants of the Northern Parts of Britain or Scotland*, reprinted (Edinburgh, 1879), 320–5.

[21] Cf. comment in Dumville, *Councils*, 21: 'In so far as we can see conciliar events of the mediaeval Gaelic world, they came in the same variety of forms apparent elsewhere: wholly ecclesiastical gatherings; ecclesiastical meetings presided over by royalty; and meetings with a substantial lay element.'

[22] M. Deanesly, *The Pre-Conquest Church in England* (London, 1961), 213.

[23] Hector Boethius, *Scotorum Historiae*, 2nd edition (Paris, 1574), fos. 200v–201v, 250v–251v; *The Chronicles of Scotland compiled by Hector Boece*, translated into Scots by John Bellenden 1531 (Scottish Text Society, 1938–41), ii, 51–3, 152–3; H&S, II, i, 122–4.

following valid sources now lost as he spelled these out,[24] the dating and context of such evidence are too uncertain to be a secure base for historical deductions. In any case it is not at all clear that Boece thought that councils were involved in framing such legislation. Two other sets of laws supposedly of ecclesiastical as well as civil significance are merely listed from Boece by Innes without any details under the years 878 and 1020.[25] Even less is known about them. But when citing the tenth-century 'Chronicle of the Kings of Scotland' Innes does invite attention to an occasion in 906 when King Constantine II and Bishop Cellach I of St. Andrews met at Scone (near Perth) to confirm some Scottish ecclesiastical customs;[26] but whether or not a church council was assembled for the occasion is unknown. These examples demonstrate clearly the tradition of royal leadership in such matters. Certainly there is no hint of disputatious clergy arguing with knowledge and understanding for their points of view in intellectually vibrant clerical assemblies to parallel the controversies of the *Romani* (internationalists) and *Hibernenses* (nativists) in seventh-century Ireland.[27] The church in the various parts of Scotland does not appear at this stage of its development to have had a life of its own apart from the general administration of the country.

This background explains the apparently anomalous activities of St. Margaret, the Anglo-Saxon wife of King Malcolm III Canmore from *c.* 1070 until her death in 1093 (and the seventh in Innes' list), as the dominant figure in the running of church councils in the country to which she had come as a foreigner and a refugee from the post-1066 Norman rulers of England. From the *Life of Margaret* probably by the Benedictine monk Turgot,

[24] In the opinion of Dr. Nicola Royan, a recent scholar of Boece's work, this is more likely than used to be thought by scholars who regarded such material as merely 'spurious' (ibid.; *SES*, i, p. xviii, n. 1).

[25] Boethius, *Historiae*, fos. 208v–209, 245v; Bellenden, *Chronicles*, ii, 69–70, 140.

[26] *ES*, i, 445. Innes cites the same source (i, 291) for a supposed council at Forteviot near Perth *c.* 860; but no council is in fact mentioned in this text. For a discussion of possible translations of this source, see M. O. Anderson, 'Dalriada and the creation of the kingdom of the Scots', in *Ireland in Early Mediaeval Europe*, ed. D. Whitelock and others (Cambridge, 1982), 127. For this Bishop Cellach see *Series Episcoporum*, VI, i, 77–8.

[27] Dumville, *Councils*, 27.

who as prior of Durham from 1087 became her confidant, and written in two versions which are now thought to be datable 1093 x 1095 and 1104 x 1107,[28] we suddenly have access to details of thinking and action at the Scottish court on a scale and at a level not available to Scottish historians for an earlier period. Princess Margaret, a great-niece of King Edward the Confessor, must presumably have known Malcolm when he visited the Confessor's court in 1059.[29] The two of them certainly had some experience of church affairs outside Scotland, and once Margaret had become Malcolm's second wife, they formed a formidable partnership, not least because though Malcolm was illiterate, he was able to act as an interpreter between his Gaelic-speaking subjects and his English-speaking wife.[30] What must have been strikingly novel (as Turgot explains it) was the lead which Malcolm allowed his wife to take in summoning frequent church councils (*crebra concilia statuit*), at which she in person argued in detail in favour of changing the ways of the Scottish church to harmonise better with the practices of the universal church (*universalis ecclesia*).[31] As a consequence of the way she stirred up controversy, two sides emerged to develop their understanding of the reasons for their opposing points of view in a way that cannot be traced in Scotland since the days of the synod of Whitby in the seventh century. Margaret brought Anglo-Norman monks and priests to help her set in motion a process whereby in time they isolated the Hiberno-Scots and won the argument against them more and more.[32] A pattern was being set which had its consequences 150 years later when the leaders of the Scottish church were to choose to follow

[28] D. Baker, '"A Nursery of Saints": St Margaret of Scotland reconsidered', in *Medieval Women*, ed. D. Baker (Oxford, 1978), 119–41, especially 129–32. For Latin texts of two different manuscripts of the *Life* see *Pinkerton's Lives of the Scottish Saints*, ed. W. M. Metcalfe (Paisley, 1889), ii, 135–96 and 199–209, and *Symeonis Dunelmensis Opera et Collectanea*, ed. J. Hodgson Hinde (Surtees Society, 1868), i, appendix III, 234–54. For material relevant here see text from the Hinde edition in H&S, II, i, 156–9. For translations see *Ancient Lives of Scottish Saints*, ed. W. M. Metcalfe (Paisley, 1895), 295–321, and *ES*, ii, 59–88.

[29] *Scottish Annals from English Chroniclers 500 to 1286*, ed. A. O. Anderson [*SAEC*] (London, 1908), 86.

[30] *Life of Margaret*, cc. 6, 8 (*ES*, ii, 68, 70).

[31] *Life of Margaret*, c. 8 (H&S, II, i, 156; *ES*, ii, 70).

[32] Cf. D. Bethell, 'Two letters of Pope Paschal II to Scotland', *SHR*, xlix (1970), 33–45, especially 43.

the example of English churchmen at Salisbury and Lincoln in devising statutes for the Scottish church.[33]

Turgot emphasises the record of one undated council meeting in particular that lasted three days,[34] perhaps because it was held in the last years of Margaret's life when he was himself around and able to take notes of the arguments on both sides.[35] He provides no details of the attendance at this council, which probably met at a time when Bishop Fothad II of St. Andrews[36] may have been the only man of episcopal rank then in office in the Scottish kingdom. There were people present capable of developing arguments based on the general canon law as well as the Bible. The themes which Turgot mentions are not, however, the great issues of the day associated with the controversies raised by the contemporary Pope Gregory VII (died 1085), such as simony and clerical marriage and the liberties of the church which the state should respect. Indeed Turgot selects just five themes from among the many so-called 'abuses' tackled by the council: these are unrelated to each other, and do not appear to have formed part of a coherent code of reform. It was more a matter of an on-going process of piecemeal reform, as individual practices of the Scottish church were challenged one by one. In our source we learn of no defeats suffered by Margaret – the balance of argument is always reported in favour of her prevailing with the international point of view.

The five themes are: (1) the Lenten fast should be observed for forty days from Ash Wednesday rather than for thirty-six days starting in the following week; (2) it is wrong to abstain from taking the bread and wine of the Eucharist on Easter Day out of a sense of unworthiness; (3) certain undefined barbarous rites in the celebration of mass are to be abandoned; (4) Sunday work is condemned; (5) marriage with a step-mother or a brother's widow is condemned. In addition Turgot claims that at this one council Margaret secured also the condemnation of many other matters that were contrary to the rule of faith and the statutes of ecclesiastical observances (*contra fidei regulam et ecclesiasticarum*

[33] See below pp. 56, 59.
[34] *Life of Margaret*, c. 8 (*ES*, ii, 70–4).
[35] Innes' suggested date *c.* 1074 is improbably early.
[36] *Series Episcoporum*, VI, i, 80.

observationum instituta).[37] She herself is credited with the knowledge as well as the skill required to grasp why and how in the name of the universal church local Scottish practices should be reformed; but we may conclude that she did not stand alone: there were others (presumably including Turgot) of sufficient number and weight to help her to carry the day. No doubt there was a backlash after this over-bearing lady and her husband had both died in 1093; but things were on the move as a permanent result of her initiatives. We now know that by twenty years later some similar themes to those which Turgot says she handled were being referred 1112 x 1114 by King Alexander I and Turgot again (now himself bishop of St. Andrews) to Pope Paschal II for advice.[38] Scotland was now alive to the advantages of making contact with the papacy as the authority for the resolution of matters which were debatable questions of church law and practice. The king was still involved, and there was no word as yet of independent church councils where there would be a sufficiency of informed clergy capable of taking corporate responsibility for interpreting the Divine Will for the Scots in their church. But once communication with Rome had been broached from a country so far away from the centre of the Western Church, it was only a matter of time before the initiative from Scotland would be reciprocated by positive action from the papacy to bring Scotland into line with the other national churches that had been accustomed for years to accept papal guidance in the name of orthodoxy and convenience. The theory of the pope as Christ's vicar on earth was now widely regarded as having practical advantages, and Scotland was ready to share in them.

[37] H&S, II, i, 158, no. 6.
[38] Bethell, 'Two letters', *passim*.

2

Legatine councils 1125–1192

A need to organise formal church councils in Scotland in accordance with Roman ideas regarding such meetings became apparent in the 1120s. It was the result of Scottish involvement, partly involuntary, partly voluntary, in affairs and developments outside Scotland. As in other parts of Europe the customary freedom of each 'national' church to go largely its own way became circumscribed as the principles and practice of 'Gregorian' reforms pushed local churches towards standardised relationships, with the pope often giving the lead in setting standards and seeking to enforce them. Scotland was to experience for the first time visits by a series of papal legates in the course of the twelfth century, and legatine councils became a novel feature of the Scottish scene.[1]

The first of these was intended in 1125, when on 13 April Pope Honorius II was sending his legate John of Crema, cardinal priest of St. Chrysogonus, to Scotland, and ordered the new king David I to receive him with honour and compel the bishops of his land to attend a council which he was to call.[2] The problem which this legate was sent to tackle was one which had been forced on the Scots (unknown to them) as early as 1072. In April–May of that year the two first appointees by William the Conqueror to the archiepiscopal sees of Canterbury and York since his conquest of

[1] For a fuller account of visits of papal legates and nuncios to Scotland than is offered here see P. C. Ferguson, *Medieval Papal Representatives in Scotland: Legates, Nuncios and Judges-Delegate, 1125–1286* (Stair Society, 1997), cc. 2 and 3.

[2] H&S, II, i, 211; R. Somerville, *Scotia Pontificia* [*Scot. Pont.*] (Oxford, 1982), 28, no. 11; *SAEC*, 158–9. Cf. Ferguson, *Papal Representatives*, 31–4

England in 1066, who had been quarrelling for two years over their respective rights, were brought to an agreement at Winchester and Windsor in the presence of the king and a papal legate. The archbishop of York was said to be subject to the authority of the archbishop of Canterbury in his capacity as 'primate of all Britain', but York was recognised as having (metropolitan) authority over the bishop of Durham and all regions north of the River Humber to the extreme limits of Scotland (*usque ad extremos Scotie fines*).[3] This was only one definition of the respective rights of these two archbishops, who were to continue quarrelling until the mid-fourteenth century;[4] but it turned out to be one of lasting importance for Scotland. The use of the word 'Britain' in 1072, when no such political or ecclesiastical unit existed, is an indication that those Anglo-Norman litigants of that time were looking back specifically to the instructions of Pope Gregory I in 601 to Augustine the first archbishop of Canterbury as preserved in the writings of Bede,[5] which had been based on long-out-of-date information about the imperial Roman province of Britain when laying down a plan that there were to be two metropolitan archbishops, each with twelve suffragan bishops, in the island which Gregory hoped was now to be re-evangelised. Gregory had made no reference to the Christian church which in 601 already existed outside the northern limits of the old Roman province of Britain, i.e. in the regions which by 1072 had come together under the authority of the king of Scots, which would appear to be what in that year was meant by 'Scotia'; he probably had little knowledge of it and its lively missionary impetus based on Iona, which was to rival the Augustinian mission as a source of inspiration for more than half a century until its expansion was effectively halted at the synod of Whitby in 664.[6] But in any case during the centuries between 601 and 1072 no attempt is known to have been made to subordinate the Scottish church to the English one. Now for reasons connected with attaining a workable compromise between the two sees of Canterbury and York under

[3] *Councils & Synods* [*C&S*], I, ii, ed. D. Whitelock, M. Brett and C. N. L. Brooke (Oxford, 1981), 601–4; *SES*, i, p. xxv.

[4] E.g. see J. C. Dickinson, *The Later Middle Ages* (London, 1979), 66–8.

[5] Bede, *History*, 104–7, bk. i, c. 29.

[6] Ibid., 294–309, bk. iii, c. 25.

new direction, the backing of both King William I and Pope Alexander II (through his legate) was given to the novel idea that Canterbury had some general primatial, and York some direct metropolitan, authority over the church in 'Scotia'. King Malcolm III of the Scots and his bishops were not consulted; but when in August 1072 he submitted to William at Abernethy (near Perth in Scotland) and became William's man,[7] it is possible that the ecclesiastical agreement made earlier in the year was brought to his unwilling attention, for in York tradition Bishop Fothad of St. Andrews was remembered as coming to York at his king's request to profess obedience there.[8]

It is likely that in these early days of the 'Gregorian' reform the implications of the offices of 'primate' and 'metropolitan' were not precisely appreciated.[9] Certainly there is no evidence of Scottish bishops being called to councils summoned by Canterbury or York.[10] But after 1072 York did gradually try to exact professions of obedience (whatever that meant) at times when bishops in addition to Durham sought consecration at their hands. The archbishops in the late eleventh and early twelfth centuries, indeed, looked successfully beyond 'Scotia' to arrange the consecrations of a series of bishops in Orkney in 1073, 1100 x 1108 and 1109 x 1114,[11] and in The (Western) Isles in 1103 x 1108, 1109 x 1114, 1134 x *c.* 1138, 1152 and 1154.[12] (In the latter case one consecration at York may have taken place as late as *c.* 1217 x 1226,[13] even though in 1154 both Orkney and The Isles were among the dioceses which had by papal authority been placed under the metropolitan jurisdiction of the archbishop of Nidaros

[7] *SAEC*, 95.

[8] Hugh the Chantor, *History of the Church of York*, ed. C. Johnson (Edinburgh, 1961), 31; *SES*, i, p. xxv, n. 2.

[9] Cf. *Dictionnaire de Droit Canonique* [*DDC*] (Paris, 1935–65), vii, col. 214; vi, cols. 875–7.

[10] *C&S*, I, ii, *passim.*

[11] B. E. Crawford, 'Bishops of Orkney in the eleventh and twelfth centuries: bibliography and biographical list', *Innes Review*, xlvii (1996), 1–13, especially 8–10.

[12] D. E. R. Watt, 'Bishops in the Isles before 1203: bibliography and biographical lists', *Innes Review*, xlv (1994), 99–119, especially 110, 107, 115–17.

[13] D. E. R. Watt, *Fasti Ecclesiae Scoticanae Medii Aevi ad annum 1638*, second draft (St. Andrews, 1969), 200.

[Trondheim] in Norway.[14]) There is no doubt that both these island areas were at this period politically part of the kingdom of Norway, though it may well be that the participants at the conference of Winchester/Windsor in 1072 were not very exactly informed on where the 'extreme limits of Scotland' lay, and were intending that what are now called the Northern and Western Isles of Scotland should be open to the aggressive expansion of York's authority if it could be managed.

Within the kingdom of Scotland itself York made less progress. When Turgot prior of Durham was chosen to be bishop of St. Andrews in 1107 by the new king Alexander I (with the agreement of King Henry I of England), there followed two years of controversy before he was consecrated at York in August 1109, probably without having to recognise York's metropolitan authority.[15] This was a sign of trouble to come. King Alexander's brother David arranged for Michael, a 'Briton' (i.e. a native of Cumbria or Strathclyde, an area which stretched from north of Glasgow to south of Carlisle) to be consecrated at York 1109 x 1114;[16] but the same David ensured that Michael's successor John was consecrated by Pope Paschal II *c.* 1114 x 1118 while the see of York was vacant,[17] and by 1115 King Alexander was turning to Canterbury for a new bishop of St. Andrews, rejecting the right of York to consecrate such bishops. But when in response the monk Eadmer was sent to Scotland from Canterbury in 1120, Alexander went a step further and refused to allow him to take up the see if he persisted in his wish to proffer obedience to Canterbury in order to receive consecration there, with the result that Eadmer had to return to Canterbury without obtaining the see.[18] Alexander and his brother David had hardened their position in reaction against aggressive efforts at this time by Thurstan the new archbishop of York aimed against this possible intrusion of Canterbury into the affairs of his province, which led him to try to insist that all the bishops of the Scottish kingdom acknowledge his superior authority. He engaged papal support for his case, so that unwelcome pressure came to be brought to bear on the Scottish

[14] *Diplomatarium Norvegicum* (Kristiania, 1849–1919), viii, no. 1.
[15] *Series Episcoporum*, VI, i, 81.
[16] Ibid., 54.
[17] Ibid., 55.
[18] Ibid., 82.

bishops. As early as 1100 x 1101 Paschal II had in general supported the metropolitan rights of York over them.[19] Now Calixtus II issued a series of instructions during 1119–22 to the Scottish bishops (and especially the bishop of Glasgow) to submit to York;[20] but his instructions were not obeyed.

By April 1125 there was a new king in Scotland, David I, and a new pope, Honorius II. The latter had been a close adviser of his predecessor,[21] and judged the time ripe for sending Cardinal John of Crema as the first known papal legate ever to be sent to Scotland.[22] Before his death King Alexander had arranged the election of Robert prior of Scone to the vacant see of St. Andrews.[23] The question of his consecration raised urgently the claims of York, and Crema was instructed to have discussions over the matter, and report back for a final decision to be made in Rome.[24] He had much business to do in Normandy and England as well. His visit to King David at Roxburgh is well attested, probably in July–August 1125;[25] but though the evidence states that he performed his duty as legate ('officio legationis peracto'), it does not confirm that he held a formal legatine council at Roxburgh, and this contrasts with the certain information that he did hold such a council at Westminster for three or four days from 8 September onwards.[26] It is therefore probably correct to argue that Crema was not able to hold a council as he had been instructed to do,[27] and certainly the Scottish church did not receive at this date a body of legatine canons (including some derived from the recent First Lateran General Council of March 1123) in the way that the English church did at Westminster. It seems likely[28] that the Scottish kings viewed this interference from Rome at the instance of York with hostility, though Alexander had not

[19] *Scot. Pont.*, 19, no. 1.

[20] Ibid., 22–8, nos. 4–10; cf. *Series Episcoporum*, VI, i, 36.

[21] *The Oxford Dictionary of Popes*, ed. J. N. D. Kelly (Oxford, 1986), 166.

[22] See above p. 9.

[23] *Series Episcoporum*, VI, i, 83.

[24] *Scot. Pont.*, 28, no. 11; *SES*, i, pp. xxvi–xxvii; *SAEC*, 158–9.

[25] *The Chronicle of Melrose* [*Chron. Melrose*], ed. A. O. Anderson and others (London, 1936), 32; *SES*, i, p. xxvii; H&S, II, i, 211; *C&S*, I, ii, 730–2.

[26] *C&S*, I, ii, 733–41.

[27] See Duncan, *Scotland*, 259; cf. *SES*, i, p. xxvi.

[28] As argued by M. Brett, *The English Church under Henry I* (Oxford, 1975), 23, n. 1.

been able to prevent Bishop John of Glasgow from having to go there in 1122 to answer for his defiance of York authority.[29] This bishop was now sent as David's envoy to the curia, where by Christmas 1125 he was arguing that Scotland was not part of the realm of England, and seeking the erection of St. Andrews into a metropolitan see.[30] No doubt these points had been made with the legate at Roxburgh earlier in the year. York pressed on with litigation at Rome against all the bishops of Scotland;[31] but in the event relations were cooled down for the time being when a compromise was arranged between King Henry and King David (who were brothers-in-law) at Windsor and London at Christmas 1126.[32] This led to the consecration of Robert bishop of St. Andrews by Thurstan archbishop of York, apparently in the presence of King David, at Roxburgh on or just before 17 July 1127, with both sides suspending their claims regarding the respective rights of York and St. Andrews for the time being.[33]

It was presumably part of the bargain made between David and Thurstan at this time that arrangements were made for the erection of a new diocese within the kingdom of Scotland based on the old see of Candida Casa or Whithorn in Galloway, where there had been Anglian bishops in the eighth century.[34] This revived see comprised the greater part of the semi-independent lordship of Galloway, and its first bishop was instructed by the pope on 9 December 1128 to go to York for consecration; this he did apparently willingly, as his successors were to do for the next two hundred years.[35] The very success of York here must surely be taken as evidence of a general agreement for the detachment of this one region of the kingdom of Scotland from the church in Scotland, and the acceptance of a small degree of York authority

[29] *SAEC*, 149–50, 154.

[30] Hugh the Chantor, *History*, 126.

[31] *Scot. Pont.*, 29, no. 13.

[32] Hugh the Chantor, *History*, 129.

[33] *Series Episcoporum*, VI, i, 83; H&S, II, i, 214–15. Note that this settlement appears not to have included the position of John bishop of Glasgow, against whose continued refusal to proffer obedience York continued to obtain papal mandates (*Scot. Pont.*, 30–1, nos. 15, 17).

[34] *Series Episcoporum*, VI, i, 19–24.

[35] *Scot. Pont.*, 29–30, no. 14; Watt, *Fasti*, 128–30.

there. It is likely that the revived very extensive see of Glasgow had been finding it difficult to establish effective control in the more distant parts of the lordship west of the River Urr, so that their loss was something of a relief. Certainly the fact that Glasgow retained control over the part of the lordship between the Rivers Urr and Nith is evidence for a compromise deal.

If this was part of the price which David was willing to pay in 1126 to stop York's pretensions over St. Andrews, another part which he was then probably not at all unwilling to play was the permanent detachment of Cumbria south of the Solway boundary from the sprawling diocese of Glasgow as the new diocese of Carlisle, for which Archbishop Thurstan consecrated a bishop in 1133.[36] This area had been politically detached from Scotland and incorporated in the Anglo-Norman kingdom by William II since 1092. It was a simplification of the bishop of Glasgow's fight against York to have this region, which appeared to have been attached to England on a permanent basis, detached from his area of responsibility. Again it must have been done with the agreement of King David, and it may well have taken some years to arrange: it could all have been part of the compromise made in 1126–7.[37] It is noteworthy that when in 1136 King David took advantage of the civil war in England which had followed the death of Henry I in 1135 to occupy English Cumbria once more and treat it as part of Scotland for twenty-one years, he did not try to restore the area to Glasgow diocese.[38] He must surely have been happy to accept the erection of Carlisle diocese in the first place.

The next papal legate after John of Crema who had power to summon Scottish as well as English clergy to synods if he so chose was William of Corbeil archbishop of Canterbury 1123–36, who was so empowered by Pope Honorius II on 25 January 1126.[39] Though he held at least two legatine councils in England, there is no evidence that he ever sought to exercise authority over the

[36] *SAEC*, 168–9; *Handbook of British Chronology* [*HBC*], 3rd edition, ed. E. B. Fryde and others (London, 1986), 235.

[37] Cf. discussions in Brett, *Henry I*, 25–7; G. W. S. Barrow, *The Kingdom of the Scots* (London, 1973), 142–4.

[38] Cf. Barrow, *Kingdom*, 147–8.

[39] *Scot. Pont.*, 28, no. 12; *C&S*, I, ii, 742–3. See also Ferguson, *Papal Representatives*, 34–5.

Scottish church.[40] His scope for even trying to do this was probably much restricted as a consequence of the papal schism of 1130–8, when after some initial hesitation England chose to adhere to Innocent II,[41] while it is possible that David I and the Scottish bishops favoured Anacletus II from the outset, as they certainly did after 1135, when Innocent supported Stephen against Matilda and David was on Matilda's side.[42] With the death of Anacletus in January 1138 the schism effectively came to an end. Innocent marked this by sending a French Cluniac monk, Alberic (whom he had created cardinal bishop of Ostia in April 1138) as legate to England and Scotland.[43] He arrived in the north of England soon after the battle of the Standard, when David and his forces had been severely beaten on 22 August 1138 as they invaded England on behalf of Matilda by an army collected by Thurstan archbishop of York on behalf of Stephen. Chronicles kept almost contemporaneously in the Northumberland abbey of Hexham tell of his visit there and then to Carlisle. At this time Cumbria was being held by the Scots, and it was at Carlisle that Alberic met King David 'with the bishops, abbots, priors and barons of his land'. Meetings were held over three days 26–28 September 1138. In the language of the contemporary Richard of Hexham Alberic is said to have negotiated (*tractavit*) with the Scots over the business of his legation.[44] When this came to be summarised by John of Hexham twenty to thirty years later, Alberic's part is described in much more masterful terms: 'he corrected what required correction and issued legislation (*statuit*) where it was needed.'[45] In the circumstances it seems more likely that it was a period of negotiation as in the case of the legatine visit of 1125, and as then there is a contrast with the regular legatine council held by Alberic

[40] *C&S*, I, ii, 743–54, 757–61; cf. *SES*, i, p. xxvii. He retained his legateship until his death in 1136 (cf. H&S, II, i, 29), with apparently a gap from February 1130 (death of Pope Honorius) until February x March 1132 (Ferguson, *Papal Representatives*, 35).

[41] *C&S*, I, ii, 754–7

[42] Barrow, *Kingdom*, 176; Brett, *Henry I*, 26. The bishop of Glasgow was certainly in 1136 accused of schism by Pope Innocent (H&S, II, i, 29).

[43] See *C&S*, I, ii, 766–79 for the English aspects of his mission; cf. *Scot. Pont.*, 31–2, nos. 19–20. See also Ferguson, *Papal Representatives*, 36–7.

[44] H&S, II, i, 31–2; *SES*, i, pp. xxvii–xxix; *SAEC*, 210–12.

[45] H&S, II, i, 32; *SES*, i, p. xxix; *SAEC*, 211; *C&S*, I, ii, 767–8.

for the English church at Westminster in December 1138, from which a list of reforming canons survives.[46] It appears that the Scottish king and church were not yet ready for legatine actions of this kind, for no formal *acta* or canons survive from Alberic's visit.

The list of items of business which are known to have been dealt with at Carlisle is as follows:

1. It was noted that the Scots had favoured Pope Anacletus. They now acknowledged Pope Innocent and his legate.
2. John of Hexham (the source compiled some years after the event) records that King David was persuaded to accept Bishop Adelulf of Carlisle back into his favour; presumably they had been at loggerheads since David's occupation of Cumbria after the death of Henry I, though Adelulf was in fact simultaneously bishop and prior of the Augustinian house at Nostell in Yorkshire from which Robert bishop of St. Andrews had first come to Scotland *c.* 1120.[47]
3. Bishop John of Glasgow (whom Pope Innocent II had continued to persecute)[48] was recalled from his retirement in the monastery of Thiron in France to his episcopal duties once more. In the contemporary source this is described as a joint act by both king and legate; in the later account it is said to have been just a legatine act under papal authority. Here the legate was reversing two decades of papal policy, which had been exercised so much in favour of York and against Glasgow.
4. The legate begged the king to make peace with King Stephen; but all that he could secure was a short truce until 11 November 1138, while the siege of Wark Castle on the Northumberland side of the river Tweed continued.
5. The legate persuaded the king's men from Galloway[49] to promise that by the same date in November they would

[46] *C&S*, I, ii, 774–9.

[47] John Le Neve, *Fasti Ecclesiae Anglicanae 1066–1300*, ii (London, 1971), 19; Barrow, *Kingdom*, 170–2.

[48] H&S, II, i, 28–30.

[49] The Hexham chroniclers in fact call the men from this region 'Picts', to distinguish them from the Scots from 'Scotia', i.e. the land north of the river Forth (cf. G. W. S. Barrow, *Feudal Britain* [London, 1956], 116, n. 2).

> return female captives whom they had taken in England (particularly in Lancashire),[50] and to spare such non-combatants in future.

There is nothing here about reform of the Scottish church and clergy, which was to be one category of business conducted at the legate's council in England. Alberic's function was more that of a go-between; and the chronicler ends by saying that he reported to King Stephen what had been done at Carlisle. Though ten English representatives were sent to the Second Lateran Council of April 1139,[51] no Scots are known to have attended. They have not been traced either at Pope Eugenius III's council at Rheims in March 1148.[52] The Scottish church was still prepared to accept papal authority only when it suited.

The early 1150s were a time when new metropolitan sees were created both in Ireland (where the previous two archbishoprics were increased to four in March 1152) and in Norway (where the archbishopric of Nidaros was split off from Lund 1153–4). When Cardinal John Paparo passed through the north of England on his way to Ireland in connection with this business in September 1151, and back again after Easter 1152, the question of raising St. Andrews to a metropolitan see was raised again, and Paparo agreed to report on the matter to the pope.[53] This time the dioceses of Orkney and The Isles in the Norwegian kingdom were to be added to the list of Scottish sees that were to become subordinate to St. Andrews. But then these two sees were confirmed as suffragans of Nidaros soon afterwards, and the St. Andrews proposal lapsed once again. At least this story is evidence of the continuing determination in Scotland to keep free of entanglements with either York or Canterbury. The St. Andrews proposal at this date was probably a response to revived papal support for York in bulls of June 1151;[54] and there was also possibly a threat from Canterbury, where Archbishop Theobald (1139–61) held

[50] *SAEC*, 187.

[51] *C&S*, I, ii, 779–81.

[52] N. M. Haring, 'Notes on the council and the consistory of Rheims (1148)', *Medieval Studies*, xxviii (1966), 39–59.

[53] *John of Salisbury's Memoirs of the Papal Court*, ed. M. Chibnall (Edinburgh, 1956), 72; cf. *SAEC*, 227.

[54] *Scot. Pont.*, 38–9, nos. 29–30.

the office of papal legate for England from 1150 onwards, and perhaps for Scotland also under Pope Anastasius IV (1153–4), though he is not known ever to have tried to act in Scotland.[55] The duty of the Scottish bishops to obey York was emphasised yet again by Hadrian IV, the English pope 1155–9.[56] Then when Bishop Robert of St. Andrews died early in 1159,[57] King Malcolm IV sent an embassy (including William bishop of Moray) to the Roman court to raise certain matters about the see of St. Andrews. These were answered by the new pope, Alexander III, on 27 November 1159.[58] The king's proposals are nowhere specified in the surviving evidence, but are generally supposed to have again been concerned with the elevation of the see of St. Andrews to metropolitan status.[59] Alexander rejected the king's proposals anyway, but according to a complicated scheme appointed the bishop of Moray as legate in the whole kingdom of the Scots until he or someone else acceptable to the king should become bishop of St. Andrews, when the new holder of that see was to hold the legation thereafter. In the event Arnold abbot of Kelso was chosen as bishop, and on 20 November 1160 was consecrated at St. Andrews on the pope's behalf by the bishop of Moray as legate.[60] Though Bishop William seems to have returned to Scotland armed with the usual wide legatine powers of correction and legislation, the pressing need had primarily been to achieve a solution to the St. Andrews appointment. No doubt this first grant of legatine powers to a bishop resident in Scotland was a reflection of Pope Alexander's difficulties as he faced a troublesome schism at Rome and needed all the support that he could get.[61] The bishop of Moray remained legate into 1161;[62] then the new bishop of St. Andrews took over the office as had been arranged in November

[55] John Le Neve, *Fasti 1066–1300*, ii, 4 and n. 7; *C&S*, I, ii, 820.

[56] *Scot. Pont.*, 40–2, 47–8, nos. 34, 40.

[57] *Series Episcoporum*, VI, i, 84.

[58] *SES*, i, p. xxx; *SAEC*, 240–1; *Scot. Pont.*, 49–50, no. 43.

[59] Cf. *Regesta Regum Scottorum* [*RRS*], i, ed. G. W. S Barrow (Edinburgh, 1960), 11, 14; but for doubts regarding the purpose of this embassy see *Scot. Pont.*, 47–8, no. 40, and Ferguson, *Papal Representatives*, 41.

[60] *Chron. Melrose*, 36.

[61] Kelly, *Dictionary of Popes*, 176–7.

[62] *RRS*, i, nos. 175, 180, 182; see also *A Scottish Chronicle known as the Chronicle of Holyrood* [*Chron. Holyrood*], ed. M. O. Anderson (SHS, 1938), 135–6.

1159,[63] and as legate consecrated a new bishop for the diocese of Ross.[64] But neither William nor Arnold is known as legate to have performed any function in Scotland other than the consecration there of bishops on the pope's behalf; no councils were held; the device of the legateship appears to have been a temporary means of keeping York at bay, and Arnold's legatine authority came to an end, perhaps later in 1161, certainly before his death soon afterwards on 13 September 1162.[65] This must surely have again been the result of pressure by York at the curia of Pope Alexander, who by 21 September 1162 was again ordering the Scottish bishops to submit to the metropolitan authority of York.[66]

But the Scots were not ready to accept such a retrograde step (from their point of view). Once Richard the next bishop of St. Andrews had been elected early in 1163,[67] and there was presumably doubt once again over how he was to be consecrated without proffering obedience to York, Gregory bishop of Dunkeld went to the curia of Pope Alexander (now in France), and is the first Scottish bishop known for certain to have attended a papal council, namely that held in May 1163 at Tours; there he significantly won the right to sit among a group of other exempt bishops rather than like the bishop of Durham beside the archbishop of York as one of his suffragans.[68] The king and bishops of Scotland must have been learning of the advantages which were to be obtained by active lobbying at the papal curia against York's continuing aggression.[69] There were now precedents favouring both sides of the dispute; and precedents were necessary to secure a clarification of law and practice.

[63] E.g. *RRS*, i, no. 226.

[64] *Chron. Melrose*, 36.

[65] Ibid.; *Chron. Holyrood*, 140–1; *Scot. Pont.*, 51, no. 45.

[66] *Scot. Pont.*, 51–2, no. 46.

[67] *Series Episcoporum*, VI, i, 86.

[68] T. A. Reuter, 'A list of bishops attending the Council of Tours (1163)', *Annuarium Historiae Conciliorum*, viii (1976), 122–5; R. Somerville, *Pope Alexander III and the Council of Tours 1163* (California, 1977), 27–9, 34–5, 37, but following the interpretation of G. W. S. Barrow in *SHR*, lviii (1979), 196. Perhaps Abbot Geoffrey of Dunfermline was also present (Somerville, ut. cit., 29–31; cf. *RRS*, i, 17). See also *Scot. Pont.*, 54–5, nos. 48–9.

[69] Scottish monasteries were by now commonly obtaining bulls of protection for and confirmation of their privileges and property from successive popes (e.g. *Scot. Pont.*, nos. 31, 32, 35, 37, 41, 47, 49, 50–3).

But York was not ready to give up. It was in the context of the dispute between King Henry II and Archbishop Thomas Becket of Canterbury that Roger de Pont L'Évêque archbishop of York was appointed legate, not for England, but in some sense for Scotland, probably in the spring of 1164.[70] The terms of his appointment are not known, but at some date before mid-September 1164 he came to the castle at Norham on the English bank of the River Tweed in an attempt to exercise his authority over all the clergy of Scotland. He appears to have wanted them to come to a council under his auspices (though this is not specifically stated in the sources); but it was some other kind of clerical assembly that met within Scotland, for it was *de consensu cleri* that Ingram archdeacon of Glasgow led a delegation to Norham to reject Roger's demands and appeal to the Roman court. Soon afterwards (probably on 13 September) Ingram was elected to the see of Glasgow, and on going to the curia of Pope Alexander at Sens in France with the full support of King Malcolm IV obtained consecration there on 28 October 1164, despite strong objections raised by messengers from York.[71] York's chagrin was complete for the present when the pope authorised the bishops of Scotland by special commission to consecrate Richard as bishop of St. Andrews, a ceremony which took place at last on 28 March 1165.[72] Scotland appears now to have in Pope Alexander III a firm defender against the pretensions of York.[73]

But political developments could have their effect on ecclesiastical relationships. Following the capture of King William by

[70] *Materials for the History of Thomas Becket* (Rolls Series, 67 [1875–85], v, 85–8; *C&S*, I, ii, 894; *Scot. Pont.*, 71–2, no. 68; cf. *Johannis de Fordun Chronica Gentis Scotorum* [*Chron. Fordun*], ed. W. F. Skene (Edinburgh, 1871–2), i, app. II, p. 405. Cf. Ferguson, *Papal Representatives*, 43–52, 59–61, where it is argued (especially on pp. 47–8) that the legation was for the province of York only, which to Roger meant the inclusion of all Scotland.

[71] *Chron. Melrose*, 37. cf. *Chron. Holyrood*, 145–7; Walter Bower, *Scotichronicon* [*Chron. Bower*], ed. D. E. R. Watt (Aberdeen, 1987–98), iv, 291; *Scot. Pont.*, 57–8, no. 54; *Series Episcoporum*, VI, i, 59–60.

[72] Ibid., 86; *Scot. Pont.*, 60–1, no. 57.

[73] But note that in 1166 Archbishop Roger was still known to John of Salisbury as papal legate for Scotland (*Scot. Pont.*, 72). He appears to have retained this office throughout the pontificate of Alexander III, possibly mainly because it provided him with exemption from the legatine powers of the archbishop of Canterbury rather than status in relation to York's traditional pretensions over the Scottish church.

the English at Alnwick on 13 July 1174 came the treaty of Falaise/Valognes of 8 December 1174, under which the Scottish clergy were required to swear fealty to Henry II and acknowledge that 'the church of England shall also have the right in the church of Scotland which it lawfully should'.[74] But just at the same time Jocelin abbot of Melrose was securing from Pope Alexander III on 16 December 1174 a mandate for his consecration as bishop of Glasgow, which was duly put into effect at Clairvaux in France.[75] The pope had already been issuing bulls of protection for the see of Glasgow on 5 April 1170, 27 February 1172/3, and 25 March 1173;[76] and now the new bishop was granted protection on a novel scale on 15 March 1174/5 and 30 April 1175, the last one taking the see of Glasgow perpetually under Rome directly, with exemption from any other authority as 'our special daughter with no intermediary'.[77] With the pope behind them in this way, the Scottish bishops could bravely face up to Henry II. It is true that at York in August 1175 six Scottish bishops (including Jocelin of Glasgow) had to swear fealty to the English king in terms of the treaty of December 1174; but they did not perform homage as King William had to do, and they secured postponement of the question of subjecting themselves to the church of England.[78] Before the time came for them to face up to this, Hugh Pierleone cardinal deacon of Sant' Angelo had arrived in England on a legation that lasted from October 1175 to July 1176, sent mainly to deal with matters which were still outstanding since the disputes of Henry and Becket.[79] But he is not listed among those who attended a royal council held at Northampton at the end of January 1175/6,[80] when the same six Scottish bishops were ordered to submit themselves to the church of England. They faced

[74] *Anglo-Scottish Relations 1174–1328: Some Selected Documents*, ed. E. L. G. Stones (Edinburgh, 1965), 2.

[75] *Scot. Pont.*, 73, no. 69; *Chron. Melrose*, 41; *Series Episcoporum*, VI, i, 61.

[76] *Scot. Pont.*, 65, no. 62; 67–8, no. 65; 70–1, no. 67.

[77] Ibid., 75–7, nos. 74, 76.

[78] *SAEC*, 259–60; *Annals of the Reigns of Malcolm and William, Kings of Scotland* [*AMW*], ed. A. C. Lawrie (Glasgow, 1910), 201–3.

[79] *C&S*, I, ii, 994.

[80] This was not a legatine council held by Pierleone himself (*SES*, i, pp. xxxii–iii, and H&S, II, i, 241). The sources make it pretty clear that the legate was elsewhere at the time (*AMW*, 206–11). See also Ferguson, *Papal Representatives*, 51, n. 122.

up to the demands of the archbishop of York (with Bishop Jocelin emphasising his recent privilege that gave his see 'special daughter' status), and then took advantage of a subsequent dispute between him and the archbishop of Canterbury over who was to receive their submission to obtain permission from Henry to go home without submitting to either.[81] Both York and the Scottish bishops now approached the pope, the former with palpably forged evidence;[82] and the Scots on 30 July 1176 secured a vitally important bull of protection (*Super anxietatibus*), which lamented that they had been compelled to swear fealty to Henry II, and relieved them from obedience to the metropolitan authority of York: the Roman pontiff himself was in future to be their metropolitan until any further settlement that might arise if York chose to pursue the matter.[83] Alexander was later to make it clear that his purpose at this time was to secure liberty for the Scottish church and kingdom.[84]

The pope had anticipated his letter of 30 July 1176 by appointing a legate to visit Scotland, Ireland and Norway (meaning apparently the diocese of The Isles based on the Isle of Man). This was Vivian cardinal priest of St. Stephen on Monte Celio, who had earlier in 1169 been employed as a legate in northern France seeking peace between Henry II and Becket.[85] According to one source he was sent at the request of King William to help with the question of the enforced subjection of the Scottish church to the English; in another chronicle his remit was: 'ad causas ecclesiasticas audiendas et determinandas.'[86] Arriving in England on 22 July 1176, he was delayed for some time before King Henry would give him a safe-conduct to travel north, which was granted only after he had promised not to harm that king's interests. It is not known what he did in Scotland in the last months of 1176; but then he moved via Whithorn in Galloway to the Isle of Man

[81] *SAEC*, 264–5; *C&S*, I, ii, 997–8.

[82] H&S, II, i, 244–5; cf. *RRS*, ii, 225–6, no. 157; see R. Somerville, 'Pope Alexander III and King William I', *Innes Review*, xxiv (1973), 121–4. Note that Archbishop Roger was still at this date holding the office of legate (cf. above n. 73).

[83] *Scot. Pont.*, 79–81, no. 80.

[84] H&S, II, i, 255; *Scot. Pont.*, 97–8, no. 101

[85] *C&S*, I, ii, 918, 926. See Ferguson, *Papal Representatives*, 53–5.

[86] *AMW*, 214; H&S, II, i, 246.

for two weeks over Christmas, and thence to Ireland after 6 January 1176/7. There at a council held at Dublin he gave firm continuing papal backing to Henry's recent conquest of Ireland.[87] He returned to England for another safe-conduct to go to Scotland again, which was granted at Winchester on 3 June 1177.[88] Then on 1 August he held a council of the Scottish prelates at Holyrood Abbey beside Edinburgh – the first fully-fledged legatine council known in Scotland.

No list survives of those who attended, nor any account of the business done: a contemporary chronicler states simply that the council was concerned 'de statutis ecclesiae', and a later one claims that by apostolic authority he acted 'plurima renovans antiquorum decreta et nova quaedam statuens praecepta',[89] which is just the expected formal language for the occasion. On the Isle of Man he is known to have regularised the marriage of King Godred,[90] and presumably he took the opportunity to tidy up similar matters in Scotland. It is interesting that he failed to force Christian bishop of Whithorn (i.e. Galloway) to attend. Christian claimed that as he had been consecrated by Roger archbishop of York,[91] he owed obedience to him as a legate within his province by grant of Pope Alexander (rather than to Vivian).[92] Cardinal Vivian suspended him, presumably because he did not accept the validity of Christian's claim. Vivian left with a reputation for harshness and greed; no doubt the discipline which he enforced and the levies which he was required to make towards his living costs were novelties in Scotland, which may have been surprising and unwelcome. The Melrose chronicler was particularly critical,[93] but this can be explained by the fact that he had certainly gone beyond papal policy in ordering that Cistercian monasteries (of which Melrose was one) should pay teind on lands which they worked but held from others, an instruction which the pope in January

[87] *Expugnatio Hibernica*, ed. A. B. Scott and F. X. Martin (Dublin, 1978), 174, 180–2, and notes 301–2 and 322–3.
[88] *SAEC*, 269.
[89] *AMW*, 216; *Chron. Fordun*, i, 266.
[90] H&S, II, i, 247.
[91] In 1154 (*Series Episcoporum*, VI, i, 25).
[92] *SAEC*, 269; *AMW*, 216; cf. above nn. 70, 73, 82.
[93] *Chron. Melrose*, 41–2.

1177/8 recognised as an error that had to be countermanded.[94] It was clearly a controversial visit.

In the course of 1178 a papal nuncio was sent to the same sections of the church as Cardinal Vivian had visited (Scotland, Galloway [mentioned separately[95]], The Isles and Ireland) with a summons to the Third Lateran Council at Rome which was planned for the following Lent.[96] An English chronicler reports that several Scottish bishops and abbots passed through England on their way to this council, which in fact met 5–19 March 1179;[97] but the name of only one Scottish bishop (Gregory of Ross) is found in the official sederunt list,[98] though two other Scots apparently made their way to Rome for their consecration to the sees of Brechin and Dunblane respectively while the council was sitting.[99] It is clear, however, that the Scottish bishops as a whole were now directly in touch with the reforming conciliar activities of the Roman see. It was the least that Pope Alexander would expect from the group of bishops who had been glad to have him as their metropolitan.

But he must have been learning about the time of the council that King William was by no means prepared to allow a Scottish church that had been freed from threats of control from York to be free to manage its own affairs without regard for royal interests. The celebrated dispute over the bishopric of St. Andrews after the death of Bishop Richard in May 1178 led to a decade of difficulties over the respective claims of John the Scot (who was elected by the Augustinian canons of St. Andrews without consulting the king) and Hugh the king's chaplain (who was nominated by the king and consecrated by some Scottish bishops at St. Andrews

[94] *Scot. Pont.*, 82–3, no. 83; *SES*, i, p. ccxlv, no. XIV.

[95] This presumably indicates that the Roman court had by this time accepted the plea of the bishop of Galloway not to be regarded as a bishop of the Scottish church.

[96] H&S, II, i, 249–50; *SAEC*, 270; *AMW*, 222–3. The nuncios were sent out from spring 1178 onwards (R. Foreville, *Latran I,II,III et Latran IV* [Paris, 1965], 135).

[97] H&S, II, i, 250.

[98] Foreville, *Latran*, 390.

[99] C. Burns, 'Two Scottish bishops consecrated at the Third Lateran Council', *Innes Review*, xi (1960), 68; cf. N. F. Shead, '. . . A correction', *Innes Review*, xxvii (1976), 162; *Series Episcoporum*, VI, i, 16–17, 37.

before the end of 1178).[100] There were to be many twists and turns in the subsequent dispute until at last in 1189 the king was able to arrange for the appointment to St. Andrews (and the acceptance there) of a bishop of his choice (Roger, his own chancellor); but successive popes had been involved from early 1179 once John the Scot had appealed to Rome against the 'intruder' Hugh, and they sent legates to Scotland at three stages of the dispute:

1. After annulling the election of Hugh,[101] Pope Alexander sent Alexis (or Alexius), a subdeacon of the Roman church, to Scotland as his legate to enquire into the validity of John the Scot's election to the see of St. Andrews;[102] he is said to have been appointed legate in Scotland, Ireland and The Isles to hear and determine ecclesiastical cases.[103] Arriving in Scotland through England with a safe-conduct from King Henry II, he was unwillingly admitted to the country by King William.[104] He held a legatine council with the 'bishops, abbots, priors and other prelates of the kingdom' at Holyrood Abbey, near Edinburgh, and after discussion ordered

[100] Watt, *Fasti*, 291–2; D. E. R. Watt, *A Biographical Dictionary of Scottish Graduates* (Oxford, 1977), 485–8; cf. *Chron. Holyrood*, 164, n. 4, Duncan, *Scotland*, 270–4, and Ferguson, *Papal Representatives*, 56–63 for the outlines of this story. It can be argued that the contradictory evidence for the year in which this election took place (e. g. *Chron. Bower*, iii, 373 [1177], and iv, 325 [1178] – the author is apparently following different sources) can best be explained in terms of 1177 rather than 1178 (A. D. M. Barrell, 'The background to *Cum universi*: Scoto-papal relations, 1159–1192', *Innes Review*, xlvi [1995], 120; cf. Ferguson, *Papal Representatives*, 56, n. 153). But the corollary of this view, that John the Scot was elected bishop at the legatine council held by Cardinal Vivian at Holyrood in August 1177 (see above p. 24) is such an unusual circumstance that it would surely have been mentioned in the voluminous contemporary evidence for this celebrated election and its aftermath; but it is not.

[101] *Scot. Pont.*, 88, no. 90.

[102] A general safe-conduct issued to him by the pope on 8 September 1178 to travel on papal business north of the Alps (*Neues Archiv*, vii [1882], 166–7) must surely relate to earlier business (cf. *Scot. Pont.*, 89, n. 1). See Ferguson, *Papal Representatives*, 57–9.

[103] *SAEC*, 271; *AMW*, 228. In an undated act in which he gives his decision in a dispute between the archbishop of York and Guisborough Priory in the North Riding of Yorkshire (which may date from either his journey north to Scotland or his return south), he mentions that he had legatine authority within England so long as he was engaged in establishing peace between the English king and the Irish (*Cartularium Prioratus de Gyseburne*, ii [Surtees Society, 1894], 49–50); but he is not known to have visited Ireland.

[104] *SAEC*, 273; *Chron. Melrose*, 43.

John's consecration there on 15 June 1180 by Matthew bishop of Aberdeen in the presence of three other bishops – and with the consent of a fifth bishop who was ill, but consented by letter.[105] At the same time he placed the diocese [*episcopatum*] of St. Andrews under interdict to try to secure obedience to his actions. But along with John and Matthew Alexis had to leave the kingdom very soon afterwards in fear of the wrath of the king, who continued to support Hugh.[106] Before he left, he reversed (in an undated act) one of Hugh's acts as bishop of St. Andrews dating from after the date of the annulment of his election; and we find him defining his legatine authority as given to him by the pope on the whole business of the church of St. Andrews, with full power to decide disputes.[107] He also ordered Hugh's excommunication for refusing to hand over the episcopal insignia, an act which he probably issued at the Holyrood council.[108] It was all a brave show of papal authority in Scotland, but certainly not one which solved the problem of the king's determination to have Hugh still as bishop of St. Andrews.

2. It was probably in the last months before his death on 30 August 1181 that Pope Alexander made a further attempt to use a legate to impose his will on King William. He chose to revive memories of the 1160s regarding the claims of Roger archbishop of York over the Scottish sees. Though his legatine powers over Scotland[109] appear to have lain dormant for nearly twenty years, they were now recalled or renewed after some contact with Alexis,[110] and he was ordered to threaten an interdict on the whole kingdom of Scotland and excommunication of the king if he kept refusing to accept Bishop John.[111] Since Roger was himself quite

[105] *SAEC*, 273, 276; *AMW*, 229, 232; *Chron. Melrose*, 43.

[106] *SAEC*, 274–5; *AMW*, 234; *Scot. Pont.*, 96, no. 100. See discussion in Ferguson, *Papal Representatives*, 58, n. 165.

[107] W. Holtzmann, *Papsturkunden in England*, i (Berlin, 1931), 451, no. 181 (cf. *Scot. Pont.*, 88, no. 91 for a later papal confirmation); the phrase is: 'qui [i.e. the pope] nobis super toto negotio ecclesie Sancti Andree et in causis decidendis plenitudinem potestatis commisit.'

[108] *Scot. Pont.*, 89–90, no. 92.

[109] See above nn. 70 and 73.

[110] *SAEC*, 272; *AMW*, 235.

[111] *Scot. Pont*, 97–9, no. 101. Note how in this letter the pope threatens to move towards a return of Scotland to its previous subjection, presumably to York (text in *AMW*, 230–1).

near to death (he was to die on 26 November 1181),[112] he was to use Hugh de Puiset bishop of Durham as his agent. Hugh did act in a negotiating capacity with King William at Redden near Roxburgh, probably August x September 1181, but was frustrated in his aim of getting John accepted, and had to break off relations by issuing the threatened sentences of interdict and excommunication.[113] It was another impasse.

3. A more flexible attitude was displayed by the next pope, Lucius III (1181–5). After receiving envoys from Scotland, he opened discussions again by lifting the interdict and excommunication on 17 March 1181/2.[114] About the same time he commissioned two new legates (Roland bishop-elect of Dol [in Brittany] and Silvan abbot of Rievaulx in Yorkshire) to go to Scotland to reopen the whole question of the dispute between Hugh and John, and revise Pope Alexander's judgment if it turned out that he had made a mistake or been deceived.[115] These legates duly came to Scotland and moved among the interested parties *c.* June 1182 before meeting the king himself at Roxburgh. There the king (rather than the legates) is said to have presided over a general discussion for three days (*tribus diebus generale concilium tenuit cum legatis domini Lucii pape*); but since no settlement was reached that suited all the parties, the matter was referred back to the Roman court.[116] As legates these envoys would have come with judicial powers from the pope like Alexis in 1180; but this time they did not preside over a legatine council; instead they behaved more as negotiators than as judges. As such they ultimately had some success, for their visit certainly helped towards the compromise settlement of the St. Andrews affair that was reached at the papal court in the following year.[117]

It would have been about this time that it is most likely that Lucius issued a bull 'confirming the liberties of the Scottish

[112] *HBC*, 281.

[113] *SAEC*, 279–80; *AMW*, 239–41.

[114] *SAEC*, 281–2; *AMW*, 243–5; *Scot. Pont.*, 103–4, no. 110.

[115] *Scot. Pont.*, 111–13, no. 117. This abbreviated text does not make it clear whether or not these envoys had legatine status; but in Scotland they were regarded by a contemporary chronicler as having that status (see next note). Cf. Ferguson, *Papal Representatives*, 61–3.

[116] *Chron. Holyrood*, 168–9; *SAEC*, 282–5; *AMW* 246–8.

[117] *SAEC*, 285–6; *AMW*, 249–50.

church', which is known to have existed still a hundred years later in 1282, but has since disappeared.[118] This was probably a reissue of *Super anxietatibus* of 1176,[119] perhaps redrafted to list by name the dioceses in Scotland whose bishops at this date were keen to ensure that there would never again be a revival of York's claim to metropolitan authority over them, i.e. the dioceses of St. Andrews, Glasgow, Dunkeld, Dunblane, Brechin, Aberdeen, Moray, Ross and Caithness – but not Whithorn/Galloway (whose loyalty to York was steadfast) nor Argyll (which had not yet been founded[120]). It was a time when there was a ten-year vacancy in the see of York, which helped to snuff out once-and-for-all the pretensions of that see to authority over the bishops of Scotland that had bedevilled relationships since 1072. And there is merit in the suggestion[121] that it was the consecration of an archbishop at York again in August 1191 which made it opportune to obtain from Pope Celestine III on 13 March 1191/2 the famous bull *Cum universi* which identified the said nine dioceses as the *Scoticana ecclesia* that as a whole was now regarded as a special daughter of the Apostolic See. Careful limits were laid down to ensure that papal authority in Scotland in matters of interdict or excommunication was to be exercised only by the pope himself or by a legate sent directly from the Roman court; legates [for lesser business] were to be either Scots or persons specially selected and sent from the Roman court by the pope; and appeals under the canon law arising from Scottish cases were not to be heard anywhere outside Scotland except at the Roman court.[122] Though York is not mentioned, it is clear that any claim to its metropolitan rights in Scotland (except Galloway) had now been demolished. The constitutional arrangement for a Scottish church comprising nine exempt dioceses, with no metropolitan except the pope, was

[118] *Scot. Pont.* 122, no. 131.

[119] See above n. 83.

[120] *Series Episcoporum*, VI, i, 11–12.

[121] Duncan, *Scotland*, 275.

[122] *Scot. Pont.*, 142–4, no. 156; *AMW*, 275–6. It has been argued (most recently in Barrell, 'The background' [see above n. 100], 128–38) that an earlier version of the bull *Cum universi* was issued by Pope Clement III in March 1188/9 and only re-issued by Celestine III in 1192 (as it was to be again by Innocent III in 1200 and Honorius III in 1218); the matter is ambiguous, but does not affect the story here.

now confirmed, and was to be unchallenged until 1472. This unique organisational phenomenon in Western Christendom had gained final recognition, at a time when there was no king in England available to protest.[123]

[123] Richard I did not return from crusading and imprisonment until March 1193/4 (*HBC*, 36).

3

Interim arrangements 1192–1225

FOR the time being the only way in which the prelates of this group of exempt dioceses could be called together was by a legate or other formal emissary acting on behalf of the pope; and between 1192 and the Fourth Lateran Council of 1215 examples occur of action by both kinds of legate that were envisaged in the *Cum universi* bull. That bull defined the sphere of activity of any such legates as the kingdom (*regnum*) of Scotland rather than the church (*ecclesia*) of Scotland, so that there was no need to change this definition as changes were made over the years in the dioceses regarded as part of that kingdom. It was probably almost immediately after 1192 that the diocese of Dunkeld was split into two by the formation of the diocese of Argyll in its western parts.[1] The position of the diocese of Galloway remained ambiguous. Though its bishops recognised the metropolitan authority of York until 1355,[2] it was long before then regarded in Roman eyes as grouped with the other dioceses of the Scottish kingdom for purposes of papal taxation. This was to be clearly demonstrated in the 1270s in the accounts kept by the papal collectors of the tax of a tenth authorised by the Second Council of Lyons in 1274.[3] Then once the Western Isles had been ceded politically by Norway to Scotland in 1266,[4] the diocese of The Isles (or Sodor) was by the time of the

[1] See *Series Episcoporum*, VI, i, 11–13 for ? 1192 x 1203 as the date for the erection of the see of Argyll.

[2] Watt, *Fasti*, 128.

[3] *Miscellany of The Scottish History Society* [*SHS Misc.*], vi (SHS, 1939), 26, 74–5.

[4] *The Acts of the Parliaments of Scotland* [*APS*] (Edinburgh, 1814–75), i, 420–1.

1291 taxation raised by Pope Nicholas IV being treated similarly by Rome along with the other dioceses of the Scottish kingdom,[5] even though it too continued until the mid-fourteenth century to accept at least some degree of metropolitan authority outside the kingdom, in this case that of Trondheim (or Nidaros).[6] But it was with the bishops of the kingdom as a whole, whether technically exempt from metropolitan authority or subject to it, that the popes found it convenient and practical to deal.

The legatine mission of John of Salerno, cardinal priest of St. Stephen on Monte Celio,[7] 1201–2 has left fuller documentation than is available for any of the earlier legatine visits to Scotland. It is not known who took the initiative in arranging this legation: if it was Pope Innocent III, it was clearly with the co-operation of King William, for John stayed long in Scotland, and the king is known to have settled at least one property dispute at his urging.[8] As with the legates sent in 1176 and 1178 his commission was to Ireland as well as Scotland.[9] His activities must therefore have been of interest also to King John, and he was allowed to exercise his legatine authority while travelling through England in the early autumn of 1201, when he perhaps held a council at London at the end of August.[10] He was at Perth by 3 December 1201, when he witnessed and sealed a grant in favour of Coupar Angus Abbey.[11] This must have been done on the eve of the legatine council which

[5] *The Register of John de Halton, Bishop of Carlisle, A.D. 1291–1324* (Canterbury and York Society, 1913), i, 153, etc.

[6] Watt, *Fasti*, 197.

[7] He ranked as a cardinal 1191–1208 (C. Eubel, *Hierarchia Catholica Medii Aevi*, 2nd edition [Munster, 1913–23], i, 4, 47). See Ferguson, *Papal Representatives*, 65–71.

[8] *RRS*, ii, 412, no. 440.

[9] See his own description of his office, e.g. *AMW*, 333. There was no mention in his official style this time of The Isles or Norway (cf. SES, i, p. xl, n. 2; and see below p. 40 for practice in 1220); but the grant of exemption to the newly founded Benedictine monastery on Iona in Sodor diocese on 9 December 1203 (*Le Liber Censuum de l'Église Romaine*, ed. L. Duchesne, P. Fabre and G. Mollat, 3 vols. (Paris, 1889–1952), i, 80; *Medieval Religious Houses Scotland* [*MRHS*], 2nd edition, ed. I. B. Cowan and D. E. Easson [London, 1976], 59) may well have followed a report by him (cf. below p. 34, at n. 21)

[10] *C&S*, I, ii, 1074–5.

[11] *Charters of the Abbey of Coupar Angus*, ed. D. E. Easson (SHS, 1947), i, 24–5, no. 11.

he is known to have held there for three days, one of which was 6 December.[12]

In the near-contemporary Chronicle of Melrose this council was remembered for his ruling on many matters that were to be observed.[13] This was probably the first time that the recently-recognised Scottish church had experience of the efforts being made from Rome to bring its local customs into harmony with the canons of the Western church that were being progressively codified. In at least three acts arising from this council (including that dated 6 December) reference was made to canons of the Third Lateran Council of 1179.[14] One theme that had been raised at Perth concerned problems regarding the proper status of churches belonging to the exempt Tironensian monastery at Kelso that lay in the two dioceses of St. Andrews and Glasgow (which provides a good example of the utility of a legatine visit to a country that had no metropolitan to impose inter-diocesan uniformity in such matters). The chronicle tradition preserved by Walter Bower in the mid-fifteenth century[15] specified from all the business done at this council only that it ordered that priests who had been ordained on a Sunday were to be removed from office: this was just one of the stricter rules for the conferment of priestly orders which were being formulated by the late-twelfth-century popes, and which were no doubt being included in the many different collections of canons that were in 1234 to be superseded by the papally-authorised *Decretals* of Gregory IX.[16]

The chronicle accounts of the composition of this council are pretty general, namely 'bishops, abbots and prelates, and other clerks of high estate both religious and secular'.[17] From two documentary witness-lists[18] it is clear that at least six bishops were

[12] *AMW*, 332–3; *Chron. Bower*, iv, 429.

[13] *Chron. Melrose*, 51 (*ibidemque multa constituit observanda*).

[14] *AMW*, 333–7; cf. canons 4 and 8 of the Third Lateran Council (*Decrees of the Ecumenical Councils*, ed. N. P. Tanner [London and Washington DC, 1990], 213–14, 215).

[15] *Chron. Bower*, iv, 429.

[16] X 1.11.1, see *Corpus Iuris Canonici* [CIC], ed. E. Friedberg (Leipzig, 1879–81), ii, col. 118.

[17] *The Original Chronicle of Andrew of Wyntoun* [*Chron. Wyntoun*], ed. F. J. Amours (Scottish Text Society, 1903–14), v, 46.

[18] *AMW*, 334; *Coupar Angus Chrs.*, i, 24–5, no. 11.

present (St. Andrews, Glasgow, Aberdeen, Dunkeld, Moray and Ross),[19] and seven abbots (Kelso, Arbroath, Lindores, Kilwinning [all O.Tiron.], Melrose [O.Cist.], Holyrood and Jedburgh [O.S.A.]), the dean of Glasgow, and the archdeacons of Lothian and Glasgow; but this selection of prelates is probably limited to those concerned with the particular bits of business which they were witnessing.

At some stage during his visit (before the death of Roger bishop of St. Andrews on 1 July 1202) Legate John joined with the king in supervising an agreement between Earl Duncan (of Fife) and the church of St. Andrews regarding the patronage of certain churches.[20] He also arranged for the name of another leading nobleman, Gilchrist earl of Mar, to be inserted in the list of those privileged to pay census to the pope.[21] In the case of monasteries named in such a list there is implied an element of protection by the Holy See that was somehow worth paying for, with sometimes a degree of exemption from local episcopal jurisdiction;[22] but what was the appeal of such expenditure for a layman is not clear. At some date in 1202 (probably after 25 March) he deposed an abbot of Dunfermline, O.S.B., and apparently arranged a replacement;[23] and at some unknown date he appropriated a church to the revenues of Scone Abbey.[24] Then he made for Ireland, taking with him Radulf abbot of Melrose to be installed there as bishop of Down.[25] He held two councils at Dublin and Athlone sometime in 1202,[26] and became involved in the complicated problems associated with the election of an archbishop of Armagh, regarding which he had to write to the pope for

[19] Note that there is no sign of a bishop of Galloway (see above p. 24).

[20] *Calendar of Entries in the Papal Registers relating to Great Britain and Ireland: Papal Letters* [*CPL*], ed. W. H. Bliss and others (London, 1893–), i, 14; full text of this papal confirmation dated 17 June 1203 is in *Die Register Innocenz' III*, vi (Vienna, 1995), 148, no. 91.

[21] *Liber Censuum*, i, 232; see also *CPL*, i, 476. Cf. Ferguson, *Papal Representatives*, 71, n. 41.

[22] Cf. W. E. Lunt, *Financial Relations of the Papacy with England to 1327* (Cambridge, Mass., 1939), 85–129, c. 2.

[23] *Chron. Bower*, iv, 429.

[24] *Liber Ecclesie de Scon* [*Scone Liber*] (Bannatyne Club, 1843), 65–6, no. 102.

[25] *Chron. Melrose*, 51; *Chron. Bower*, iv, 429.

[26] *The Annals of Loch Cé* (Rolls Series, 54), i, 227.

guidance on how to proceed.[27] He returned to Scotland while awaiting the pope's instructions (which seem not to have been issued until September), being apparently on his way back when at Lochmaben in Dumfries-shire he settled a local church patronage dispute in favour of the bishop of Glasgow on 10 July 1202.[28] He was presumably at Scone near Perth 18/20 September, when his agreement was given to the king's request for the translation of William Malveisin from the see of Glasgow to that of St. Andrews;[29] and either before or after that date he is reported to have spent 'fifty nights and more' at Melrose Abbey, involved for so remarkably long a time in fruitlessly trying to resolve disputes between the monks there and those of Kelso; the local chronicler lamented that he accepted gifts from both parties without settling the dispute before he left.[30] This sour note probably derives from that fact that when the king took at least part of the matter up later, he was to decide firmly in favour of Kelso.[31] The legate did, however, resolve some outstanding differences between Kelso and the new bishop of St. Andrews by mediating between them at some unknown date and place (presumably late in 1202) in a large assembly of clergy from the dioceses of St. Andrews and Glasgow.[32] Again it was in Scotland only a legate whose authority could cross diocesan boundaries. By Christmas 1202 he had left Scotland again, and was at York on his way back to Ireland.[33] Rome was still addressing him as legate there on 20 February 1203; but he left later in the year without resolving the issue at Armagh.[34]

The exercise of legatine authority on a different scale (but still within the terms of *Cum universi*) is illustrated in 1213.[35] In April of that year Pope Innocent III issued general letters conveying

[27] *Pontificia Hibernica*, ed. M. P. Sheehy (Dublin, 1962–5), i, 116–21, no. 52.

[28] *AMW*, 334–5. In contemporary England such a case would have come before the royal court.

[29] *AMW*, 343; *Chron. Bower*, iii, 393.

[30] *Chron. Melrose*, 51.

[31] *RRS*, ii, 412–13, no. 440.

[32] *Liber S. Marie de Calchou* [*Kelso Liber*] (Bannatyne Club, 1846), ii, 333–4, no. 434.

[33] Ferguson, *Papal Representatives*, 67, n. 16; cf. 66, n. 5.

[34] *Pontificia Hibernica*, i, 121–2, no. 53, and 120, n. 8.

[35] For discussions of the varying powers of different types of legate see *DDC*, vi, cols. 371–4, and *New Catholic Enyclopaedia*, viii, 607.

legatine authority for preaching and collecting money in various provinces of the church for the crusade: in Scotland this duty was imposed on Bishops William Malveisin of St. Andrews and Walter de St. Albans of Glasgow jointly.[36] It was presumably sometime later in the same year that these two bishops held a legatine council at Perth in terms of this particular commission, and as a result many took the cross.[37] Here is an example again (as in 1159) of legatine powers being entrusted to Scots living in their home dioceses, when no one was being sent *a latere*, i.e. from the curia itself. The fifteenth-century chronicler Walter Bower was particularly well informed about events in Scotland in the early years of the thirteenth century,[38] and from him we learn about the composition of this legatine council: it comprised bishops, prelates and clergy, and also (as was said to be customary – but whether this means then or when the chronicle was written is unclear) some people from other walks of life ('aliorum statuum') at the king's command. The precise implications of this phraseology are irrecoverable: when crusading was in question, the main point was to get through to the laity; but it would be likely that they were summoned to legatine councils only when business of this kind was on the agenda. The royal interest in what went on in church councils held within Scotland was surely nothing new: the king in practice always defined the parameters within which the *Scoticana ecclesia* was allowed to run its affairs or associate itself with wider church standards and ideals.

On 19 April 1213 Pope Innocent issued his summons to a general council of the church to meet at in the church of the Lateran at Rome two-and-a-half years later on 1 November 1215. The bishops of Scotland as a group were on the distribution list. By implication all but one or two were to come in person, together with some abbots and priors and representatives of the cathedral chapters.[39] In the event just four bishops from Scotland are known

[36] *CPL*, i, 38; cf. Lunt, *Financial Relations*, 423–4 for discussion of similar legatine powers granted to two Englishmen to work within England. But see Ferguson, *Papal Representatives*, 72–3 for doubts regarding the legatine status of these two bishops.

[37] *Chron. Bower*, iv, 473.

[38] Cf. ibid., iv, pp. xxiii–xxiv.

[39] *CPL*, i, 38; Patrologiae Cursus Completus Series Latina, ed. J. P. Migne (Paris, 1844–55), 216, col. 825; Foreville, *Latran*, 328–9.

to have attended the month-long deliberations (William Malveisin of St. Andrews, Walter de St. Albans of Glasgow, Brice de Douglas of Moray, and Adam of Caithness). One abbot (Henry of Kelso) probably went also, together with some unnamed representatives of other prelates.[40] It is strange that the Melrose chronicler omitted the name of Bishop Adam from this list, for he had until as recently as 1213 x 1214 been abbot of Melrose;[41] perhaps he was unwilling to record the unfortunate fact that Bishop Adam along with the bishops of Glasgow and Moray was to become so involved about the time of the council in the Scottish policy of opposition to the papally-protected King John of England and his successor King Henry III to the extent that the three of them were to have to return in Rome in 1218 to seek absolution from the excommunication which they had incurred;[42] or perhaps it was painful to recall that it was as a consequence of trying to put into effect the Lateran Council's backing for the payment of teind that Bishop Adam was in 1222 to be murdered by some of the indignant peasant farmers of his diocese.[43] Just as Archbishop Stephen Langton of Canterbury was to have to remain abroad after the meeting of the council until May 1218,[44] so for unknown reasons did the bishop of Glasgow until 1217 and the bishop of St. Andrews until January 1218.[45] But all four of the Scottish bishops who had attended the council must have eventually brought home an awareness of the newly-defined standards of faith and order in the church which the seventy-one canons of the council contain.[46]

[40] Ibid., 392; cf. ibid., 253, where these Scottish bishops have been seen as sitting in the 'wake' of the archbishop of York (cf. ibid., 390 for arrangements in 1179); cf. *Chron. Melrose*, 61; see *RRS*, ii, 32–3, 379 for name of the bishop of Glasgow, and Watt, *Fasti*, 214 for name of the bishop of Moray.

[41] J. Dowden, *The Bishops of Scotland* (Glasgow, 1912), 233–4.

[42] *Chron. Melrose*, 71; *CPL*, i, 55, 59; Watt, *Dictionary*, 377, for the bishop of St. Andrews. The supporters of of the barons against King John were excommunicated at the council (*Selected Letters of Pope Innocent III concerning England* (*1198–1216*), ed. C. R. Cheney and W. H. Semple (Edinburgh and London, 1953), 221–3, no. 85).

[43] Duncan, *Scotland*, 528.

[44] *Chron. Melrose*, 70.

[45] Ibid., 61, 70.

[46] Tanner, *Decrees*, 230–71; *English Historical Documents 1189–1327*, ed. H. Rothwell (London, 1975), 643–76.

A chance to make moves towards putting at least some of these canons into effect in Scotland came when King Alexander II took the initiative in re-establishing normal relations with the papacy.[47] He probably supported his chancellor William de Bosco and Bishop Douglas of Moray when in November 1218 they secured through agents personal absolution for their anti-English activities,[48] and at the same time arranged for the instructions being drafted for Pandulf the new papal legate to England to include a review of an old treaty between the late Kings William and John that was now unwelcome.[49] The pope also renewed on 21 November 1218 the *Cum universi* privilege of 1192 which confirmed the right of the Scottish church to independence under Rome.[50] Recent interference from England by the legate Guala Bicchieri had been justifiable in terms of that privilege, for he had been the pope's authorised agent when engaged in defending the rights of the English monarch during the minority of the young King Henry III; but the rules of 1192 emphasised that in normal circumstances the Scottish church was free to follow Rome in its own way. Once a political settlement was reached between the kings of England and Scotland under the guidance of the legate Pandulf at York on 15 June 1220 and sealed by a royal marriage a year later on 19 June 1221,[51] the way was once again clear.

In fact the first council of prelates known to have assembled in Scotland after the Lateran Council was a consequence of the decision in c. 71 of its canons that 'all clerics, both those under authority and prelates, shall give a twentieth of their ecclesiastical revenues for three years to the aid of the Holy Land, by means of the persons appointed by the apostolic see for the purpose'.[52] Innocent III had subsequently appointed collectors for this tax in various provinces of the church, and after his death in July 1216 Honorius III pressed on with its assessment and collection on a

[47] *Chron. Fordun*, i, 288.

[48] *CPL*, i, 59; A. Theiner, *Vetera Monumenta Hibernorum et Scotorum Historiam Illustrantia* (Rome, 1864), 6–7. Cf. Ferguson, *Papal Representatives*, 80, n. 91.

[49] *CPL*, i, 59–60; Theiner, *Monumenta*, 7.

[50] Stones, *Documents*, 14–16, no. 5.

[51] Duncan, *Scotland*, 525–6.

[52] Tanner, *Decrees*, 269; Rothwell, *Documents*, 674; cf. *Chron. Melrose*, 60–1, where the writer shows knowledge of the official record.

scale previously unknown in Christendom. In England the successive legates Guala and Pandulf seem likely to have been made responsible overall, and much was collected in the years 1217–20; and by 24 July 1220 the bulk of this money had already been sent to the Holy Land.[53] There must have been a parallel exercise in Scotland too over a similar period of time; but all that we know about it is a brief note from a lost chronicle preserved in Bower's *Scotichronicon*[54] to the effect that in '1220' a papal nuncio called 'dominus Egidius' held a meeting of 'all the prelates of Scotland', where he collected ('recepit') the three-year twentieth as had been ordered at the recent Lateran Council. This nuncio has customarily been identified with Giles de Torres of Spain, cardinal deacon of SS. Cosmas and Damian since 1216.[55] But it seems more likely (as argued in the new edition of the *Scotichronicon*) that he was the Master Giles de Verracclo, papal subdeacon and chaplain, who was a brother of the Pandulf who was legate in England, and who like Pandulf is known to have been handling papal funds before 22 September 1220, in his case at Paris.[56] This would be in harmony with the known policy of Honorius to use from 1218 onwards members of his household to supersede or supervise local collectors.[57] It is significant that the contemporary Melrose chronicler makes no mention of the collection of this twentieth other than to say that it was ordered by the Lateran Council:[58] the explanation lies in the apparent exemption of Cistercian abbeys from this tax.[59] In fact this meeting of prelates called by a papal

[53] Lunt, *Financial Relations*, 242–7.

[54] *Chron. Bower*, v, 113, and notes at 241–2. Cf. Ferguson, *Papal Representatives*, 84–5.

[55] *SES*, i, p. xlii; cf. Eubel, *Hierarchia*, i, 5, 49. For the activities of Cardinal Gil Torres see P. Linehan, *The Spanish Church and the Papacy in the Thirteenth Century* (Cambridge, 1971), especially 276–95.

[56] *CPL*, i, 76; cf. ibid., 58; for his surname and death in 1241 (probably still in papal service), see A. P. Bagliani, *Cardinali di Curia* (Padua, 1972), ii, 523–4; perhaps held archdeaconry of Ely between 1219 and 1228 (John Le Neve, *Fasti 1066–1300*, ii, 51); he is styled 'germanus' to Pandulf in 1226 (*Regesta Honorii III* [Rome, 1888–95], ii, no. 6032; cf. also nos. 4815, 5995).

[57] Lunt, *Financial Relations*, 244, 246.

[58] As above n. 52.

[59] Lunt, *Financial Relations*, 243. The Melrose chronicler is not specific, but does say that members of some religious orders were exempt ('exceptis quibusdam religiosis' [*Chron. Melrose*, 61]).

nuncio (whose powers were presumably limited to his tax-collecting duties) was recorded in Scotland only in the fifteenth century from a source that is now lost.[60]

Already by 31 July 1220 a more authoritative papal legate (specifically *a latere*) had been appointed to visit Ireland, Scotland and The Isles,[61] presumably with the agreement of the legate Pandulf in England and of King Alexander II in Scotland. This was Master James, another member of the papal household (this time a chaplain and penitentiary), who was also an Augustinian canon of St. Victor near Paris.[62] Some outstanding problems from both Ireland and Scotland which had been brought to the papal court for solution were on 6–8 August 1220 referred to him for solution, including on-going litigation which had been raised by St. Andrews cathedral priory against their bishop (William Malveisin) and others.[63] These disputes had been troublesome for some years,[64] but were presumably not the only reason for sending a legate. Perhaps the king had sent his clerk Thomas de Stirling to ask for the legate to be sent, since Master James was instructed to grant him the favour of a dispensation to hold several benefices at once, and on 15 December 1220 local mandatories in Scotland were alternatively instructed to act in this matter if the legate had not yet arrived in Scotland.[65] In fact he seems to have reached Scotland about Christmas 1220,[66] and he certainly held a 'general council' of 'the prelates of the whole realm' at Perth for four days

[60] As above n. 54.

[61] *CPL*, i, 74; Theiner, *Monumenta*, 15–16, no. 35.

[62] *Chron. Melrose*, 72; the identity of this man is discussed in Bagliani, *Cardinali*, i, 118–19. He appears to have been with the legate Pandulf in London on 22 September 1219, when the king of The Isles submitted to the pope (Theiner, *Monumenta*, 11, no. 26). He is given the surname 'Penciail' in *Annals of Loch Cé* (Rolls Series, 54), i, 263–4. Cf. Ferguson, *Papal Representatives*, 85–8.

[63] *CPL*, i, 74–5; Theiner, *Monumenta*, 16–17, nos. 36–9 (no. 39 is misdated); see discussion in Barrow, *Kingdom*, 215–16.

[64] Watt, *Dictionary*, 378–9.

[65] *CPL*, i, 77; Theiner, *Monumenta*, 18, no. 42; Stirling became archdeacon of Glasgow in 1222 (Watt, *Fasti*, 171) and was later king's chancellor (*HBC*, 181).

[66] *Chronicon de Lanercost* [*Chron. Lanercost*] (Maitland Club, 1839), i, 29, wrongly dated 1221. He had first visited Ireland (Ferguson, *Papal Representatives*, 86, n. 133).

starting 9 February 1220/1.[67] There is no specific record of what was done at this council rather than at other times during the legate's visit to Scotland. He appears to have solved the St. Andrews litigation, of which no more is known. He became involved in an attempt that was made to have the current marriage of Alan, lord of Galloway and constable of Scotland, to an unnamed lady set aside on the grounds of consanguinity. The initiative seems to have come from the couple, perhaps as part of a political act against the reigning King Alexander, who had little or no support from either Alan or his brother Thomas.[68] The legate may well have discussed this matter at his council, for he claimed the support of several Scottish bishops when he wrote to the pope for instructions in this case; he was told in reply to assemble the bishops of the realm and take such action as seemed best. But as Alan's proctor was returning from Rome with these instructions, he met the legate already on his way back from Scotland, so that this procedure was not possible. Instead three English bishops were on 30 March 1222 instructed to proceed in this matter.[69] It may be that even a legate had to seek further instructions in this case because of the particular circumstances of the see of Galloway to which Alan belonged as lord of Galloway. That see was a suffragan of York, and as in 1176–7[70] there may have been a claim that his authority as legate to Scotland did not qualify him to deal with a Galloway case. Alternatively there may have been problems in interpreting the procedures laid down in canons 50–2 of the Fourth Lateran Council which dealt with cases of consanguinity. Whatever the problem, this case was one which even a legatine council could not solve without further papal instructions. Perhaps the need for co-ordinated action by the Scottish bishops which emerged over this case brought home to them as well as to the legate and the pope the difficulties that could arise for a group of exempt dioceses without a metropolitan as confirmed in the bull *Cum universi*. Surely the report of the legate James after his experiences in Scotland in 1221 must have

[67] *Chron. Melrose*, 72, 75; *Chron. Bower*, v, 113.

[68] Duncan, *Scotland*, 529–30; see *The Scots Peerage*. ed. Sir J. Balfour Paul (Edinburgh, 1904–14), i, 419–22 and iv, 139–43 for this family.

[69] Theiner, *Monumenta*, 20–1, no. 48; cf. *CPL*, i, 87.

[70] See above p. 24.

been material in preparing the way for the revised papal privilege that was to come in 1225.

The hand of Legate James can be traced in three other matters, even though they cannot be shown to have been mentioned at the Perth council. He advanced the Augustinian priory of Inchaffray in Dunblane diocese to the status of an abbey.[71] He was at Kelso in Roxburghshire on 17 April 1221 when he gave papal confirmation to an endowment for the bishop of Moray's table.[72] But he had his detractors because of the actions of some members of his entourage, and he got little sympathy from the pope for this.[73] At the same time during this visit he was being urged by King Alexander to perform an unprecedented coronation ceremony. The pope was quick to forbid this unless and until the young English king and his counsellors should agree to it.[74] If this reveals the ulterior motive behind an initial request from the king for a legate to visit Scotland, James's visit must have ended in disappointment when the pope chose to maintain his policy of providing every protection for the rights of the young English king, and even to emphasise how 'it is said that' the Scottish king was subject to (*subesse*) the English king.[75] The pope was not yet ready to support Scottish political pretensions.

[71] *Chron. Bower*, v, 113.

[72] *Registrum Episcopatus Moraviensis* [*Moray Registrum*] (Bannatyne Club, 1837), 16–17, no. 22.

[73] *CPL*, i, 83.

[74] Ibid.; see full text in *SES*, i, p. xlv, n. 2 (from *Raynaldi Annales*). This text is undated, but was copied into the papal registers along with other letters of the papal year ending July 1221. It must surely date from at least three to four months after James's arrival in Scotland; cf. different dating suggested in *ES*, ii, 443.

[75] Cf. Duncan, *Scotland*, 526.

4

Establishment of the Scottish provincial council 1225–1239

POPE Honorius was, however, soon to respond to suggestions from the Scottish bishops that his recognition in 1218 of their exempt status directly under Rome required the development of special administrative arrangements to make this workable when Scotland was so far away from the papal curia. Most other dioceses that came directly under Rome were in Italy and so easily subject to papal supervision. There was a handful of other single dioceses that were similarly exempt from the usual metropolitan authority, but nowhere outside Italy were there as many as ten dioceses together without a metropolitan.[1] It had been recognised by canon 26 of the Fourth Lateran Council that though bishops of exempt dioceses should if possible approach the pope in person for confirmation after election to their sees, proper supervision of this kind was not practicable in the case of candidates for distant posts.[2] The sending of legates so far away as Scotland (as in 1221) was presumably not possible on a frequent basis. It is probable therefore that it was from discussions then between the Legate James and the Scottish bishops that there emerged the suggestion that they should ask the pope to agree to issue a special privilege suitable for the unusual circumstances, authorising the bishops of Scotland to hold their own provincial council as a layer of authority between the individual dioceses and the distant Roman

[1] See list in *Liber Censuum*, ii, 104–6 dating from the late twelfth century.

[2] Tanner, *Decrees*, 247; Rothwell, *Documents*, iii, 656–7.

see. The outcome was the pope's mandate letter addressed to the bishops of the kingdom of Scotland as a group dated 19 May 1225:[3]

> Honorius, bishop, servant of the servants of God, to his venerable brethren all the bishops of the kingdom of Scotland, greeting and apostolic benediction. Certain of you have recently informed us that since you did not have an archbishop by whose authority you could hold a provincial council,[4] it has the effect that in the kingdom of Scotland, which is so remote from the Apostolic See, the statutes of the general council are disregarded and very many irregularities are committed which remain unpunished. Now since provincial councils should not be overlooked, at which careful consideration should be given under fear of God to the censure of transgressions and the correction of manners [*mores*], and the rules of the canon law should be rehearsed and preserved, especially the statutes of the same general council, by this Apostolic letter to you we command [*mandamus*] that, since you are known not to have a metropolitan, you hold a provincial council by our authority. Dated at Tivoli [near Rome] 19 May in the ninth year of our pontificate [1225].

There is no doubt that this instruction to the Scottish bishops was drafted in the light of the general rules for annual provincial councils which the Lateran Council had recently instructed metropolitan archbishops to hold throughout the church; and we know that by 1237 at least the Scottish church was thought at Rome to recognise only the Roman church as its 'mother and metropolitan with no intermediary'.[5] Canon 6 had laid it down that reports on matters requiring correction or reform were to be assembled

[3] Translated here from the Latin in *SES*, ii, 3, which follows the text in *Registrum Episcopatus Aberdonensis* [*Aberdeen Registrum*] (Spalding and Maitland Clubs, 1845), ii, 3; another text with minor variants is in *Moray Registrum*, 332, no. 257. This letter of justice in the form of a papal mandate (note the main verb *mandamus*) does not correspond closely with the various types of mandate used by Pope Honorius III which have been identified in J. E. Sayers, *Papal Government and England during the Pontificate of Honorius III (1216–1227)* (Cambridge, 1984), ad indicem; but for a not dissimilar papal mandate of 1223 to the English clergy see *Royal and other Historical Letters illustrative of the Reign of Henry III* (Rolls Series, 27), i, 211–12, no. 190.

[4] For the general rule that only a metropolitan archbishop could hold or authorise a council, see Gratian's *Decretum*, D. 18 c. 4 (*CIC*, i, col. 54).

[5] *ecclesia Scoticana Romanam ecclesiam solam matrem et metropolitanam nullo medio recognoscit* (Theiner, *Monumenta*, 35, no. 90).

throughout the year in each diocese of each province. After these reports had been dealt with at a provincial council, each local bishop was to hold his own synod annually to ensure that the decisions made at provincial level were enforced. And canon 30 had ordered an annual review at each meeting of the provincial council into the way patronage over ecclesiastical benefices was being exercised by heads of churches and corporate chapters, with the council having the power to remove erring patrons and substitute others.[6] In 1225 it was still early days after the heady weeks of the Lateran Council ten years before, and the bishops of St. Andrews and Glasgow in office were still the same men who had taken part in that council. The fact that the initiative for a new and unprecedented administrative mechanism in the Scottish church came from them is a measure of the continuing urge for reform with which the Lateran Council had enthused church leaders in many branches of the Western church.[7]

The text of Honorius' mandate of 1225 has essentially a disciplinary air. The meetings of the provincial council are to be occasions for reminding the participants of both recent and more long-standing rules of the canon law. The council is to provide a single ecclesiastical court for the Scottish kingdom, which is clearly a big and most desirable step forward in a country of bishops all equal to each other. The scope of the council's jurisdiction is defined in very general terms, with a presumption of first instance as well as appellate cases. And when it comes to 'correction of manners' (a phrase taken from the Lateran canon 6), the Latin word *mores* is ambiguous: it could alternatively have meant 'morals' or 'customs'; but whatever the modern equivalent in English, it has been pointed out that it could include matters such as matrimonial disputes within its definition.[8] Provincial councils were meant to be a permanent feature of the church's legislative, judicial and administrative

[6] Tanner, *Decrees*, 236–7, 249; Rothwell, *Documents*, 648, 658.

[7] But cf. the cautious comment that has been made regarding the effects of the Council in England: 'A certain effort was undoubtedly made, but it was in most cases too tentative to bring about a fundamental and spiritual reformation in the English church' (M. Gibbs and J. Lang, *Bishops and Reform 1215–1272* [Oxford, 1934], 130).

[8] C. R. Cheney, *English Synodalia in the Thirteenth Century* (Oxford, 1941/1968), 28–9; cf. 8.

authority in the various local branches of the church. It has been argued that the mandate for Scotland in 1225 was intended to authorise a single council meeting;[9] but this was clearly not the case, for in terms of the Lateran Council thinking such councils were meant to meet annually. We should not start, however, by assuming that the Lateran legislation was necessarily fully effective. It was not widely enforced in France, where, for example, in the province of Rouen only nine provincial councils were held in the twenty-five years 1245–70.[10] And in England in the hundred years after 1215 there were perhaps only eighty-one councils held for Canterbury province or all England, apart from fifteen exceptional legatine ones.[11] Hostiensis in the 1250s was to assert that few metropolitans kept the rule.[12] But the rule was meant to be a more manageable and moderate one than previous canons which had ineffectively ordered the holding of provincial councils even more frequently than once a year.[13]

It was apparently not considered necessary to define the composition of the council that was now authorised. The Lateran canon 6 had mentioned simply that metropolitans were to meet with their suffragan bishops. We must therefore consider the evidence for any meetings of the bishops of Scotland as qualifying for inclusion in a list of councils held under the authority of the mandate of 1225: we shall soon find that those meetings which have left traces behind them have normally included also various regular and secular clergy in addition to the bishops. This may well have been the accepted practice in the legatine councils of the previous hundred years, so much so that it did not have to be spelled out in terms of who had the duty to attend or of those who had this privilege. Less understandable is the fact that the papal mandate made no mention of how the first meeting of the new council was to be called. Nor were any arrangements laid down for how it was to conduct its business, either at its meetings, or in the execution of its decisions. All we can assume is that a first

[9] *SES*, i, p. l, n. 1.

[10] O. Pontal, *Les Statuts Synodaux* (Turnhout, 1975), 28; cf. 9–30.

[11] *HBC*, 592–4. For Spain see P. Linehan, 'Councils and synods in thirteenth-century Castile and Aragon', in *Councils and Assemblies*, ed. G. J. Cuming and D. Baker (Cambridge, 1971), 101–11.

[12] Cited in E. W. Kemp, *Counsel and Consent* (London, 1961), 44.

[13] *DDC*, iii, col. 1272.

meeting was called somehow in 1225 or soon afterwards, and that the consitutional arrangements for which there is later evidence were soon agreed.

The first hint of a possible meeting of the council comes in some evidence that was looking back from 10 October 1232, when an agreement was reached between the bishop of Moray and the landed magnate David de Strathbogie concerning among other things the right of parish priests to enjoy common pasture for their animals throughout their parishes. This right is said to have been 'defined and laid down by the bishops of the kingdom of Scotland in their council'.[14] The date of this council is unknown, but must have been between 1225 and 1232. Interestingly enough the bishop of Glasgow is known to have been busy on 21 July 1225 and 8 January 1227 persuading the earls of Carrick and Lennox respectively to agree to respect the same right of pasture on their estates 'in accordance with the traditions of the Holy Fathers and the statutes of Holy Church';[15] but here the language of the documents is too vague to allow it to be suggested that this bishop too is referring to an early meeting of the new provincial council.[16] It may well be, of course, that some of the individual statutes of the provincial council which are now known in codified form dating from the 1240s (see below) were in fact first passed very early in the council's history; but since proof of such possibilities is not available, it is better to consider now the evidence for councils which were definitely held.

The first dated council that can be traced was held at Dundee in '1230'.[17] It was attended by at least six bishops, two abbots, two archdeacons (of St. Andrews and Dunkeld) and two *magistri*

[14] *est provisum et constitutum de episcopis regni Scoticani in concilio eorundem* (*Moray Registrum*, 29, no. 35).

[15] *Registrum Episcopatus Glasguensis* [*Glasgow Registrum*] (Bannatyne and Maitland Clubs, 1843) i, 117, 119, nos. 139, 141.

[16] The reference in 1232 has been taken as indicating that canon 92 of the later collected Statutes of the Scottish Church had already been passed (D. B. Smith, 'A note on a Moray charter', *SHR*, xix [1922], 115–17; cf. D. M. Williamson, 'The Legate Otto in Scotland and Ireland 1237–40', *SHR*, xxviii [1949], 23); but all three references in this paragraph must surely provide background to canon 92 rather than be a product of it, for its content is clearly different.

[17] *Miscellany of the Scottish History Society*, viii (*SHS*, 1951), 5–6, no. 1.

(who were probably in the followings of the bishops of St. Andrews and Glasgow respectively). We know about this occasion only through an amicable agreement reached 'in concilio' between the abbeys of Arbroath O.Tiron. in Angus and Balmerino O.Cist. in Fife over the leasing of the revenues of a parish church, which was witnessed by the distinguished group listed above. The meeting of a council was apparently an occasion for settling a tricky problem between abbeys in the same diocese of St. Andrews but belonging to two different orders.[18]

Then on 1 July 1238 a 'council' was held at Perth which was attended by at least four bishops (at a time when the bishop of St. Andrews was dying elsewhere[19]), four abbots, the archdeacon and dean of Glasgow, and a doctor of theology.[20] Bishop Clement of Dunblane was much engaged about this time in securing better endowments for his see,[21] and one product of this council was a decision in a dispute between him and the earl of Menteith over financial arrangements affecting both Dunblane Cathedral and a new Augustinian priory which the earl was founding at Inchmahome in Dunblane diocese.[22] Though the matter appears to be an internal one affecting that diocese only, perhaps Bishop Clement was glad of the backing of his ecclesiastical colleagues to help him impose an advantageous deal on the earl.

The next year saw a visit to Scotland of a papal legate once again. This was Cardinal Otto da Tonengo, who was based in England as legate from July 1237 until January 1241, and who in November 1237 held his celebrated legatine council at London, when he published a series of thirty-one constitutions of lasting importance for the English church.[23] His separate commission as a legate to Scotland was apparently an afterthought, for it was dated only on 7/10 May 1237 when Otto was already on his way

[18] *MRHS*, 66–7, 72–3.

[19] Watt, *Dictionary*, 379.

[20] Peter de Ramsay (ibid., 460–3).

[21] Ibid., 101.

[22] *Liber Insule Missarum* (Bannatyne Club, 1847), pp. xxix–xxxii; W. Fraser, *The Red Book of Menteith* (Edinburgh, 1880), ii, 328; cf. *MRHS*, 91–2.

[23] *C&S*, II, i, 237–59; D. M. Williamson, 'Some aspects of the legation of Cardinal Otto in England, 1237–41', *English Historical Review* [*EHR*], lxiv (1949), 159–60. See Bagliani, *Cardinali*, i, 76–97 for this cardinal. See Ferguson, *Papal Representatives*, 89–96.

to England.[24] This was a time when Bishop Clement of Dunblane was active at the papal court, and it would have been in character for him to encourage the pope to make this arrangement and perhaps offer to help to make it work.[25] Probably King Alexander was quite suspicious of it, for in recent years the pope had been responding more favourably to English diplomacy at the curia than to his own.[26] But one of the legate's first concerns was to carry out a papal mandate dated 24/27 March 1237 to make peace between the kings of England and Scotland;[27] and this he achieved at York on 25 September 1237 when both kings reached what was to be a lasting agreement in his presence.[28] It would not be surprising, however, if Alexander was unwilling at that stage to have the legate visit Scotland, even if a story about his hostile attitude reported by the chronicler Matthew Paris is not believable.[29]

As it turned out the legate stayed on in England much longer than originally expected; but he did in the end find the time to visit Scotland between 21 September and early November 1239.[30] He held a council at Holyrood Abbey beside Edinburgh on 19 October 1239.[31] One motive for his visit was certainly financial. The pope was much concerned to raise money throughout the Western church for the crusade, and on 31 March 1238 had

[24] Theiner, *Monumenta*, 34–5, no. 90; cf. erroneous summary in *CPL*, i, 161–2. A suggestion in Duncan, *Scotland*, 287 that 'a legatine council was desirable because provincial ones could not be held' appears to derive from a misreading of this evidence.

[25] Cf. Watt, *Dictionary*, 101.

[26] Theiner, *Monumenta*, 29, no. 73; Stones, *Documents*, 17–18, no. 6.

[27] Theiner, *Monumenta*, 34, nos. 87–8; *CPL*, i, 160.

[28] Stones, *Documents*, 19–26, no. 7; cf. Duncan, *Scotland*, 533–4.

[29] Ibid., 287; see also Williamson, 'Legate Otto', 21. Paris also says that when Otto did arrive in Scotland in 1239, the king was at first hostile and then kept away (*SAEC*, 346; *SES*, i, p. lvii, n. 1); cf. Williamson, 'Legate Otto', 26.

[30] The apparently contradictory evidence (noted in Williamson, 'Legation of Cardinal Otto', 172), which places Otto at an unidentified place called 'Dinoflet' on 22 September 1239, is resolved by the identification of this place with 'Diniflee' or Temple Dinsley in Hertfordshire and the date as 23 August (i.e. '10 kal. Sept.' rather than '10 kal. Oct.) in Cheney, *Synodalia*, 22, n. 3.

[31] *Chron. Melrose*, 86–7; cf. *Chron. Lanercost*, i, 48, where it is reported that at this council the legate granted an idulgence of ten days to persons showing devotion to the Virgin.

authorised Otto to take money from those in Scotland who had taken the crusading vow, but were not able to go in person: if they now paid up, they might still enjoy the benefits of the crusader's indulgence while being freed from their vows.[32] It was probably a roundabout way of raising more money from people who never in fact intended to go to Palestine,[33] though in the official language of the bull the pope would appear to be extending to Scotland a privilege which had been requested by King Alexander, and the money was supposed to help the expenses of other crusaders who did go in person. In any case this was a task which Otto could perform by correspondence with Scotland or through an agent whom he sent there: it did not require his personal presence there. In fact on 27 August 1238 Peter de Supino, an Italian papal clerk who had already in 1237 worked for Otto in England as a collector of papal revenues, but who was now back at the Roman court, was given a letter of introduction by the papal chancery addressed to the bishop of St. Andrews,[34] and it may be assumed that he was being sent to Scotland on financial business. The letter was presumably never used, since it survives in the English royal archives; and in any case the see of St. Andrews was to be vacant for more than a year.[35] Meanwhile a need developed for Otto himself to negotiate with the Scottish clergy over what was probably a papal request for a subsidy. This would be in the category of a 'charitable' (rather than a mandatory) tax, when the clergy could not be forced to pay, but rather had to be consulted and cajoled into paying. No evidence survives of the purpose or exact character of this proposed tax, but very likely it was similar to that requested in November 1238 from the English and French clergy for the relief of the Latin Empire of Constantinople,[36] or, less likely because of the timing, to that requested in October 1239 from the English clergy for a war against the excommunicated Emperor

[32] Theiner, *Monumenta*, 38, no. 96; *CPL*, i, 169.

[33] Cf. Lunt, *Financial Relations*, 430–1.

[34] *Calendar of Documents relating to Scotland* [*CDS*], ed. J. Bain (Edinburgh 1881–1986), i, 558–9, no. 4; see Lunt, *Financial Relations*, 147; cf. Bagliani, *Cardinali*, i, 95–6.

[35] Watt, *Fasti*, 292.

[36] Lunt, *Financial Relations*, 194–6: a thirtieth for three years was requested in England, but refused.

Frederick II.[37] Just as Otto held councils in England to seek agreement to such taxes (with more success in the second case than the first), so this was part of his business at Holyrood in October 1239. The surviving Scottish chronicles do not mention this; but the English chroniclers say that he collected 'no small amount of money', from a tax described variously as a thirteenth or a twentieth.[38] The exact nature of the tax levied in Scotland is unknown; but from the record of a lawsuit dated 29 March 1240 'on payment of the money promised to the lord legate by the separate parish churches of the kingdom of Scotland',[39] it was clearly a tax of general incidence, and probably levied at some regularly defined fraction of the valuation of each benefice. Much of the collection was supervised during 1240 by Otto's assistants, including Peter the Red, and a considerable sum of money appears to have been removed from Scotland by them before the end of that year.[40]

The other kind of business done at the Holyrood council was by implication the publication of constitutions or canons chosen by Otto as suitable for the needs of the Scottish church. This had happened on his legations to Germany and Denmark,[41] as well as at his famous London council of 1237. His constitutions for Scotland were not preserved as an identifiable group, unlike the parallel case in England, where many copies were made of his legislation, and it was to be constantly referred to and studied for the rest of the Middle Ages.[42] As in England, however, the main act of publication would have been just the reading out of the legate's constitutions at his council, with those present obtaining written copies as best they could.[43] Bishop David de Bernham of

[37] Ibid., 197–205; cf. view expressed in Williamson, 'Legate Otto', 21.

[38] *Flores Historiarum*, ed. H. R. Luard (Rolls Series, 95), ii, 233, 240; cf. *SAEC*, 346.

[39] *Registrum de Dunfermelyn* [*Dunfermline Registrum*] (Bannatyne Club, 1842), 137, no. 221.

[40] *SAEC*, 346; cf. Lunt, *Financial Relations*, 203–5, 612. See also below, 93, n. 45.

[41] Bagliani, *Cardinali*, i, 83–4.

[42] Williamson, 'Legation of Cardinal Otto', 160.

[43] Ibid., 164. She goes on to say: 'They were authoritative formulations for England of the general law of the church, which filled in the gaps and strengthened the sanctions of the existing legislation' (ibid., 165).

St. Andrews (who had presumably attended the legate's council as bishop-elect)[44] in 1242 at one of his own diocesan synods referred to 'what was recently laid down by our venerable father Otto, by the grace of God legate to Scotland, regarding the residence and ordination of vicars', and clearly was assuming knowledge in his listeners of the penalties which Otto had laid down for offences against his rulings on these matters.[45] We are left to assume that Otto may have made a constitution for Scotland along the same lines as canon 10 of his London legislation, though it cannot have been identical. Similarly from the unusual activity of the same Bishop Bernham in dedicating parish churches 1240–49[46] we may assume that a constitution on this subject was included at Holyrood, though whether or not it was exactly the same as canon 1 of the London legislation is unknown. A more direct textual comparison is possible between four constitutions of the collected General Statutes of the Scottish Church (discussed in chapter 5 below), i.e. nos. 16, 17, 18 and part of 51 with canons 5, 8, 16 and 18 of the London legislation,[47] for in these cases there is a close resemblance. Probably more traces of Otto's constitutions at Holyrood remain to be identified; but meanwhile we can agree with Williamson: 'Perhaps the most important effect of Otto's visit is to be seen in the activities of David de Bernham and possibly other reforming bishops; synods and visitations were best calculated to attack the abuses of the church.'[48]

Very little is known about Otto's other activities in Scotland during his visit compared with his record in England.[49] He granted a personal dispensation for illegitimacy to a young secular clerk who was later to become a bishop;[50] he granted a somewhat general indulgence, perhaps to Holyrood abbey;[51] he regularised a change of abbot for the exempt Kelso abbey, at Melrose in Roxburghshire on 8 October 1239,[52] and granted this abbey a

[44] Watt, *Dictionary*, 42.
[45] *SES*, ii, 62, no. 134.
[46] Watt, *Dictionary*, 43.
[47] *C&S*, II, i, 247–9, 252–3.
[48] Williamson, 'Legate Otto', 24
[49] See his itinerary in Williamson, 'Legation of Cardinal Otto', 171–3.
[50] Watt, *Dictionary*, 5–7, s.v. 'Albin'.
[51] *Chron. Lanercost*, i, 48.
[52] *Chron. Melrose*, 86–7.

financial privilege as he was leaving Scotland on 2 November;[53] and he heard the evidence in a patronage case affecting the bishop and chapter of Dunkeld until the parties agreed to accept arbitration.[54] It must have been convenient and welcome to have the distant authority of Rome thus briefly available in Scotland to give immediate responses to Scottish requests for privileges or justice. As has been said regarding the legate's stay in England: 'The machinery of papal authority . . . can be seen, therefore, to be running with almost perfect smoothness, and the papal representative is everywhere accorded that respect which is evidently to be paid to the pope himself.'[55]

[53] *Kelso Liber*, ii, 338–9, no. 442.

[54] *Charters of the Abbey of Inchcolm*, ed. D. E. Easson and A. Macdonald (SHS, 1938), 15–17, no. 18. All these activities are analysed in Williamson, 'Legate Otto', 24–26. His court could deal with first instance cases (cf. Williamson, 'Legation of Cardinal Otto', 149).

[55] Ibid., 146.

5

Diocesan and provincial statutes of the mid-thirteenth century

AS part of the Europe-wide thirteenth-century phenomenon of a move from administration by oral methods to administration by writing,[1] we find that church councils at all levels tended to follow the lead of the general councils and give time to considering again and again various attempts to put into writing useful definitions of received custom and proposed reforms.[2] The sixth Lateran canon of 1215 had not specifically mentioned statute-collecting and statute-making as a purpose for the provincial councils and diocesan synods that it encouraged; but as a necessary adjunct of more energetic administrative and judicial procedures in local councils we find that everywhere there was a rash of statute-publication in harmony with the fashion of the age. This was particularly a thirteenth- and early fourteenth-century interest in England, France, Germany and Italy, in association with the general codification of the law for the whole Western church in the *Corpus Iuris Canonici* (especially the *Decretals of Gregory IX* of 1234).[3] Scotland was no exception, and has its collections of synodal and provincial statutes which,

[1] Cf. M. T. Clanchy, *From Memory to Written Record* (London, 1979), *passim.*

[2] Cf. Pontal, *Statuts*, 56; C. R. Cheney, *Medieval Texts and Studies* (Oxford, 1973), 141–2.

[3] Cheney, *Synodalia*, 34–6; Pontal, *Statuts*, 39–51; cf. R. C. Trexler, *Synodal Law in Florence and Fiesole, 1306–1518* (Studi e Testi, 268; Vatican, 1971), for discussion of the earliest-known synodal statutes for two exempt dioceses in Italy dating from 1306 and 1310.

as in France,[4] survive in manuscripts which are not concerned to draw clear distinctions between the two. As in England at any rate, there is little evidence of similar interest in conciliar assemblies once the thirteenth century was past,[5] though bishops were always having to define in one way or another how things were to be done or how people were to behave.

When we consider the surviving collection of statutes emanating from the thirteenth-century Scottish church, there is only one fixed point to which everything else must somehow be related. There survives in Lambeth Palace in London, in a single manuscript copied 'very soon after 1500',[6] a set of some thirty-one statutes (as split up by Joseph Robertson for his edition of 1866) issued by David de Bernham bishop of St. Andrews for the archdeaconry of Lothian in his diocese at a synod at Musselburgh near Edinburgh on 5 May 1242.[7] Here is further evidence that at least one Scottish bishop took seriously some of the Legate Otto's exhortations.[8] He seems to have been interested also in the text of a set of statutes collected for Lincoln diocese by the famous Bishop Robert Grosseteste, apparently in 1239,[9] for the Lambeth manuscript has copied into it just before Bernham's statutes a list of the rubrics to Grosseteste's statutes,[10] and it is reasonable to assume that this information was already available in St. Andrews when Bernham was collecting his diocesan statutes; but only some very faint echoes of the full texts of Grosseteste's statutes can be identified in those of Bernham.[11] It is indeed remarkable how few are these parallels; and, when looking wider for other possible sources copied by Bernham, we can find only two of his statutes echoing the language of the Salisbury statutes of 1217 x 1219

[4] Pontal, *Statuts*, 65–6.

[5] Cheney, *Texts*, 150, and Cheney, *Synodalia*, 43; cf. Pontal, *Statuts*, 50.

[6] Opinion of N. R. Ker in his *Medieval Manuscripts in British Libraries*, i (Oxford, 1969), 93 on dating of Lambeth Palace MS. 167. This whole collection probably represents what was currently in force before Archbishop Forman issued his statutes 1516 x 1521 (*SES*, i, pp. cclxx–cclxxxv; see below p. 170).

[7] These are statutes nos. 109–39 in *SES*, ii, 53–63 and Patrick, *Statutes*, 57–67. The year-date is supplied in *Chron. Bower*, v, 177.

[8] See above pp. 51–2.

[9] *C&S*, II, i, 265–78.

[10] This list is complete apart from nos. 1, 2 and 43 (*SES*, ii, 51–2, no. 108; cf. *C&S*, II, i, 276–8).

[11] Bernham nos, 129, 132, 135, 137; cf. Grosseteste nos. 31, 15, 30.

(reissued for Durham diocese 1228 x 1236) which were popular among contemporary English bishops as a model worth following.[12] The pervasive influence on the continent of the Paris statutes issued by Bishop Odo de Sully *c.* 1204 does not appear to have spread to St. Andrews either.[13]

It has been observed (in an Italian context) that a code of synodal constitutions might consist of laws already long in force, or might represent a body of new laws added to a traditional corpus, or (as in Fiesole in 1306 and Florence in 1310) could be entirely new, without taking texts from any earlier material.[14] In Bernham's case reference was on occasion made to passages in the codified general canon law derived for example from Gratian's *Decretum*,[15] or from the canons of the Third and Fourth Lateran Councils;[16] and no doubt the Legate Otto had brought an emphasis on current legal thinking with him to Scotland. But in his preamble Bernham says that he wished first to call to mind some of the statutes made by his predecessors (*ex antiquis patribus*), and then to add some new statutes of his own.[17] And, although some other influences behind his phraseology may yet remain to be detected, it seems probable that this collection of statutes does sum up Scottish traditions of long standing, with the addition of some unidentifiable items expressed in words which the dynamic Bernham took the trouble to draft himself. Since this whole collection was being copied still in the early sixteenth century, it was presumably still of current interest some 250 years after it had first been issued.

But the contemporary significance of Bernham's statutes for St. Andrews becomes clearer when it is realised not only that most

[12] See *C&S*, II, i, 57–96; cf. Bernham nos. 111 and 138 with Salisbury nos. 21 and 36. See discussion in Cheney, *Synodalia*, 62 ff.

[13] Pontal, *Statuts*, 82. See details of French legislation in *Les statuts synodaux français du XIIIe siècle*, ed. O. Pontal, two volumes (Paris, 1971–83). Dr. Pontal has kindly compared these statutes issued by various French councils *c.* 1204–60 with the Scottish statutes of the same period, and reports that though many of the topics covered in the two countries were the same, no textual similarities have been traced to suggest that the Scottish bishops were copying the work of the French bishops at this time.

[14] Trexler, *Synodal Law*, 9.

[15] No. 114.

[16] Nos. 126; 111 and 128.

[17] *SES*, ii, 53.

other Scottish bishops of his day may well have been similarly inspired by Otto's visit to issue their own synodal statutes, but that one other collection does in fact survive which can be directly compared with his. This is the corpus of another thirty-one statutes (as set out by Robertson) associated with the diocese of Aberdeen.[18] It is found in a single manuscript, a register of Aberdeen cathedral which was probably begun in the time of Bishop Adam de Tyningham in the 1380s.[19] To start off this new register copies were made of various records from the thirteenth century including a collection of 'General statutes of the Scottish church' (*Statuta generalia ecclesie Scoticane*) and a rental of 'second tenths' due to the bishop of Aberdeen from the royal revenues of the sheriffdoms of Aberdeen and Banff.[20] It is clear that the rental at any rate was being brought up to date as it was being copied,[21] and so it is possible that the statutes likewise were being modernised rather than just copied. But when we come later to study the part of this collection that relates to the whole Scottish church, we shall find that the text corresponds exactly with a genuine thirteenth-century text which also survives;[22] and so this is one reason for treating the other part of the collection which appears to contain Aberdeen synodal statutes as a probably unaltered copy of thirteenth-century material also. It must be noted that this part from no. 56 onwards is not separated off from the earlier part as 'synodal' rather than 'provincial': the whole collection in this manuscript follows from the initial rubric without a break. But Joseph Robertson was surely right to see nos. 56–86 as synodal and emanating from Aberdeen diocese (though there is no specific proof of this latter point – it is just that they are found

[18] *SES*, ii, 30–43, nos. 56–86; Patrick, *Statutes*, 30–45; see also *Aberdeen Registrum*, ii, 23–36, nos. 55–83 (i.e. divided into twenty-nine statutes).

[19] National Library of Scotland, Adv. MS. 16.1.10. See description of this manuscript in G. R. C. Davis, *Medieval Cartularies of Great Britain* (London, 1958), 129. For Tyningham see Watt, *Dictionary*, 551–5.

[20] *Aberdeen Registrum*, ii, 4 ff.; i, 55 ff. Note the facsimiles at these references which show that both sections of this manuscript are in the same hand.

[21] The 'Mariota de Kardeny' or Cardeny mentioned as holding part of the thanage of Aberdeen (ibid., i, 56) was favoured with royal grants only from the accession of Robert II in 1371 onwards (e.g. *Registrum Magni Sigilli Regum Scotorum* [*RMS*], edd. J. M. Thomson and others (Edinburgh, 1882–1914), i, 184, no. 506).

[22] See below pp. 61–2.

today copied into an Aberdeen register). The separating rubric which should come before no. 56 has been lost, but the circumstances thereafter are those of one diocese only with its bishop and synod rather than those of the whole Scottish church.[23] Just as in the Lambeth manuscript some synodal statutes relating only to St. Andrews diocese follow more general statutes for the wider Scottish church, so in the Aberdeen case. And the point is indubitably established when the content of nos. 56–86 is considered: as in the St. Andrews case there is much concern with details of the administration of the sacraments and little interest in matters of church liberties or teind as in the provincial statutes.

But these Aberdeen statutes offer two contrasts with the St. Andrews ones. First they have no specific date attached to them. As we have them today, they are presumably in the form in which they were issued by some bishop at some date. But it is clear that he was building on the earlier statutes of at least one predecessor,[24] so that the collection as it now stands probably represents an accretion of statutes over a period of years rather than the reforming work of one man at one time. But they do clearly belong to the same general era as the St. Andrews statutes, most obviously from the similar use of material derived from the Third and Fourth Lateran Councils,[25] though there is no obvious sign of the visit of the Legate Otto. Most striking is a second main contrast with the St. Andrews statutes in Aberdeen's wholesale borrowing from the Salisbury statutes of 1217 x 1219. This is a complex matter which it is not relevant to analyse here; but in at least twelve statutes there is greater or lesser dependence on Salisbury precedents, sometimes interwoven in a most complex way and often with minor changes or additions.[26] At some stage someone made a very positive effort to bring the customs of Aberdeen diocese up to date. It must have been after 1217, and probably well before mid-century, by which time 'the statutes of Salisbury lose the pre-eminent importance which they at first possessed'.[27] The lack of

[23] See nos. 64, 71, 74.

[24] No. 74; cf. no. 76.

[25] No. 65 refers to III Lateran c. 7, and nos. 58, 63, 66 and 80 refer to IV Lateran cc. 21, 14, 15, 16, 19, 51, 39.

[26] Nos. 56, 58–64, 66, 72, 80, 82.

[27] Cheney, *Synodalia*, 89.

reference to the Legate Otto leads to placing at least the bulk of this synodal collection in the 1220s or 1230s, and nothing has been found which *requires* any single statute in it to be dated later. Certainly this was an active period in the development of diocesan organisation at Aberdeen;[28] and perhaps the collection can be tentatively associated with Bishop Gilbert de Stirling (1228–39).[29]

Can this argument be strengthened by showing that some of the Aberdeen statutes influenced the drafting of the St. Andrews statutes of 1242? The answer seems to be negative. It is true that some topics are dealt with in similar ways (which is hardly surprising).[30] But much more striking are the rules for the conduct of the sacraments, which differ substantially,[31] not least because Aberdeen in these cases has taken over Salisbury definitions of good practice while St. Andrews has not. Since both sets of statutes seem to have had a long history before them, we must conclude that the traditions of liturgical practice were markedly different in these two dioceses.

This is a basic fact to bear in mind as we go on to consider our main theme of the statutes of the Scottish provincial council. The logic of canon 6 of the Fourth Lateran Council was for reform to flow down from above, from the general council through annual provincial councils to annual diocesan synods. Scotland from 1225 had the possibility of sharing in this pattern of authority, and may well have experienced a more regular series of provincial council meetings than occurred in England or France.[32] But in fact everywhere it is likely that it was the bishop in his synod who provided the most effective continuous expression of authority by choosing which items of church law and custom to emphasise by written precept, by oral exhortation, by administrative, penitential or judicial procedures; and when it comes to analysing surviving statutes it seems best to start in Scotland as elsewhere with the position that varying diocesan codes (whether in customary or

[28] Cf. Watt, *Fasti*, 5.

[29] Cf. Watt, *Dictionary*, 524.

[30] E.g. Aberdeen nos. 56, 80, 83, 86 and St. Andrews nos. 111, 136–7, 121 and 124, 131.

[31] E.g. Aberdeen nos. 56, 58, 60–2 and St. Andrews nos. 118, 119, 115, 117, 119.

[32] See below p. 82; cf. also above p. 46.

written form) existed in the early thirteenth century before any provincial statutes could be framed to establish a common pattern for the group of ten exempt dioceses. And since there was no metropolitan in an authoritative position to impose a common pattern on his suffragan bishops, but only a council of equals producing suggestions for good practice, it must remain a question for further enquiry how far each bishop was willing to absorb provincial statutes into his own diocese inasmuch as they suggested modifications to its individual customs.[33] This therefore should be the framework for our study now of such evidence as survives of the provincial statutes of the Scottish church in the thirteenth century.

There are three manuscripts to be considered. The first of these provides the *terminus ad quem* which fixes the thirteenth century as the era of an identifiable code of provincial statutes, even if it was to be copied also in manuscripts of much later date. This is the Ethie MS.,[34] which comprises the fragmentary remains of the earliest-known cartulary of Arbroath abbey in St. Andrews diocese. On fos. 14v, 16 and 16v (old foliation) appear part of what the rubric (in a different hand) calls *Statuta Concilii Scoticani*, and these leaves have been dated as 'in a hand not later than the reign of Alexander III' (1249–86).[35] In the same gathering of the original manuscript is fo. 19 (still attached to fo. 16), which contains part of a valuation list of benefices in St. Andrews and other dioceses.[36] This section is datable *c.* 1282,[37] and since the hand of the list appears to be the same as that which added an extra sentence in the top margin of fo. 16v of the statutes,[38] it may

[33] Cf. below pp. 75–6.

[34] The manuscript is now deposited in the Dundee City Archives (GD.130/25/17). It is called after Ethie Castle in Angus near Arbroath, where it was discovered in the mid-nineteenth century.

[35] *Liber S. Thome de Aberbrothoc* [*Arbroath Liber*] (Bannatyne Club, 1848–56), i, xxxiii; this judgment is accepted by Robertson (*SES*, i, pp. cxcii–cxciii, where as a frontispiece there is a facsimile of fo. 14v).

[36] Printed in *Arbroath Liber*, i, 240–7, starting with 'Ecclesia de Nyg'.

[37] Church of Garvock is said here to belong to Arbroath abbey (ibid., 247), probably in such a way as implies a recent acquisition. It was given to the abbey in August 1282, as confirmed by the bishop of St. Andrews in September 1283 (ibid., 271–3, nos. 314–17).

[38] As noted in *SES*, ii, p. ix, at no. 49.

be argued that the date of the hand of the statutes must be earlier than this. No *terminus a quo* can be so firmly suggested from the manuscript itself; but at least we do have here a clear thirteenth-century origin for a code of statutes with a formal preamble, and then for the text of nos. 1–5 and 32–50 (excluding 39) and parts of nos. 6, 31 and 51 in the modern printed edition. As it happens none of the statutes derived from the Legate Otto's London Council of 1237[39] survives here; but on general grounds we may take 1237 x 1282 as the outside dates of this source, with the 1260s or 1270s as its probable date. It survives just as a list of provincial statutes with no diocesan statutes now attached, so that no local implications can be drawn from it beyond the simple fact that it was the abbey of Arbroath that wished to have these statutes to hand for easy reference.

The second source in the order of writing is the Aberdeen cathedral register already mentioned.[40] The manuscript at this section probably dates from the 1380s. It begins on fo. 25v with a copy of the relevant papal bull of 1225, followed by a paragraph not found elsewhere entitled 'Mode of procedure in the council of the Scottish clergy'.[41] Then on fo. 26 comes the rubric 'Here begin the general statutes of the Scottish church'[42] and the same preamble as in the Ethie MS. in the same hand as the bull, followed by a series of statutes as numbered 1–38 and 40–55 in the printed editions.[43] Since the text then runs on into a series of diocesan statutes (as discussed above), it appears that these provincial statutes were preserved and copied at Aberdeen because they were considered there to be as authoritative as the statutes of the local bishop. Presumably they were brought to Aberdeen by a bishop who had participated in a provincial council; or more probably this version represents a list of statutes brought in this way from

[39] See above p. 52; cf. below p. 67.

[40] See above p. 58 at n. 20.

[41] *Modus procedendi in concilio cleri Scoticani*; printed in *Aberdeen Registrum*, ii, 4, and *SES*, ii, 4; see also Patrick, *Statutes*, 2–3. This paragraph is certainly in a different hand, but is not, it is suggested, of later date (cf. Robertson's opinion in *SES*, i, p. cxciii, n. 6).

[42] *Incipiunt statuta generalia ecclesie Scoticane*. Cf. the facsimile in *Aberdeen Registrum*, ii, 4, where 'fo. 29' is an error for 'fo. 26'.

[43] I.e. in *SES* and Patrick, *Statutes;* numbering in *Aberdeen Registrum* is different and runs from 2 to 54.

several councils over a number of years and preserved locally with additions from time to time. Since the Ethie MS. provides a control for about only a half of this whole series of statutes, it must be possible that some of them date from council meetings held after its date, say between the 1270s and the 1370s (more analysis of this later).

The third source is the Lambeth MS. 167 already discussed, written 'very soon after 1500'.[44] This contains a general collection of the laws of Scotland of all kinds,[45] ending with a section of some twelve folios (fos. 237–248v) all under the rubric 'Incipiunt statuta ecclesiastica' and ending with the colophon 'Explicunt statuta ecclesiastica etc.'. The series begins with fourteen miscellaneous statutes not found elsewhere:[46] then without any break come the preamble and the full series of provincial statutes parallel to those found in the Ethie and Aberdeen MSS., but with the major difference that they run on with eight further statutes not found in just this form elsewhere.[47] At the end comes the index to Grosseteste's Lincoln diocesan statutes mentioned above, which leads to the section of the manuscript containing the St. Andrews diocesan statutes.[48] As in the Aberdeen case therefore, provincial and diocesan statutes have been preserved together and there is something of a blur between the two. But we clearly have here materials which are likely to have all been copied from a source or sources preserved at St. Andrews in the early sixteenth century. We have in this manuscript the provincial statutes as brought back to St. Andrews and added to there over the years; and where such additions cannot be traced in the Ethie and Aberdeen MSS., we may suppose that they may have been introduced as late as the fifteenth century.

What can be learned from a comparison of these three manuscripts? First it must be admitted that variations in the order in which the statutes are set out and in the way in which the text is

[44] See above n. 6.

[45] See analysis of this manuscript in *APS*, i, 202–3.

[46] Printed as nos. 87–100 in *SES*, ii, 44–7, and Patrick, *Statutes*, 46–50.

[47] Printed as nos. 101–8 in *SES*, ii, 48–52, and Patrick, *Statutes*, 51–6.

[48] See above n. 10. It is curious and interesting that just one item in this index is changed: for the original rubric no. 37, 'Ne quisquam eorum audiat in scolis vel doceat leges seculares', this manuscript has the variant 'Quod audiant et doceant leges clericales' (*C&S*, II, i, 274, n. 2, and Patrick, *Statutes*, 54, n. 2).

divided into separate statutes may simply be the result of scribal initiative or error.[49] But some conclusions about the way in which these collections accrued do emerge from an analysis of at least some of the differences between the manuscripts.

It is possible to assume from the placing of nos. 87–100 in the Lambeth MS. that this placing was the same in the exemplar from which the Lambeth MS. was copied, that is that they were entered before the main code introduced by a preamble, and that this was so because they come from an earlier date than the main code. This may be too simple a view, but what is to be said for it? Modern editors have been unable to advise whether these statutes derive from the provincial council or from some diocesan synod (presumably that of St. Andrews).[50] In favour of the former possibility it may be observed that nos. 87 and 97–9 deal with details of teind, a subject that is not dealt with in the known synodal statutes of St. Andrews and Aberdeen,[51] but which is covered in similar fashion in detail in the code that is certainly provincial.[52] It would seem likely that the provincial council would have been at once from 1225 a useful forum for spelling out tricky points of interpretation in a practice which had already affected Scotland for the best part of a hundred years.[53] The definitions of mortuary fee in nos. 88 and 100 probably date from two different occasions, but they would similarly be a suitable subject for provincial definition; the reference in no. 100 to the duties of the 'prelate of the church' in cases of intestacy is not the language of a bishop devising his own diocesan statute, but must surely be the phraseology of a provincial statute; and such a statement of this rule could have preceded the provincial decree about the excommunication of offenders against it, which was going to form part of no. 51 of the code. The definition of a priest's right to pasture

[49] E.g. in the Lambeth MS. the last sentence of no. 88 has erroneously come to be attached to no. 28; nos. 37 and 38 are one statute in the Lambeth MS., but two statutes in the other two MSS.; no. 18 is divided into three statutes in the Lambeth MS., but stands as one in the Aberdeen MS.; no. 48 is omitted in the Lambeth MS. at its proper place and inserted instead among some fourteenth-century synodal statutes as no. 162.

[50] *SES*, i, pp. clxxxiv, n. 1, cxciv; Patrick, *Statutes*, 50.

[51] No. 70 [69] of the Aberdeen code is merely a general statement on this topic.

[52] See particularly nos. 34–8, 40–5.

[53] Duncan, *Kingdom*, 298.

for his animals in his parish found in no. 92 seems to fit well with the pronouncement on this topic which the bishops of Scotland are known to have made in council between 1225 and 1232.[54] More puzzling is no. 93 about the times when parts of churches are not open to laymen, for the mention of times when 'our chapters' are meeting reads more naturally (though not necessarily) as the language of a single bishop than of the bishops together in council; and the statute as a whole has a fairly clear parallel in no. 81 of the Aberdeen synodal statutes. The simple statute no. 94 on sanctuary is also rather similar to the Aberdeen statute no. 67, though both seem to ante-date the more sophisticated distinctions set out in the provincial code no. 26. Of the rest nos. 89–91 deal with the sacraments in a style familiar in the synodal statutes, but nos. 95–6 are sufficiently general about payments due to the clergy to be quite probably provincial in origin. In sum this collection would appear to contain some statutes on varied topics which seem to have had their origin in the provincial council, but which have been preserved in the form in which they are known to us intermingled with local synodal statutes. Presumably they could have been preserved in St. Andrews diocese with the rest of the ecclesiastical materials in the Lambeth MS.; yet since they seem likely to date from the same period as the Aberdeen statutes (i.e. the 1230s), but none of them were included by Bishop Bernham in this 1242 revision of St. Andrews statutes, it may be suggested that they were originally collected in a third diocese which cannot now be identified. In this case the material used seems to have been drafted in Scotland with no obvious borrowings from abroad.

Now it is time to consider the main code of provincial statutes which in their edited form comprise a preamble and then items numbered 1–55 and 101–7. From a comparison of the three texts available it may be suggested that an early recension ran from no. 1 to no. 46 (which gives orders for the publication of *iste sentencie* three times a year in all the churches of each diocese) with the omission of the second part of no. 6, nos. 7, 10, 22–5, the second part of no. 33, and no. 39. A text without these items (and, of course, without nos. 47–55 and 101–7) runs in the same order in the Aberdeen and Lambeth MSS. and in such of the Ethie MS. as

[54] See above p. 47.

survives; but as the other items have come to hand, they have been included by insertion and addition in different ways in each of the three manuscripts. The argument here is that at some date the basic code with the preamble was distributed throughout Scotland, and then all the other items as agreed on subsequent occasions singly or in groups were inserted or added locally in different ways into copies of the basic code kept at Arbroath, Aberdeen and St. Andrews. This situation has been found also in the manuscripts of the English statutes;[55] but we need to note that in these English collections mere draft statutes which in fact were never formally enacted were sometimes mistakenly included in local collections, for 'those who attended medieval provincial councils [in England] were not careful to destroy their rough notes'.[56] This may explain the survival of certain duplicate but not wholly similar statutes on certain topics in the Scottish evidence. In general we need to heed the warning: 'An existing text commonly presents statutes in a form in which they were never published. It is, as often as not, an incomplete conflation.'[57] Whatever the date of the original code in Scotland (see later), the second parts of nos. 6 and 33, no. 35 and nos. 47–51 (but not no. 39) had certainly been added by the time the Ethie MS. was written in (say) the 1260s or 1270s; but we cannot be so definite about nos. 7, 10, 22–5, 52–5 and 101–7, since there are lacunae in this manuscript which force us to leave the question open.

What are the characteristics of this putative early recension? It has the appearance of a well-drafted code, assembling statutes methodically in a series of sections. First come rules for the conduct of the council itself (nos. 1–2), which will be analysed later. Then come generalisations about the faith and the sacraments (nos. 3–4) and the building of churches and chapels (nos. 5–6), which are nothing like so detailed as similar items in the diocesan statutes. Next comes (nos. 8–9, 11–13) a section on parish rectors and vicars, their appointment, the building of their manses, and the protection of parish benefices from increased tax assessments (probably for episcopal expenses and the like). Then come a series of statutes on the discipline of the clergy – their orderly ordination,

[55] Cheney, *Synodalia*, 47, 127; cf. Pontal, *Statuts*, 54.

[56] Cheney, *Texts*, 129.

[57] Ibid., 154.

help for secular clergy who want to become religious, arrangements for their confessions, control over their leasing of church property, control over their misuse of property in favour of their concubines and children, and rules to prevent the alienation of church revenues (nos. 14–21). Then there are rules about the liberties of the church in Scotland in general, defining the limits of sanctuary, putting procedural controls over benefit of clergy (with arrangements for the punishment of criminous clerks), putting limits on the secular courts, offering protection to crusaders, asserting the freedom of the clergy from secular distraints and court procedures (nos. 26–33). There follows a wide variety of statutes about teind, setting out general rules in quite complex detail (nos. 34–8, 40–5); and the code ends with the order for the publication of these statutes three times a year in every church of each diocese of the participating bishops (no. 46).

A code of this kind was not the product of discussion and debate: it must have been drafted with care and forethought by one man or a small group. There is no hint on who this may have been. A little combing of the canon law of the whole Western church and of useful earlier legatine constitutions can be observed. There is not surprisingly some reference to the *Decretum*[58] and the *Decretals*,[59] and there are references to the Lateran Councils.[60] Some canons published by the Legate Otto in the Council of London in 1237 provide close parallels for nos. 16–18:[61] perhaps they had been repeated by Otto at Holyrood in October 1239,[62] but it is significant that the text of no. 17 was enlarged in comparison with the London version by the insertion of a sentence protecting the rights of religious orders. These were in all probability statutes devised in Scotland in line with Scottish customs and requirements, which owe very little indeed to outside precedents (though, of course, there may remain textual relationships with other collections of statutes which have not as yet been spotted).[63]

[58] The Preamble is derived from D. 15 cc. 1–2 (*CIC*, i, cols. 34–5).

[59] Cf. no. 29 with X 3.49.5 (*CIC*, ii, col. 655).

[60] No. 13 refers to III Lateran c. 7; no. 31 to either I Lateran c. 10 or IV Lateran c. 71.

[61] Cf. no. 16 with London c. 5, no. 17 with London c. 8, and no. 18 with London c. 16 (*C&S*, II, i, 247–9, 252–3).

[62] See above p. 51.

[63] Cf. above pp. 56–7.

This corresponds with what has been observed in other countries. Most canons of general or provincial councils were apparently provoked by local problems in various parts of the church for 'law, like population, recruits from below'.[64] The Fourth Lateran Council may have encouraged a filtering down process from a centralised law code; but just as influential was the process of defining local custom from the bottom upwards, whether in great variety in diocesan synods or on a regional basis at provincial level; and 'custom is made: it does not germinate spontaneously'.[65] There was constant interaction between the law of local churches and the law of the universal church,[66] and the one has little meaning without the other. It has been well argued that the mere existence of codified canon law imposed very little restriction on local bishops if they did not choose to be active in its propagation, for much of the canon law 'rested at any given moment on degrees of consensus among lawyers, reaching from unity to wide divergence between different camps'.[67] There were certainly some courses of action not open to them, no doubt, but local legislators had ample freedom it seems to take local conditions into account. 'The resultant constitution is best comprehended as a result of legal tradition and local pressures, not as the result of the decretal.'[68]

Presumably one function of provincial legislation was to produce more generally useful and applicable statutes than the individual bishops were currently enforcing in their separate dioceses. A comparison of this code with the Aberdeen and St. Andrews statutes (the latter alone being firmly dated) may help not only to illustrate this hypothesis, but also to establish the relative dates of these surviving collections. The picture is an extension of that delineated above in connection with items of provincial legislation (preserved perhaps in an unidentified diocese) which appear to date from the 1230s, in which simple rules on teind and

[64] Cheney, *Texts*, 185.

[65] Ibid., 201.

[66] Pontal, *Statuts*, 80.

[67] Trexler, *Synodal Law*, 13–14. The argument provides the background to an analyis of diocesan statutes, but in two exempt dioceses where the bishops were in practice acting as their own metropolitans (as the provincial council did in Scotland).

[68] Ibid., 14.

sanctuary were found to have been elaborated by a seemingly later provincial code.[69] Rules of the 1230s forbidding the holding of secular courts on church premises are in the code elaborated as a separate item.[70] The old rule protecting benefices from new assessments is found in both the Aberdeen statutes and the code, perhaps gaining wider emphasis from its inclusion in the latter.[71] Rules for checking on the proper qualifications of stranger clergy found in the St. Andrews statutes are matched in the code by rather more comprehensive rules about clergy moving from one diocese to another.[72] But perhaps most helpful is a comparison of the fairly loose rules for limitation of the leasing of churches found in both the Aberdeen and St. Andrews collections with the more drastic adoption in the code of the Legate Otto's five-year limit.[73] This last example is clearly a case of tightening up – indeed of adopting one of Otto's canons which Bishop Bernham had apparently deliberately chosen to omit from his 1242 synodal collection; and it provides the best argument for suggesting that the code was put together not merely later than the Aberdeen statutes, but also later than the St. Andrews ones of 5 May 1242.

But there is another support for this argument. At some time in 1242 (i.e. after 25 March 1242), quite probably *c.* 15 July when the bishops of St. Andrews and Dunkeld are known to have been with King Alexander at Scone,[74] 'all the bishops of Scotland' are said to have held a council of the clergy at Perth. The king attended at the clergy's request, and with him came 'all the earls and barons' of Scotland. The clergy complained of harassment by fighting men over teinds and the privileges of the church. The king entered the council and forbade any knight or baron under heavy penalties to interfere with the customary rights of the church (*sacrosancte ecclesie consuetudinem*).[75] It hardly seems likely that this was the occasion for the initial publication of the complex code of

[69] See above pp. 64–5.
[70] Cf. nos. 68, 81 and 93 with no. 29.
[71] See nos. 65 and 13.
[72] Cf. no. 130 with no. 14.
[73] Cf. nos. 79 and 132 with no. 17.
[74] *Glasgow Registrum*, i, 147, no. 181.
[75] *Chron. Bower*, v, 180–1. Note that the extract from this source printed in *SES*, i, p. lix, n. 1 conflates passages from two different manuscripts, as the modern edition makes clear.

provincial statutes which we are considering,[76] for it was a time of stress and disturbance in the country.[77] But teind and church privileges are in fact two of the main themes of this code. Was it therefore drafted after Otto's visit in 1239 and long enough before July 1242 for opposition to it to have been aroused by then? This hardly seems likely in the time available; and in any case it has already been argued from the evidence of the statutes themselves that this code must have been put together subsequent to 5 May 1242. It seems therefore preferable to date this code 1242 x 1249, and regard it as having been promulgated at some other meeting of the provincial council held in that period under the protection of the king, who at least from 1244 was able in the last years of his reign to keep his magnates in check.[78] There was at least one tradition handed down to the fifteenth century to the effect that in this last period the church rejoiced to have such a defender who brought them prosperity.[79] It would be in such circumstances that it was possible and not too risky to spell out written definitions of what the church regarded as its privileges, and to go into detail on the contentious matter of teinds, even to the extent of boldly admitting that teind had not hitherto been paid on some commodities and activities which were now declared to be tithable.[80] In sum the code in its first recension shows the Scottish church riding high as it asserted its rights and privileges in the last years of the reign of a king who was willing to provide the necessary backing for their claims.

The very existence of these provincial statutes therefore may well have led directly to the reaction of the magnates against clerical pretensions once the king had died in July 1249 and the country was in the throes of a royal minority. The new reign of the young Alexander III seems to have started with the magnate council of regency giving lip-service (but not written commitment)

[76] This was once the accepted view (cf. *SES*, i, p. xiii, n. 2); and it is still sometimes suggested (Duncan, *Scotland*, 295).

[77] See, for example, D. E. R. Watt, 'The minority of Alexander III of Scotland', *Transactions of the Royal Historical Society*, 5th series, xxi (1971), 2–3.

[78] Ibid., 3–6.

[79] *Chron. Bower*, v, 279, n. 47. But cf. Duncan, *Kingdom*, 290 for an argument that the king exercised a 'strong hand' over the clergy, and that after his death their aim was 'to re-occupy the field they had lost thirty years before'.

[80] No. 34.

to acknowledging the privileges of the church as under the late king. But then came a whole series of incidents when clerical privilege was attacked. It was probably about 19 June 1250 (when the relics of the newly-canonised St. Margaret were being translated at Dunfermline Abbey) that seven bishops met to protest to the regency government about a case where the prior of St. Andrews had been despoiled of church property by unnamed laymen, without any ecclesiastical judicial process.[81] By 31 May 1251 the pope was responding to a long series of accusations against the regency government which had reached him from the Scottish church about interference with church privileges in Scotland since the death of King Alexander II.[82] The pope then ordered three English bishops as judges-delegate to take action on these complaints on his behalf. It is unlikely that they did so; but the complaints themselves are a valuable dated source for a study of how certain statutes in the code of 1242 x 1249 had been causing trouble, and of how some at least of the additional surviving provincial statutes came to be introduced.

It is true that there are some ways in which the regency government was said to have been interfering (or allowing interference) with church privileges which are *not* connected with specific matters mentioned in the corpus of statutes: there had been attacks on traditional church jurisdiction in cases involving patronage of benefices, honouring of oaths and the persons of married clerks; and papal judges-delegate had been prevented from carrying out their mandates. In such an atmosphere it is not surprising to find objections to payments of certain kinds of teind (particularly of hay, mills and pasture) such as had been prescribed recently in statutes nos. 41, 34, perhaps 40 and 92; and there was objection to statute no. 96 (on the payment of money fines for ecclesiastical offences). No doubt the bishops had already to hand such definitions on those topics as they needed; but a number of new provincial statutes which are to be found as additions to the code of 1242 x 1249 in the surviving manuscripts appear to be a response to the problems of 1249–51. No. 33 is strengthened by an additional clause in the *ipso facto* excommunication of those

[81] *SES*, ii, 241–2; for dating see Watt, *Dictionary*, 42.
[82] *SES*, ii, 242–6; *Moray Registrum*, 334–8, no. 260.

who disturb church privileges.[83] This theme of provincially-ordered routine excommunication four times a year of a variety of classes of offender including perjurers (such as had been a menace to churchmen recently) is taken up in statutes nos. 51–2.[84] Such arrangements had been made before at diocesan level (see nos. 69 and 122), but a more widespread approach must now have seemed necessary. And linked with this in the Lambeth MS. is statute no. 55, which tries to prevent the continuance of what is said to be the recent abuse of lay pressure on prelates to relax sentences of excommunication. The Ethie MS. has another group of three new statutes relevant to other problems of 1249–51 in nos. 50, 47 and 48.[85] These condemn beneficed clergy who have been helping laymen to attack church privileges, and who are guilty of plotting against, or resisting, the lawful authority of their bishops, archdeacons and deans. Thus there seems to be some evidence of a group of provincial statutes which have come to be added to the earlier code as a result of the persecution suffered in the years 1249–51. They are unlikely to have been drawn up as early as the protest on just the one case made apparently in June 1250.[86] Perhaps they were issued in self-defence while the appeal for help was being sent to the pope early in 1251. But most likely they date from sometime in 1252, i.e. after the interference of King Henry III of England had led to the marriage at Christmas 1251 of the young King Alexander III with Henry's daughter Margaret, which in turn was accompanied by a change of regency government in Scotland. With the removal of some of their persecutors the bishops were free to set out some new statutes to try to prevent their return. By 1252 or so this may well have seemed a better way of tackling their problems than the earlier

[83] In the Ethie MS. this addition forms a separate statute following no. 34; but in the Aberdeen and Lambeth MSS. it is attached to no. 33.

[84] Part of no. 51 is taken from c. 18 of the Legate Otto's legislation at the Council of London 1237 (*C&S*, II, i, 253) with small verbal changes which may well date from his council at Holyrood in 1239.

[85] In the Ethie MS. no. 50 is repeated in two sections placed separately in the manuscript, which may indicate that the council dealt with this matter on more than one occasion. No. 48 appears to have been omitted from the Lambeth MS. in this context (perhaps in error), though it is found later in that manuscript as no. 162 among some St. Andrews synodal statutes of the fourteenth century.

[86] See above p. 71.

plan of getting the pope to invite three English bishops to interfere in a masterful way in Scotland. At least for a few years from early 1252 onwards not all the bishops were excluded from government as had been the case earlier in the regency,[87] so that a council could meet peacefully and constructively.

Now we have to consider the remaining statutes which cannot so clearly be allocated to 1242 x 1249 or *c.* 1252. No. 49 is of especial interest since it is recorded in three versions. The shortest version occurs in the text of the Ethie MS., where a basic rule was set out for ensuring that itinerant pardoners did not exceed their commissions. Then a sentence forbidding them to visit any church more than once a year is added in the margin, and the statute as a whole is found in the texts of the Aberdeen and Lambeth MSS.; and from its position in all three manuscripts it seems likely that in its corrected form it was issued with the rest of the *c.* 1252 material even if it is not obviously related to the problems of 1249–51. But in the Aberdeen MS. alone a further section is added regarding an indulgence for a limited period (with no year specified) to help the building fund for Glasgow Cathedral. Robertson was surely right to see this as probably a synodal statute of Aberdeen diocese,[88] which was apparently included like an example for a formulary in just the one collection of statutes, presumably at any time between *c.* 1252 and the date when the manuscript was written in the 1380s.

Another statute that was probably issued with the *c.* 1252 collection is no. 53, which is found in both the Aberdeen and Lambeth MSS.; and though the Ethie MS. has a lacuna at this point, it is reasonable to argue from a case dated 1267 that this statute is likely to have been issued before then.[89] It lays down the duty of bishops to back up one of their number (if so requested) in publishing and executing individual acts of excommunication. It is interesting to see how here the bishops are wanting to stick together so that excommunication can be made fully effective.

[87] The bishops of Glasgow and Dunblane, and probably also the bishop of St. Andrews, were particularly associated with the ruling group of magnates from early 1252 to September 1255 (Watt, 'Minority', 10–14; cf. Stones, *Documents*, 30–1, and Watt, *Dictionary*, 42).

[88] *SES*, ii, p. ix.

[89] *Chron. Bower*, v, 361, ll. 22–45; cf. *SES*, ii, 267.

But there are significant special rules when the offender is associated with the king or the queen or (much more drastically) with a common assembly (*communis congregatio*) of the magnates of the kingdom. In such cases the originating bishop is left with the difficult duty of persuading those important people to abandon the person who is excommunicated, so that presumably the other bishops are not willy-nilly to be involved in such politically explosive cases. This putting of the magnates on the same level of exception as the king and queen must surely point to a timing for this statute associated with the circumstances of the minority of the young king, and so it would fit well with the others allocated above to *c.* 1252 as another aspect of the ways in which the bishops in their council were then trying to establish a better working relationship with the regency government than had been their experience 1249–51.[90]

Four other matters were apparently dealt with at some date that was similarly later than the code of 1242 x 1249, because they have been added to the core of statutes which lies behind the Aberdeen and Lambeth MSS., even if in quite different ways.[91] Since the Ethie MS. again does not help us here, these items cannot certainly be dated to the later thirteenth century, and they do not appear from their content to be datable on other grounds. No. 22 takes up a theme that is just briefly mentioned in a St. Andrews synodal statute of 1242 (no. 127) and forbids the involvement of secular and regular clergy in lay business affairs in such a way that they might be called to account (echoing perhaps similar rules laid down in III Lateran c. 12, IV Lateran c. 42, and the 1222 Council of Oxford c. 12, though not copying the specific wording of these precedents[92]). Nos. 24 and 25 deal with certain detailed problems which had arisen in the interpretation of the privileges enjoyed throughout Christendom by exempt religious orders such

[90] A possible objection to this suggested dating is the protection against interdict offered later in the statute to the chapels, or chaplains (another reading), of the king and queen *and their children*, for *c.* 1252 the king and queen were themselves both children; but it may be suggested that such a definition is common form in these statutes with an eye to the normal necessarily privileged position of the royal family (cf. nos. 104, 154). See also pp. 82–3, n. 20 below.

[91] Nos. 22, 24, 25 and 54 in the order of the Aberdeen MS. all come together after no. 50 in the Lambeth MS. (with nos. 101–3 as a substitute for no. 54).

[92] Tanner, *Decrees*, 218, 253; *C&S*, II, i, 110.

as the Knights Hospitaller, the Cistercians and others. No. 54 is very different, dealing with the punishment of women, bishops and priests when it is a case of fornication between women and their fathers in God to whom they have come for confession. In the Aberdeen MS. it is just a question here of citing word for word two sections from Gratian's *Decretum*,[93] while in the Lambeth MS. three sections (nos. 101–3) follow the same source at greater length.[94] It seems impossible to find out just when the provincial council ordered that special attention should be drawn to these particular canons of the church at large. There must, however, have been due cause for the provincial council to discuss these matters: presumably this reflects what were felt to be difficulties in administering these general rules of the church in Scotland in particular.

More difficult to interpret are two groups of statutes which survive positively in only one manuscript tradition and not as heretofore in this discussion in at least two. These are items which have the appearance of provincial statutes, but were not recorded in all the localities of Scotland with equal attention. There are four items which are not included in the Lambeth MS. The first of these is in the Ethie MS. as well as the Aberdeen MS., and so is datable, say, 1252 x 1282: but the Ethie MS. fails us for the other three, so that all we can be sure of is that they were traditionally preserved at Aberdeen and interspersed with the statutes which appear to have come from 1242 x 1249 and *c.* 1252. The first is an addition to the original no. 6 of 1242 x 1249. It is now specifically stated that the rule insisting on episcopal permission for the building of chapels is not being observed, and so the provincial council (and it is clear that this is not a synodal statute for just one diocese) orders bishops to take a much more positive attitude in order to safeguard the rights of the mother churches of parishes. Just possibly this extra rule was made necessary by the 'magnate reaction' in the first years of the minority of 1249. No. 7 was probably enacted at the same time on an ancillary topic, with the council seeking to curb the practice of holding divine services in unlicensed places. No. 10 is an undatable decree on clerical dress, except that it echoes some points

[93] C. 30 q. 1 cc. 9–10 (*CIC*, i, col. 1099).

[94] Ibid., cc. 8, 9, 10.

of IV Lateran c. 16.[95] No. 23 builds on the rules against clerical concubines by borrowing two sentences from c. 37 of the 1222 Council of Oxford, which forbade the purchase of property for the benefit of the concubines and children of beneficed clergy, and then by adding a rule forbidding the leaving of money by will to concubines.[96] Just possibly this last statute was published for Aberdeen diocese alone (though it is not so described); but certainly the first three at any rate come from the provincial council – the language of the texts is quite clear on this. It is unknowable why all four were not preserved with other provincial legislation at St. Andrews. It may be just the consequence of scribal error when the Lambeth MS. was being compiled in the early sixteenth century; but we are entitled to draw the conclusion that not all provincial legislation was equally well preserved (let alone enforced) in all the Scottish dioceses, even if it may be fruitless to speculate further on the reasons for this.

The same point is emphasised when we consider the group of statutes preserved only in the Lambeth MS. No. 39 provides a definition of a tricky point about the teind of sheep when stock are moved from one parish to another. In the Lambeth MS. this item is in fact placed before no. 37 which treats of a very similar matter; but it is not in the Ethie MS. (at least not at this place) nor in the Aberdeen MS., even though it is the kind of ruling which must have been desirable over the whole country. Then there are nos. 104–7.[97] No. 107 offers another definition of teind that is on a similar level of detail to that in no. 39; these two statutes could well have emerged from the same council. No. 106 spells out what is said to have long been customary, that chaplains should be paid a maximum salary of 7½ marks: this seems to date from an era not long after that of no. 9 of the 1242 x 1249 code which had produced the generous definition of a vicar's stipend as

[95] Tanner, *Decrees*, 243.

[96] *C&S*, II, i, 118.

[97] See above p. 75 for nos. 101–3; and p. 56, n. 10 for no. 108. There is no indication on fo. 242 of the Lambeth MS. to suggest that the additional material printed as no. 101 onwards is of a character different from the provincial statutes printed as nos. 1–55. It is thus here assumed that only no. 108 was kept at St. Andrews as of interest in connection with the diocesan statutes, and that nos. 101–7 are provincial statutes (cf. the hesitant views in *SES*, i, p. clxxxiv, n. 1 and Patrick, *Statutes*, 50).

10 marks at least.[98] No. 105 can be seen as a development from St. Andrews statute no. 130 and the provincial rule no. 14 of 1242 x 1249, which deals with control of the qualifications of foreign clergy who seek to serve as priests in Scotland, and so appears to reflect the mid-thirteenth-century problems which were beginning to arise over papal provisors. No. 104, too, is a development from both St. Andrews and earlier provincial statutes (this time nos. 122 and 51), for it adds to the long list of potential oppressors of the church who are to be warned off in advance four times a year with threats of excommunication. The particular emphasis this time is on magnates who burden both secular and regular clergy with ruinous demands for hospitality. It looks again to be perhaps the product of the early days of the royal minority after 1249.[99] There is nothing to prove that these five extra statutes found only in the Lambeth MS. date from so early after the code of 1242 x 1249 as, say, the 1250s or 1260s; but when so much in the available manuscripts comes from the mid-thirteenth century (however much later it was still being copied), there seems to be no good reason for assuming that any of it is datable much later. All that we can conclude is that the bulk of the provincial statutes that survive seem to have formed a code collected 1242 x 1249, that some others were probably issued *c.* 1252, and that yet some others come probably either from then also or from a few years later, since they do not have the same characteristic of having been similarly or at least equally well recorded both at Aberdeen and St. Andrews.

What then are we to make of the gap of the best part of three centuries until the provincial council can be shown to have again been involved in statute-making on a big scale?[100] It is relevant to note Cheney's argument[101] that in England in the later Middle Ages there was little publication of new synodal legislation as opposed to episcopal commendation of particular statutes of their

[98] Cf. discussion of English practice in Patrick, *Statutes*, 11, n. 2.

[99] Cf. Robertson's view that this statute was perhaps a product of the council of 1242 (*SES*, ii, 276; i, p. lix; and see above pp. 69–70); but the subject-matter is neither teind nor church privileges such as are said to have been under attack then.

[100] For statutes issued from 1549 onwards see *SES*, ii, 81 ff. and Patrick, *Statutes*, 84 ff. They are not part of the present study.

[101] Cheney, *Texts*, 149–50.

predecessors. He argues that ecclesiastical authorities were satisfied with what was already available. And a major plank in his discussion is the absence in England today of contemporary manuscripts containing statutes. Such copies as there once were may well have been worn out with use over a long period. Thus in the Scottish case the late dates of the Aberdeen and Lambeth MSS. may be interpreted as evidence that nothing else worth copying had been produced in the fourteenth and fifteenth centuries. Whatever else the provincial council may have been engaged in after the mid-thirteenth century, it seems unlikely to have been concerned with making statutes.[102]

[102] This argument does not apply to statute-making at the level of episcopal synods (see below pp. 130 and 170).

6

Membership and organisation of the provincial council

THE code of 1242 x 1249 in its preamble and first two statutes provides also some firm information on the composition and organisation of the provincial council in Scotland by that date, and we can gather some other hints on these topics from the thirteenth-century statutes as a whole. The body itself is at first styled a *concilium provinciale* as in the 1225 bull that had set it up.[1] It also refers to itself in two of its statutes as the *sacrum concilium*,[2] and in another as the *sacrum ecclesie Scoticane consilium*.[3] By the fourteenth century at any rate it was being mentioned in other sources as the *provinciale Scoticanense concilium*,[4] the *sacrum concilium Scoticanum*,[5] or just the *concilium Scoticanum*.[6] It was the bishops alone who in 1225 were authorised to hold a council; but by 1242 x 1249 it was the rule for all abbots and priors of independent priories to meet with the bishops.[7] Since any of these was allowed (indeed ordered) to send a proctor in his place if he had a legitimate excuse under the canon law for being absent,[8] some lower clergy would presumably be found taking part at most meetings of the council.

[1] *SES*, ii, 9, preamble and no. 1.
[2] Nos. 3, 53.
[3] No. 104.
[4] *Dunfermline Registrum*, 196–7, no. 308 (*c.* 1300?).
[5] *Moray Registrum*, 127, no. 114 (1343).
[6] *Liber S. Marie de Dryburgh* [*Dryburgh Liber*] (Bannatyne Club, 1847), 247, no. 297 (1326/7); *Aberdeen Registrum*, i, 77 (1345).
[7] No. 1.
[8] Ibid.

Pope Honorius III had laid it down on 25 February 1217 that representatives of cathedral chapters ought to be summoned and admitted to provincial councils; but by mid-century this seems to have been interpreted as a permissive rule rather than a mandatory one. And the canonist Hostiensis in the 1250s argued that the heads of religious houses and ordinary clergy had no right to attend, but should do so in their own interest.[9] On the continent the presence of abbots and representatives of chapters seems to have been normal in the thirteenth century.[10] Even laymen may have attended some councils, though apparently just as petitioners or advisers.[11] Perhaps it was as proctor for his bishop that the archdeacon of Dunkeld attended the '1230' council; but the other archdeacon and the *magistri* who were there, and the archdeaon, dean and doctor of theology found at the council of July 1238, cannot be explained on the same principle.[12] It would have been helpful and sensible from the beginning for the bishops to bring some of their cathedral dignitaries or clergy of their households with them to councils to help with particular business. And the Order of Business (*Modus Procedendi*), which is found copied into the Aberdeen register along with the provincial statutes of the thirteenth century,[13] in laying down dress regulations for those attending council meetings makes allowance for the presence of deans and archdeacons and other clergy as well as of bishops and abbots. These two last categories, however, seem at this early stage to be the only clergy summoned to these councils as of right.

The language of the statutes, moreover, is predominantly episcopal, e.g. 'each of us in his diocese will enquire . . .' (no. 6), or 'in each church of each diocese belonging to us. . .' (no. 46), or the reference to 'any one of us bishops' (no. 53). The interests of

[9] Kemp, *Counsel and Consent*, 43–5.

[10] Ibid., 45.

[11] Ibid., 35, 45–7. For a trend towards the exclusion of laymen from diocesan synods, see Cheney, *Synodalia*, 33 and Trexler, *Synodal Law*, 35.

[12] See above pp. 47–8.

[13] *SES*, ii, 4; Patrick, *Statutes*, 2–3. This item is found in National Library of Scotland, Adv. MS. 16.1.10, copied at fo. 25v in a hand that is different from that which copied the preceding bull of 1225 and the succeeding code of 1242 x 1249. But it is not necessary to argue that this is a hand of a later period (cf. Robertson in *SES*, i, p. cxciii, n. 6): this item, indeed, seems likely to have been copied from an earlier source in the 1380s with the rest, and there is every reason to suppose that it, too, dates from the thirteenth century.

the monastic heads when they were present are represented only obliquely in most of the statutes produced by these councils;[14] no doubt they put their weight behind statutes about maintaining the general privileges of the church in Scotland, and as holders of appropriated churches they would be particularly interested in making the system for the collection of teind as effective as possible. The monastic heads may perhaps have had a more committed interest in some other aspects of the council's work, such as the correction of abuses and adjudication over disputes.[15] But it seems to have been for the better running of the secular church in the dioceses that the statutes at any rate were devised; and after all it was as a substitute for part of the machinery associated in most parts of Christendom with metropolitan authority that the Scottish provincial council was invented.

The most important organisational development which presumably came just as soon as the council began meeting after 1225 was already by 1242 x 1249 part of the laudable custom of the predecessors of the men who drew up the code of statutes then.[16] This was the establishing of the office of *Conservator Statutorum Concilii* or just *Conservator Concilii*.[17] As defined in the code this office was held by one of the bishops chosen by the others. There is no suggestion that the council as a whole was involved in the choice: and this restriction may well date back to 1225 when the very first meeting of the council probably comprised bishops only (as the founding bull suggests). Nothing is said about the length of the Conservator's term of office: it is just that he is to exercise his office 'from council to council', which probably (though not necessarily) implies that elections would be held annually at every council meeting. Certainly there is no suggestion of a rota among the bishops for this office; but we just do not have any information for a hundred years after 1225[18] on who was elected to it, or re-elected, or for how long. As part of the Conservator's duties between council meetings, it was laid down that he had to

[14] Exceptions are nos. 15, 17, 22, 47, 50, 104.

[15] See above pp. 47–8 for business affecting monasteries that was resolved at councils in '1230' and 1238.

[16] No. 1.

[17] No. 2; cf. no. 1. Cf. Duncan, *Kingdom*, 293 for argument that the office of Conservator emerged perhaps as late as 1267.

[18] See below p. 85 for List of Known Conservators.

intimate to all concerned in proper fashion (*competenter*) the date appointed for the next meeting of the council. It is not stated whether or not he had discretion in choosing this date (or the place), but since no standard date was laid down for this annual meeting, it seems quite likely that he did have. It was the Conservator therefore who stood in the place of the metropolitan in taking the initiative (or not as the case may be) in calling provincial councils. It is at least possible that as an elected rather than an appointed officer he felt impelled to call councils more regularly than most metropolitans did: the pressure may well have been upon him from the other bishops to do so, since under the rules his official powers continued until the next council meeting. Alternatively he had it in his power to get rid of the burden of office as Conservator by calling a council meeting.

The functions of the Conservator at these meetings are not clearly spelled out. He is described in the Order of Business as presiding over the opening devotions of the council which he had called, but the responsibility for preaching (or getting someone else to preach) the opening sermon was from 1242 x 1249 to be in the hands of all the bishops in a rota beginning with the bishop of St. Andrews.[19] Business was then begun with what appears to be a ceremony of excommunication by all the bishops present of such persons as had been summoned but had failed to turn up and had no valid excuse. There were said to be statutes on this matter laying down how absentees were to be punished (though these are not now known apart from a general statement in statute no. 1), and these were to be read out before the excommunication was pronounced.[20] Was the Conservator still the presiding officer?

[19] No. 2.

[20] This appears to be the meaning of the last sentence of the *Modus Procedendi*. Cf. the last sentence of statute no. 1 of 1242 x 1249, which orders the punishment of absentees *auctoritate et arbitrio Concilii* (*SES*, ii, 10). Cf. also the translation in Patrick, *Statutes*, 3, which suggests that the whole corpus of the council's statutes is to be read out at the beginning of each meeting, with thereafter a general excommunication of potential offenders. But the Form of Excommunication in *SES*, ii, 5–6, no. IV does not follow the *Modus Procedendi* in the Aberdeen MS.; it comes after all the conciliar and diocesan statutes in that manuscript, and seems likely to be meant for use locally in connection with the ceremonies of excommunication that are ordered to be held four times a year under statute no. 51 of *c.* 1252. This particular form seems to have been drawn up to allow for the excommunications ordered in statutes nos. 47 and 52 of the

It would seem likely;[21] but there is as yet no evidence to show the stage in the three-day meeting of the council at which he was re-elected or a successor was chosen. Indeed it is assumed in the Order of Business that a council meeting might at least begin without the Conservator being present – in which case the senior bishop present was to take charge.

The implication seems to be that the Conservator himself was not essential as the presiding officer at meetings of the council. His job is defined positively as the executive arm of the council's decrees. Between meetings of the council he was to 'punish manifest and notorious offenders against the council and any statute made by it, and effectively to compel due satisfaction to be made by means of ecclesiastical censure according to the exigency of the law'.[22] This suggests a very active role even if he was not regarded as being the only one with responsibility for enforcing conciliar decrees. In some cases rectors and vicars, or archdeacons and deans are instructed to take action.[23] In other cases the local bishops were expected to take the initiative.[24] On the other hand there were some statutes in which the device of the regular excommunication in advance of whole categories of offender was used.[25] In one of these statutes (no. 104) it is specifically stated that absolution for offenders might be obtained only from the Conservator; and probably this is implied not only in the other statutes about such excommunications, but also in many statutes (the large majority) in which no executive officer is mentioned.[26] If this is so, the Conservator was regarded as being responsible for investigating possible infringements of even quite a petty nature in every corner of every Scottish diocese.

---

same date; but the reference therein to 'the king and queen and their son' survives perhaps from an earlier version. See discussion above pp. 72–4; and cf. below pp. 136–7.

[21] Cf. view in Duncan, *Kingdom*, 293, and see below pp. 111–12.

[22] No. 2.

[23] Nos. 7, 18.

[24] Nos. 6, 10, 11, 23, 31, 50, 55.

[25] Nos. 47, 52, 104.

[26] Cf. William Lyndwood's fifteenth-century view that in England the archbishop (as metropolitan) had concurrent jurisdiction in the dioceses of his suffragan bishops over any matter which had been dealt with in provincial statutes (cited in Cheney, *Texts*, 133–4, 174).

Throughout the statutes indeed there is emphasis on the 'authority' of the council, even if it is specifically mentioned only occasionally.[27] There is little doubt that this was conceived as a layer of authority between that of the bishops and that of the pope.[28] It is interesting that there does not seem to have been any question of obtaining papal approval of the council's acts, so that it is not the case in these exempt dioceses that the pope himself took over all the responsibilities as a metropolitan, even if he did continue after 1225 to act like a metropolitan at least in the matter of confirming episcopal elections. In a normal provincial council the metropolitan alone was the authority for issuing statutes and putting them into effect. He would usually, however, take counsel and seek consent from the members of his provincial council. It has been argued[29] from the practice in thirteenth-century France and from contemporary canonists that the advice of only the bishops was necessary, however often lesser persons might sometimes contribute to the discussion; and apparently it was 'frequently' the case that the metropolitan and his fellow-bishops regarded themselves as the head and members of an ecclesiastical corporation. In some cases therefore the bishops 'contributed to the authority of the assembly's acts';[30] and in practice it would be normal for the bishops to have considerable say in the drafting of suitable statutes for the province.[31] It was as such a corporate group that the bishops in Scotland interpreted their terms of reference in the bull of 1225 as entitling them to make statutes on a considerable scale. The operative initial phrase 'We decree' (*Statuimus*) in this case therefore is clearly not the plural form often associated with a single person occupying a high office, but is rather the sign of a corporate act. Since the Conservator was the executive arm of the council and not its master, it is a council of equals with which we are dealing. This implies that, with the possible exception of the inital code of 1242 x 1249,[32] the council's

[27] E.g. nos. 7, 33; cf. *Moray Registrum*, 127, no. 114.

[28] The position of exempt monasteries requires investigation. For the implications of exemption for diocesan synods see Cheney, *Synodalia*, 4, 10, 22–4.

[29] R. L. Kay, 'The making of statutes in French provincial councils 1049–1305', in *Dissertation Abstracts*, xx (Ann Arbor: Michigan, 1959), 1004.

[30] Cheney, *Synodalia*, 3.

[31] Cheney, *Texts*, 123–4.

[32] See above p. 67.

legislative output was not normally, if ever, inspired by a single dominant figure, but is more likely to reflect the miscellaneous difficulties which individual bishops found in their dioceses, or matters regarding which it was inconvenient or unworkable to have a variety of practices in the different Scottish dioceses. Thus we find a willingness to legislate in the form of statute no. 6 – 'each of us in his diocese will enquire. . .'. And this was parallelled by the willingness of fellow-bishops to back up one of their number who wished to have their support in extending the effectivenes of sentences of excommunication,[33] though this was accompanied by an interesting penalty clause to the effect that if any bishop failed to respond to such a request, he was to be subject to the judgment of the council and cut off from the counsels of his brother-bishops and the other prelates there. When this is considered along with the rule in statute no. 1 about punishing non-attenders who had no excuse, we can see that the council by the mid-thirteenth century was following conventions of exercising its jurisdiction even over its own constituent members. Scotland had no metropolitan, but the Scottish Council with its Conservator did a least offer a degree of consistency and cohesion as it attempted to keep the ten dioceses together, and provided an authority which could usefully be called upon as advantageously local compared with the time-consuming and expensive alternative of dealing with Rome.

List of Known Conservators

William de Lamberton (St. Andrews)?: 9 Jul. 1321 (*APS*, i, pp. 478–9)

William de Sinclair (Dunkeld): 21–22 Mar. 1325 (*Glasgow Registrum*, i, 230–1, no. 270, wrongly called 'Walter')

Walter Trayl (St. Andrews): 18 Jul. 1388 (*Moray Registrum*, 350–1, no. 267)

Alexander Bur (Moray): early 1390s? (*SES*, ii, pp. 3–4)

William Stephenson (Dunblane): 16 Jul. 1420 (*SES*, ii, p. 77, no. 166)

John de Crannach (Brechin): 28 Jun. 1445 (see below[34])

Thomas Spens (Aberdeen): 19 Jul. 1459 (*SES*, ii, pp. 79–80, no. 167)

Patrick Graham (St. Andrews): 17 Jul. 1470 (see below[35])

[33] No. 53.

[34] *Registrum Episcopatus Brechinensis* (Bannatyne Club, 1856), i, 98, no. 56.

[35] St. Andrews, University Muniments, MS. Registrum Evidentiarum et Privilegiorum Universitatis Sanctiandree, fos. 70v–72v.

7

Developments 1239–1296

THE connection of Scotland with the general councils of the church was resumed somewhat tenuously in the 1240s. Bishops Bernham of St. Andrews and Bondington of Glasgow were summond to the council called to Rome for 31 March 1241, and travelled as far as France and perhaps Italy. But the Emperor Frederick II prevented this council from assembling, and the two bishops returned home without having reached Rome.[1] Then on 27 December 1244 Pope Innocent IV called another general council to Lyons for 24 June 1245. The full list of addressees is not known, but there is sufficient evidence for a modern historian to conclude that 'le cercle des invités coincide avec la liste des archives de Grégoire IX'.[2] Bishop Bernham certainly attended this council, whose formal sessions were held on 28 June, 5 and 17 July 1245,[3] for he was one of the members of the council who attached their seals on 13 July to a series of transumpts of old privileges in favour of the papacy which were assembled and copied for greater safety,[4] and he seems to have dealt with other matters at the curia in the next few months.[5] Did Bishop

[1] See Watt, *Dictionary*, 42 for details. The summons seems to have been restricted to these two bishops (*Chron. Melrose*, 87; *CPL*, i, 195), probably in terms similar to that sent to the archbishop of Sens in France on 9 August 1240 (H. Wolter and H. Holstein, *Lyon I et Lyon II* [Paris, 1966], 249; cf. 27–8).

[2] Wolter, *Lyon I*, 51–2.

[3] Ibid., 62.

[4] Ibid., 71; D. L. Galbreath, 'Scottish seals from the Continent', *SHR*, xxvii (1948), 127–41, especially 128; C. Burns, 'Scottish bishops at the general councils of the late Middle Ages', *Innes Review*, xvi (1965), 135–9, especially 137.

[5] Watt, *Dictionary*, 43.

Bondington attend as well? It is not so certain that he did; but on balance it is likely,[6] even though he was still in office as chancellor of King Alexander II.[7] On the other hand the Master Reginald de Irewyn who is certainly found as a royal envoy to the curia in September 1245[8] (when a general privilege for settling Scottish ecclesiastical disputes within Scotland was secured[9]), may in his other capacity as one of the archdeacons of Glasgow have attended the council in June–July as a proctor for the Glasgow chapter,[10] and could have acted for his bishop as well. It is just possible that Master Richard Vairement was also at Lyons in the company of Bishop Bernham, with whom he had been associated at St. Andrews, though in the emerging collegiate church of St. Mary there rather than as a member of the Augustinian cathedral priory;[11] but it may be that it was others who secured for him the personal dispensation that was granted on 13 September 1245.[12] Perhaps both the two bishops and these two lesser clergy all came to the council as in some sense royal proctors,[13] and were successful on the king's behalf in extracting from the pope the mandate of 27 July 1245 which started the proceedings that led in 1250 to the canonisation of Queen Margaret of Scotland.[14] They

[6] He did not seal the transumpts like Bishop Bernham, but then only a representative number of council members did so (cf. Wolter, *Lyon I*, 71). He may well have sought in person the privileges for the church of Glasgow granted by the pope 13 July–7 September 1245 (*Glasgow Registrum*, i, 152–4, nos. 188–90); and he was somehow instrumental in obtaining an indult for his clerk Master Hugh on 4 August 1245 (Theiner, *Monumenta*, 44, no. 115; *CPL*, i, 219; cf. Watt, *Dictionary*, 450, s.v. 'Hugh Picard', where it is probably wrongly assumed that Bondington was not then at Lyons).

[7] *HBC*, 181; cf. Watt, *Dictionary*, 461–2, s.v. 'Peter de Ramsay').

[8] *CPL*, i, 220; see Watt, *Dictionary*, 285.

[9] *Glasgow Registrum*, i, 155, no. 192; *SES*, i, lix, n. 4; cf. *Foedera, Conventiones, Litterae et Cuiuscunque Generis Acta Publica*, ed. T. Rymer, Record Commission edition (London, 1816–69), i, 263.

[10] Watt, *Fasti*, 171, 174, s.v. 'Irvine'; see Wolter, *Lyon I*, 52 for evidence that at least some cathedral chapters were expected to send proctors.

[11] Cf. Watt, *Dictionary*, 559.

[12] *CPL*, i, 220.

[13] King Henry III of England certainly sent his proctors to this council (*C&S*, II, i, 402).

[14] *Dunfermline Registrum*, 181, no. 281. But note that agents of Dunfermline abbey were also active at the curia obtaining a series of privileges for that abbey between 24 April and 6 September 1245 (ibid., 177–83, nos. 273–80, 282–6).

may have come to Lyons to serve the pope's purposes (which centred on the deposition of the Emperor Frederick II), but they returned home with privileges valued in Scotland.

Two of the constitutions agreed at Lyons had financial implications. As at the Fourth Lateran Council it was again ordered that the clergy of Western Christendom should pay a tax of one-twentieth of their ecclesiastical revenues for three years to help the Holy Land.[15] Additionally clerks who did not reside personally in their benefices for at least six months of each year were to pay half their revenues for three years for the benefit of the fading Latin Empire of Constantinople.[16] In England news of these mandatory taxes evoked prolonged opposition, and a number of meetings were held where this opposition was voiced, including one on 1 December 1246 in London which was apparently wholly clerical in composition. In the end probably none of the twentieth was collected in England, and only a proportion of the other tax.[17] What of Scotland? The 1215 tax had occasioned a council in Scotland in 1220,[18] but this time at least the twentieth (for nothing is known about the incidence of the other tax) was collected without any known council being called locally to discuss it. By October 1247 Clement bishop of Dunblane had been appointed by Rome as collector in the kingdom of Scotland for this twentieth and other revenues for the Holy Land,[19] and it was still being collected in May 1254 by a foreign collector John de Frosinone.[20] There seems to have been no special council of clergy called either in Scotland in connection with a concurrent new demand for a charitable subsidy for the pope along the lines negotiated by the Legate Otto *c.* 1239.[21] Fr. John Anglicus, O.F.M., was appointed to work for this end in Scotland as well as England in October 1246, and was active in England by February 1247, negotiating with the bishops jointly for the payment of a round sum which the individual bishops were then to discuss with their clergy.[22]

[15] Tanner, *Decrees*, 299.

[16] Ibid., 295.

[17] Lunt, *Financial Relations*, 250–5; *C&S*, II, i, 388–401.

[18] See above p. 39.

[19] Theiner, *Monumenta*, 48, no. 128; cf. *CPL*, i, 237.

[20] *Foedera*, i, 303. For this clerk see Bagliani, *Cardinali*, i, 169 and Ferguson, *Papal Representatives*, 100.

[21] See above pp. 49–51.

[22] Lunt, *Financial Relations*, 220–2; *C&S*, II, i, 390.

He sent another Franciscan Fr. William de Basinches to Scotland, where in the course of 1247 he received every encouragement in his task from King Alexander.[23] We do not know how this papal agent consulted the Scottish clergy (as he was bound to do for this kind of levy) or whether he had any success.

Mention has been made above[24] of the meeting of seven bishops perhaps about 19 June 1250 to assert the rights of churchmen threatened in their privileges by the minority regime. Such troubled times may well have prevented the holding of annual provincial councils regularly as envisioned in the 1242 x 1249 statutes, and the split of the leading clergy into Comynite and Durwardite factions, which is so clear in 1255,[25] may have taken some years to heal. But it is perhaps surprising that it is not until 1268 at Perth that the next meeting of the council can be traced. There the bishop of St. Andrews secured the excommunication of the abbot of Melrose and a large part of the convent there (all belonging to Glasgow diocese) following a fracas on the bishop's estate at Stow in Midlothian when blood had been shed.[26] When two prelates were at loggerheads like this, their fellow-prelates would be anxious to re-establish the peace without awkward questions about the privileges of the church being raised; and there was no other church court in the country to which the case could be brought.[27]

But there must have been also a number of additional meetings of clerical councils about this time in connection with the activities of the legate Cardinal Ottobono Fieschi. When on 5 May 1265 this distinguished churchman (a nephew of the late Pope Innocent IV and himself a future pope) was appointed by the new pope Clement IV as his successor in the office of legate to England, Wales and Ireland, his powers were without explanation extended

[23] By 14 March 1247/8 the king was being reassured by the pope that he had not compromised by his helpful attitude the right of Scotland to exclude legates other than those directly from Rome (Theiner, *Monumenta*, 49, no. 131; cf. *SES*, i, p. lx, where this man's work is attached to the wrong papal tax).

[24] See above p. 71.

[25] Stones, *Documents*, 30–4, no. 10; see discussion in Watt, 'Minority', 12–15.

[26] *Chron. Bower*, v, 371; cf. Watt, *Dictionary*, 213–14, where this abbot of Melrose is wrongly identified.

[27] See below p. 94.

to Scotland as well.[28] Though his stay in England was to be a long and useful one (from 29 October 1265 to July 1268)[29] following the troubled period of the Barons' Wars, there is no evidence that King Alexander III of Scotland had been consulted about this appointment, and it is likely that the Scottish clergy were ambivalent from the beginning about the very sweeping powers delegated to him by the pope. Not the least of these was the authority to collect one-tenth of church revenues in Scotland as elsewhere to help with the business of his legation.[30] There seems to have been no suggestion that representatives of the Scottish clergy should attend the legatine councils held in England in December 1265, February and June 1267.[31] It was probably sometime in 1266 that he sent his first envoys to King Alexander, explaining that he could not come in person.[32] These envoys would have demanded procurations from the Scottish clergy for the support of 'their legate', the rate of which is reported by the chronicler John of Fordun a hundred years later as 4 marks per parish church and 6 marks per cathedral church.[33] This seems to have been a levy on a wider scale than was sought in England;[34] but the same Scottish source suggests that it was collected in Scotland up to a total of 2,000 marks, and then the king stepped in to forbid its despatch to the south, making an appeal to Rome.[35] Presumably there had been a least one church council meeting behind these actions, and again behind the reported action of the Scottish clergy in the following year (1267) in getting the king to abandon his appeal while they paid their procurations to the

[28] Theiner, *Monumenta*, 96–8, no. 245; *CPL*, i, 426–30; cf. ibid., 396. See Ferguson, *Papal Representatives*, 108–13.

[29] *C&S*, II, ii, 725.

[30] Theiner, *Monumenta*, 98, no. 246; *CPL*, i, 429; and see Lunt, *Financial Relations*, 291–2.

[31] Cf. *C&S*, II, ii, 726–8, 732–8.

[32] R. Graham, 'Letters of Cardinal Ottoboni', *EHR*, xv (1900), 82–120, especially 90, no. 4; one of the envoys was a Master Maurice (ibid., 95, no. 7).

[33] *Chron. Fordun*, i, 303.

[34] Lunt, *Financial Relations*, 550–1; cf. 555.

[35] The developed fifteenth-century version of this evidence in *Chron. Bower*, v, 357 suggests that the 2,000 marks were paid by the clergy to pay the costs of this appeal. Bower seems to have been trying to make sense of a passage by Fordun that he found hard to understand (cf. ibid., 472; and see *SES*, i, p. lxii, and Duncan, *Kingdom*, 291).

Legate Ottobono on the different basis of six pence per valued mark.[36]

Later in 1267 the legate is said to have sent another envoy to Scotland (a man of Roman origin) to obtain the king's permission for him to come to Scotland himself; but after a consultation with the clergy the king refused to let him come.[37] It may well have been this envoy who met with threats of death from some servants of the king, and also with a royal fiat that no one was to obey him.[38] Or this treatment may have been dealt out to another of Ottobono's envoys coming to Scotland in connection with a different piece of business, for, though the tenth authorised in May 1265 had probably been abortive, the legate had on 8 and 22 June 1266 been authorised to collect another tenth in Scotland for the benefit of King Henry III (in particular to pay for the debts of his queen), provided that King Alexander agreed.[39] In England the collection of this tax led to the meeting of at least one legatine council of clergy (at Bury St. Edmunds in Suffolk, February 1267),[40] and it seems likely that there was a discussion on the same matter between Alexander and the clergy in Scotland; but by 15 July 1267 it is apparent that he had refused to allow this tax to be paid.[41] It is not possible to say whether it was before or after this that the legate proposed himself for a visit to Scotland as mentioned above. Bower reports two more attempts to tax the Scottish clergy which would appear to be different from those of 1265 and 1266–7. Once Henry III's sons Edward and Edmund had taken the crusading vow in June 1268,[42] that king and Ottobono are supposed to have persuaded Pope Clement IV (who died on 29 November 1268) to write to the Scottish clergy

[36] *Chron. Bower*, v, 361, where procurations are confusingly said to have been paid also to Cardinal Hubert de Cocconato, who is not known to have been a legate in Britain at this time.

[37] *Chron. Bower*, v, 361; cf. Graham, 'Ottoboni letters', 95–6, no. 7, which perhaps refers to this embassy.

[38] Ibid., 117–18, no. 34.

[39] Theiner, *Monumenta*, 99–100, no. 249; *CPL*, i, 432–3.

[40] Lunt, *Financial Relations*, 293–4.

[41] Other arrangments were on this date made for the queen's debts (ibid., 296; *CPL*, i, 434).

[42] F. M. Powicke, *King Henry III and the Lord Edward* (Oxford, 1947), ii, 562.

ordering them to pay a tenth to the English king. King Alexander is said to have had the unanimous consent of his clergy in refusing to allow this tax to be collected, on the grounds that Scotland was making an adequate contribution of its own to this crusade.[43] King Henry is said to have tried again to collect this tenth in 1269, only for his envoys to be met with a refusal from the Scottish clergy, who decided to send their own envoys to the vacant papal court to appeal against this.[44] These further attempts to tax the Scottish church are not vouched for by any contemporary evidence, and so there is no certainty that as many as four different levies were suggested by the pope or the English king 1265–9; but it is reasonable to suppose that at least some of them must have been discussed by clerical councils of some kind in Scotland and such bodies must have grown in stature when with royal support they had the determination to refuse to pay.[45]

We can be more certain that the bishops of Scotland met in 'common council' to consider a summons (issued probably in December 1267)[46] to attend Ottobono's final legatine council in London in April 1268. Certainly in the event the legate at this council emphasised his authority in the kingdom of Scotland as well as in England, Wales and Ireland, when he introduced his famous collection of fifty-three canons, which are said to have become 'the most important single collection of local law for the English church'.[47] It is reported by Fordun[48] that he demanded the attendance in London of all the bishops of Scotland, together with two abbots and two priors to speak for the clergy of the whole realm of Scotland. The bishops are said to have 'by common council' decided to send just the bishops of Dunkeld and Dunblane to this legatine council 'lest anything in the absence of these two be ordained to the prejudice and injury of the bishops'. As a

[43] *Chron. Fordun*, i, 303; *Chron. Bower*, v, 369.

[44] *Chron. Fordun*, i, 303–4; *Chron. Bower*, v, 373.

[45] In 1356 the abbey of Fearn in Ross diocese was said to be liable to some form of ecclesiastical taxation (as opposed to royal levies) 'secundum taxacionem domus predicte per Ottobonum editam Sedis Apostolice in Scotia judicem delegatum' (*SES*, i, p. liii, n. 1). Perhaps this is an error for the Legate Otto's caritative tax of 1239 (see above pp. 50–1).

[46] *C&S*, II, ii, 738.

[47] Ibid., 747–92; cf. 739.

[48] *Chron. Fordun*, i, 303.

palliative the two bishops took with them some money which they seem to have been responsible for collecting in Scotland for the legate's procurations (i.e. expenses).[49] The rest of the clergy sent the abbot of Dunfermline and the prior of Lindores as their representatives. Presumably the bishops had held one of their customary meetings early in 1268; but how the views of the 'Scottish clergy' (*clerus Scotiae*) were obtained is quite unknown. Perhaps it is simplest to suggest that by this time (and not least as a response to the legate's recent financial demands) a representative element of lower clergy had come to be associated occasionally with the bishops and monastic heads as a part of the *concilium Scoticanum*.[50]

Once the report came back from London about the fifty-three new canons which Ottobono intended to be applied to both the secular and the regular clergy in Scotland,[51] Fordun tells us that the bishops of Scotland refused to accept them, while Bower in his later account interestingly makes it the clergy (*clerus*) of Scotland rather than just the bishops who refused to observe them.[52] We cannot now know what kind of assembly it was to which the four representatives who had been to the London council reported, though it is quite likely to have been the 'council' at Perth which is known to have acted on an inter-diocesan dispute in the course of 1268.[53] But though the abbot of Dunfermline at any rate may be presumed to have brought back accurate knowledge of Ottobono's canons,[54] the collection as a whole entered the law and practice of the church in Scotland even less than had that of the Legate Otto in 1237 or 1239.[55] For better or worse the Scots clergy were probably left to go their own way during the

[49] Watt, *Dictionary*, 281, s.v. 'Richard de Inverkeithing' (cf. above p. 91).

[50] See above p. 80, and below p. 118.

[51] *tam de secularibus quam religiosis personis Scotorum* (*Chron. Fordun*, i, 303).

[52] Ibid.; *Chron. Bower*, v, 369.

[53] See above p. 92.

[54] Otto's canon no. 18 was copied into the register of Dunfermline Abbey (*Dunfermline Registrum*, 202, no. 312) along with an earlier papal pronouncement on procurations payable to visiting prelates.

[55] See above p. 48 and pp. 51–2. There is a case in 1442 when Otto's canon 12 (on protection for church property) was cited, but by the prior of Durham in defence of the Durham cell at Coldingham in Berwickshire, when it was no doubt convenient to cite law that was currently well-known in England (*SES*, i, pp. lxiii–lxiv, n. 2).

prolonged papal vacancy that came soon afterwards (from November 1268 to March 1272), for there is no sign that the eventual new pope, Gregory X, tried to provide papal backing for Ottobono's canons in Scotland as he did in England.[56] Perhaps the provincial council was just too firm in its attitude and too well backed by their king to be overridden.

Almost at once after his coronation as pope on 27 March 1272, Pope Gregory announced on 31 March that he wished a general council of the church to assemble on 1 May 1274 at a place still to be determined.[57] The distribution-list of this letter of summons has not survived in the papal archives, but we may assume that letters were sent then to the bishops and king of Scotland. The rules were that all bishops were to come in person, except for one or two per province who were to remain behind 'for those matters which require the office of bishop'. Furthermore the bishops of each province were on the pope's behalf to select chapters of cathedral and other churches who should send proctors to the council, since matters affecting their interests were to be dealt with there. Meanwhile there was to be an enquiry in each province into matters requiring correction and reformation, so that these might be brought to the attention of the council for suitable action.[58] This summons came at a time when the Scottish episcopate had only five incumbents in office,[59] with vacancies in all the remaining seven sees, largely as the result of delays caused by the papal vacancy. The instruction to hold local enquiries, therefore, is unlikely to have been followed with energy. But by 13 April 1273 when the pope wrote round again to say that the council would again be held at Lyons and giving more details about the agenda,[60]

[56] *C&S*, II, ii, 792 (27 July 1272).

[57] *Les registres de Grégoire X et Jean XXI* (Paris, 1892–1960), 53–6, nos. 160–1 (letters to archbishop of Sens and the king of France).

[58] For English and continental responses to this instruction see *C&S*, II, ii, 804–9, and 810, n. 3.

[59] Argyll, Dunblane, Galloway, The Isles and Moray (Watt, *Fasti*, under each bishopric). Of these Galloway and The Isles were ecclesiastically subject to foreign archbishops though they were politically part of the Scottish kingdom.

[60] *Registres de Grégoire X*, 118, nos. 307–8. A letter went this time to the king of Scotland specifically; but the papal clerks seem to have thought that the right way to write to the Scottish bishops was through the Irish archbishops (full texts are printed in Mansi, *Amplissima Collectio*, xxiv (Venice, 1780), cols. 56–9).

bishops had been consecrated for Aberdeen, Glasgow and Ross, and those for Dunkeld and St. Andrews followed suit by autumn 1273. It would be in the latter part of 1273 that the Scottish bishops met at Perth and decided that the bishops of Dunkeld (Robert de Stuteville, newly consecrated[61]) and Moray (Archibald, who had been in office since 1253[62]) should remain at home;[63] and it is reported that all the others left for Lyons after 2 February 1274.[64] The six sessions of this council were in fact held between 7 May and 17 July 1274. There is documentary proof that five Scottish bishops as a national group were present in person on 13 July to seal a new constitution on the procedure for holding papal elections – Argyll, Dunblane, Glasgow, The Isles and St. Andrews.[65] The bishop of Ross had also gone to Lyons, for he died there during the council.[66] It is curiously uncertain whether the bishops of Aberdeen and Galloway were present or not, for we cannot know whether all available bishops were meant to seal a document on 13 July or just a suitably large representative group of them.[67] No names of any lesser clergy are known; but when on 18 May 1274 the non-episcopal members of the council were given permission to go home, provided that each geographical/political region left a minimum numbers of proctors behind to represent them, those from the kingdom of Scotland are listed as having to leave just one proctor,[68] so that the presumption must be that at least some were present. Certainly full knowledge of the proceedings at Lyons must have been brought back soon to Scotland.[69]

[61] Watt, *Fasti*, 95.

[62] Ibid., 214.

[63] *Chron. Bower*, v, 399.

[64] Ibid.

[65] *Innes Review*, xvi (1965), 137–9; *SHR*, xxvii (1948), 127–8.

[66] *Chron. Bower*, v, 401.

[67] Cf. *C&S*, II, ii, 810. The full list of bishops from various countries who added their seals on 13 July is given by F. Kaltenbrunner, *Actenstücke zur Geschichte des Deutschen Reiches unter den Königen Rudolf I und Albrecht I*, in *Mittheilungen aus dem Vatikanische Archive*, i (Vienna, 1889), 58–60, no. 52, appears to be selective rather than comprehensive; cf. Watt, *Dictionary*, 40, s.v. 'Hugh de Bennum'. The sees of Brechin and Caithness were still vacant (Watt, *Fasti*, 39, 58).

[68] Tanner, *Decrees*, 313; cf. Holstein, *Lyon II*, 173, 175, 191.

[69] The chronicler Bower was exceptionally able to list the achievements of this general council in some detail from sources available to him in Scotland in mid-fifteenth century (*Chron. Bower*, v, 399–401).

One customary concomitant of the thirteenth-century General Councils was the levying throughout Western Christendom of a tax for the Crusade, and at Lyons this was duly promulgated as a tenth of clerical incomes for six years.[70] We know much more about how productive this tax was in Scotland than about any other papal tax in this country during the Middle Ages, because its collection coincided with new papal administrative procedures for increased central control over the work of the tax collectors. Regular reports were demanded, and care was taken to preserve relevant correspondence and to carry through effective audits of accounts.[71] The kingdom of Scotland was on this occasion allocated a separate papal collector for herself. This was the Italian clerk Baiamund de' Vicia, who had served under the Legate Ottobono in England in the 1260s,[72] and who was commissioned to his new office on 20 September 1274.[73] He left Lyons a few days later,[74] and remained in this employment as it turned out under successive popes until his death, probably in Scotland, between 1 September 1289 and 16 September 1291.[75] It was part of his instructions to levy this tax on the basis of a much more comprehensive valuation of benefices than had previously been used, and presumably he hoped for the co-operation of the Scottish bishops who had agreed to this tax at Lyons. But there was opposition to this which was voiced at a council which the collector is said to have assembled at Perth on 6 August 1275, and he was prevailed upon to return to the Roman court with the suggestion that the *antiqua taxacio* (i.e. the current customary valuation) should be used as the basis of this tenth, but that the Scottish clergy should pay for seven years rather than just six.[76] In fact this suggestion was not acceptable, and the collection went on for some years on the basis originally laid down. The nature of

[70] Tanner, *Decrees*, 310.

[71] Lunt, *Financial Relations*, 333–4.

[72] Ibid., 627.

[73] Theiner, *Monumenta*, 104, no. 258. See Ferguson, *Papal Representatives*, 114–17.

[74] *SHS Misc.*, vi, 30.

[75] *CDS*, ii, no. 382; *Rotuli Scotiae* (London, 1814–19), i, 5.

[76] *Chron. Fordun*, i, 306; *Chron. Bower*, v, 403. The translation adopted here is different from that found in *Chron. Fordun*, ii, 301, *SES*, i, p. lxvi, and *SHS Misc.*, vi, 5.

the council at Perth is not clearly defined in the later chronicle accounts: Fordun writes both of *episcopi et clerus* and of *episcopi et abbates*; while Bower prefers *prelati et clerus*; but it would have been an assembly very like the provincial council and probably identical to it. In such circumstances it is very likely that it embraced a considerable representation of the lower clergy, who throughout the country were so closely affected by the stiffer level of taxation that was being proposed. It is interesting that, following on their success in opposing the demands of Ottobono in the 1260s, they could now force a papal collector to make a fruitless journey back to base before they would co-operate. But it is equally interesting that in the end they did co-operate with him, for this collector was able to extract very considerable sums with the assistance of the Scottish clergy thereafter.[77] Their corporate will could be effective in more than one direction.

There is useful contemporary evidence of a more routine meeting of the provincial council in the Dominican church at Perth in 1280. The bishop of Moray had been litigating with William de Fenton (lord of Beaufort in the Aird, Inverness-shire) and his wife Cecily over some land belonging to the church of Kiltarlity, and obtained on 26 March 1280 a procedural sentence of excommunication against his opponents from three papal judges-subdelegate who were involved in the case. Then on 18 August he wrote to the council of 'bishops, abbots, priors, deans, archdeacons and other prelates of churches' who were due to meet at Perth on 26 August asking for the repetition of this excommunication 'in every church of your dioceses'.[78] It was clearly an ordinary meeting of the provincial council that was being addressed, and advantage was in fact being taken of no. 53 of the provincial statutes which entitled a bishop to ask for help in this way. But it was not just his fellow-bishops that the bishop of Moray was addressing: even such essentially episcopal business was being addressed now to the same kind of larger council which seems likely in recent years to have been customary in dealing with financial matters.

[77] His accounts survive in part and have been published (Theiner, *Monumenta*, 109–16, no. 264; *SHS Misc.*, vi, 25–77; *EHR*, xxxii (1917), 59–61; cf. *SHS Misc.*, v (1933), 87–106; x, 7–9; *Innes Review*, xxii (1971), 9–10.

[78] *Moray Registrum*, 140–2, no. 127; *SES*, i, pp. lxxi–lxxii.

Valuable insight into the stage of development which the *concilium Scoticanum* had reached by the end of the thirteenth century is provided by an undated royal letter that survives in a formulary collected in the 1320s, which includes several model documents relating to the period of the interregnum in Scotland 1286–92 and to the reign of King John Balliol that followed 1292–96.[79] This particular letter is addressed to the clergy who are due to meet at Perth on 1 October (no year-date), and they are described in just the same terms as had been used by the bishop of Moray in 1280.[80] It is said to have been the custom of kings of Scotland in times past to send knights and clerics (*milites et clerici*) to 'Scottish councils' *ad allegandum proponendum et appellandum*, lest anything be done or asserted against the royal dignity or against the customs hitherto accepted in the kingdom. The king therefore now sends an undefined number of such proctors to the council (with at least two expected to attend), who are to stop business there by appealing in the king's name to the apostolic see if there is any danger of injury to the king's rights. They are also to ask for and receive something in the king's name; but the letter as preserved in the formulary breaks off without explaining what this was to be, presumably because it was of temporary rather than lasting interest.

A number of different questions arise from this text. Whatever its date, it offers a guide to the working relationship established between the council and the king, say between 1225 and the death of King Alexander III in 1286. We have noted how the king himelf came to a council meeting in 1242; and as part of the resistance mounted in the late 1260s to the financial demands of the Legate Ottobono the king helped the council to avoid having to submit by appealing to Rome.[81] Now we can see how by sending 'knights and clerks' to hold a watching brief at a council meeting the king exercised fundamental control such as everywhere in Western Christendom formed the bedrock of such 'liberties' or privileges as the organised church could in practice enjoy. And when it was

[79] *Formulary E: Scottish Letters and Brieves 1286–1424*, ed. A. A. M. Duncan (Glasgow, 1976), 31, no. 65. Cf. nos. 1, 2, 4–6, 8–9, 10, 16, 20, 37, 41, 46, 59, 67, 68, 78, 82, 84–8, 90, 97, 99, 113.

[80] See above p. 98; the only difference is that here archdeacons are listed before rather than after deans.

[81] See above pp. 69, 91.

a question of operating the mechanism established by the papal decree of 1225, it is logical that the king's weapon against any over-ambitious or recalcitrant council should be to threaten to take matters to the Roman court. This meant that the bishops were being reminded that they themelves were subject to papal authority, and that they were permitted to act jointly in council only insofar as the pope allowed them to do so. They did not have the common law of the church on their side as metropolitans had; and it is reasonable to suppose that normally a threat from the king's proctors would be enough to bring the council to heel. We cannot be sure of any case where the king had to carry out his threat; but perhaps in 1266 his temporary interference with the payment of procurations to Ottobono is to be interpreted (since a lot of money had in fact been collected) as royal interference with what the council wanted to do rather than as conniving with it for their mutual advantage.

Then there is the matter of suggesting an original date for this letter which came to be preserved in a formulary. Professor Duncan suggests '1291 x 6 (not 1295)' and sees King Edward I as its most probable author, whom failing John Balliol. The argument turns on two points: first the rather distant and detached reference to past kings of Scotland – but surely this could be the language of either Edward or John as they sought to re-estabish continuity following the vacancy on the Scottish throne from 1286 onwards. Second there is the tantalising matter of what at the end of the letter as we now have it the proctors were 'to ask for and receive'. Professor Duncan interprets that as a reference to the papal mandatory tax of a tenth for six years imposed on the clergy of England, Scotland, Wales and Ireland on 18 March 1291, the proceeds of which were to be paid to Edward in support of his planned Crusade, which was meant to set out in June 1293.[82] Though Edward in the end never went on this Crusade, the tax was certainly levied generally and collected in Scotland for four out of the six years (i.e. at twice-yearly terms probably from February 1292 to May 1295), which was longer than it was levied in England.[83] But the business of assessment and collection was on

[82] *CPL*, i, 551–5.

[83] *The Register of John de Halton, bishop of Carlisle, A.D. 1292–1324* [*Reg. Halton*] (Canterbury and York Society, 1913), i, 153; cf. 16–21, 41–6; *Coupar Angus Chrs.*, i, 139–41, no. 64; cf. Lunt, *Financial Relations*, 356.

this occasion controlled by the bishops of Caithness and Carlisle (nominated by office rather than as individuals), and it is hard to see how through the *consilium Scoticanum* Edward could 'attempt to lay hold on taxation of the church' as Professor Duncan suggests.[84] The royal proctors are likely to have 'asked for and received' something more like a promise to maintain good church–state customs than money. Thus it seems best not to see any financial aspect in this letter referring to a council which was to meet on 1 October; and it seems more likely to be an act of King John Balliol than of King Edward I, and so datable 1292 x 1295, probably 1292 x 1294.[85]

It is worth noting by the way from the records of this 1291 tax that the collectors included not only Galloway diocese in their area of responsibility, but also the diocese of Sodor, i.e. The Isles. Though the former was still ecclesiastically in the province of York and presumably had as yet no place in the Scottish provincial council, it was not only indubitably part of the kingdom of Scotland, but had been assessed for church taxation purposes along with the other Scottish dioceses both in the mid-thirteenth century and for the tenth of 1274.[86] Though The Isles became part of the Scottish kingdom in 1266, the diocese of Sodor was not taxed along with the Scottish dioceses by Baiamund de' Vicia; but the tenth of 1291 was collected at least from the Isle of Man portion of the diocese by the bishop of Carlisle, and for six years rather than just the four years on the mainland.[87] The whole diocese remained for the present under the archbishop of Trondheim in Norway as metropolitan, so that its bishop presumably had no place in the *consilium Scoticanum*. Nevertheless the bishops both of Galloway and Sodor were by the end of the thirteenth century accustomed to taking their places among the

[84] *Formulary E*, p. 31.

[85] October 1295 is unlikely, since the government of the country seems to have been taken out of King John's hands from July 1295 onwards (G. W. S. Barrow, *Robert Bruce and the Community of the Realm of Scotland*, 3rd edition [Edinburgh, 1988], 63); but formal documents were during this time still being issued in the king's name (G. G. Simpson, *Handlist of the Acts of Alexander III, the Guardians and John 1249–1296* [Edinburgh, 1960], 60).

[86] *Liber Cartarum Prioratus Sancti Andree in Scotia* [*St Andrews Liber*] (Bannatyne Club, 1841), 28, 360; *SHS Misc.*, vi, 26, 74–5.

[87] *Reg. Halton*, i, 153.

magnates of Scotland when it came to political assembies such as that at Birgham near Roxburgh in March 1290 which confirmed the abortive Anglo-Scottish royal marriage treaty,[88] or as auditors in the Great Cause of 1291–2.[89] It must therefore surely be an open question whether they were still not invited to attend the *consilium Scoticanum* as well. Mark bishop of Sodor 1275/6–1303 was a Galloway man who had been King Alexander's choice as bishop.[90] He was a sufficiently active bishop to issue a code of thirty-six diocesan statutes on 10 March 1292, which include two which are textually derived from items in the Scottish provincial code of 1242 x 1249, whilst the rest cover familiar themes in individual ways.[91] No doubt the assimilation of these islands which had for so long been under Norse rule was going to be a gradual process.

[88] *Documents Illustrative of the History of Scotland 1286–1306*, ed. J. Stevenson (Edinburgh, 1870), i, 129, no. 92.

[89] *Documents and Records illustrating the History of Scotland*, ed. F. Palgrave (London, 1837), illustrations, no. 2; cf. ibid., p. 53.

[90] Watt, *Fasti*, 201.

[91] C. R. Cheney, 'Manx Synodal Statutes, A.D. 1230(?)–1351', *Cambridge Medieval Celtic Studies* (1984), vii, 63–89, and viii, 51–63. No. 30 is taken partly from the Scottish code no. 29; no. 24 is an amalgam of Scottish nos. 51, 47 and 52, with specific reference to 'the custom of the Scottish church'.

8

The reign of Robert I 1306–1329

THE formulary letter of 1292 x 1294 is matched by a similar one dating from some occasion in the reign of Robert I, which is preserved in another formulary collected about 1330.[1] There was to be a *generale consilium* of the bishops of the realm of Scotland and 'other inferior prelates' in the Dominican church at Perth on the 'morrow of St. P.' [*sic*]. The style here is so different from that used in 1292 x 1294 as to make it likely that some years had passed. It may be that the saint's day abbreviated here is that of St. Palladius (6 July), so that this document could possibly refer to the council which certainly met at Perth on 9 July 1321,[2] and which could well have started its session on 7 July. Alternatively, because of the mention of 'the state of the kingdom and of the Scottish church' [see below], it might more probably refer to a council held in July 1326 just before the parliament of Cambuskenneth where on 15 July 1326 the laity agreed to pay a tax to the king.[3] There is no reference now to 'knights and clerks'; instead the king sends as his proctors two doctors of civil law.[4] It

[1] *The Register of Brieves*, ed. Lord Cooper (Stair Society, Edinburgh, 1946), 47, no. 67; see also *SES*, ii, 239 and Patrick, *Statutes*, 208. Professor Duncan associates it with the reign of Robert I because it includes the phrase *regia maiestas* (*Formulary E*, p. 31).

[2] See below p. 112. Cf. *Formulary E*, p. 31, where 2 August, i.e. the morrow of the feast of St. Peter's Chains (no year-date) is suggested.

[3] See below pp. 113–14.

[4] In academic usage the qualification 'iuris civilis professor' (mentioned in the text) was identical with 'iuris civilis doctor'. If this text comes from 1326, these two doctors could well have been James Ben (D. C. L.) and Walter de Twynham (supposedly D. U. J.), who had just then returned from an embassy on behalf of the king to the king of France (Watt, *Dictionary*, 37, 550).

may be concluded that he now had a more highly qualified staff available to watch over the business of the Scottish clergy at least on this one occasion; but we may not assume that this specific type of proctor was always available, since the form-letter may have been regularly followed in its other phrases without this particular type of qualification for the king's proctors being essential or even likely. The proctors now have a more positive brief than before: they are to tell the council what the king thinks they need to be told about the state of the kingdom[5] and of the Scottish church. But also they are to have the function of protesting and appealing if there is a danger of anything being done in the council which might be to the prejudice of 'the royal majesty'. The main theme is the same as in 1292 x 1294, but as a consequence of the troubled years of the struggle for independence, the king is now behaving more masterfully towards the council. There is no mention of tradition any more; the king is taking the initiative in bringing matters on to the council's agenda, even church matters; and, most significant of all, if there has to be an appeal, it is no longer to go to the pope – who had proved so fickle a friend of the Scottish kingdom over the years of troubles, and who was in the 1320s still holding out against granting recognition to the Bruce dynasty. In effect therefore the king has cut the pope out, and any appeal must be presumed to be directed to the king himself.[6] The council had in practice never been more than conditionally free, but now it must play close attention to pleasing the king. After a revolution it could hardly have been otherwise.

But this does not mean that Robert I did not have occasion to be grateful for the help which he had received from most of the bishops and leading clergy in his long fight for recognition after 1306. At least some of the bishops attended the usurper's first parliament at St. Andrews on 16/17 March 1309, when both 'the bishops, abbots, priors and others of the clergy duly constituted

[5] The phrase 'pro statu regni' in the parliament of 1328 is understood to imply consideration (by burgh representatives in this case) of a grant for the king (A. A. M. Duncan, 'The early parliaments of Scotland', *SHR*, xlv [1966], 36–58, especially 52).

[6] This seems to be the implication also in a parallel English warning letter to an English council of bishops and prelates sent much earlier in 1241 (*C&S*, II, i, 339).

in the realm of Scotland' and the lay magnates were invited to adhere to a declaration in favour of the claim of Robert Bruce to be king of Scots.[7] Perhaps six or eight bishops in all were prepared to add their seals at that time.[8] Then nearly a year later another copy of the same declaration was prepared for sealing by twelve persons at a *consilium generale Scoticanum* held (or to be held) on 24 February 1310 in the Franciscan church at Dundee.[9] The title of the assembly matches nicely the change in title observable between the royal letters of 1292 x 1294 and 1321 or 1326 mentioned above; but there are strong political reasons for questioning whether this council was ever held, not least because the small town of Dundee was in English hands at the time.[10] All that can be said is that at least some of the seal-tags on the document appear to have been used by at least a handful of bishops,[11] though this is not proof that this provincial council actually met at the time and place mentioned. Indeed it may well have been an abortive plan, from which we can learn just that this council was now seen as an assembly at which it was hoped to obtain wider adherence to the new king from the leading Scottish clergy than had proved possible at the 1309 parliament. It would be the assembly where the corporate identity of the clergy could be expected to be most widely felt.

Yet another attempt was made to obtain the adherence of the bishops to the same declaration in favour of Bruce (which must surely have been necessitated by the comparatively poor response to the two earlier attempts). This time the names of all twelve Scottish bishops were engrossed in the text (including those of Galloway and Sodor) in such a way that we can calculate that it must have been produced for sealing between October 1314 and November 1316.[12] Again, however, we cannot be sure that all

[7] *APS*, i, 459–60, as interpreted in Barrow, *Bruce*, 183–6. Cf. D. W. Hunter Marshall, 'On a supposed provincial council of the Scottish church at Dundee in February 1310', *SHR*, xxiii (1926), 280–93.

[8] Barrow, *Bruce*, 363–4, n. 100.

[9] *APS*, i, 460; Barrow, *Bruce*, 268–9.

[10] See arguments by Hunter Marshall, loc. cit.; cf. *SES*, i, p. lxxii, n. 2, for view that this was a meeting of the Estates; but see below p. 109.

[11] Hunter Marshall, loc. cit., 282.

[12] *APS*, i, 460–1; Barrow, *Bruce*, 269. October 1314 is the *terminus a quo* since it was then that Bishop Wischard of Glasgow returned from captivity in England (Watt, *Dictionary*, 590).

twelve seals were attached.[13] They may well have been; but whether this implies that all or many of these men met at a separate meeting of the provincial council in this period, or whether their seals were added at the time of some other convenient meeting or meetings such as the parliament at Cambuskenneth of November 1314 or the royal assembly at Ayr of April–May 1315,[14] or whether the seals were added piecemeal as occasion arose is now unknowable.

On 12 August 1308 Pope Clement V issued his summons to a general council to meet at Vienne on 1 October 1310. It is noteworthy that following Robert Bruce's confusing usurpation of the Scottish throne in March 1306, the papal chancery did not on this occasion write to the king of Scotland (as had probably been done for the 1274 Council of Lyons),[15] though the king of England was sent a letter as usual.[16] This time there was no general summons to bishops to attend: only a selection of prelates were invited, with the suggestion that the others might remain behind if they so wished, and appoint those who did go as their representatives.[17] From Scotland only the bishops of St. Andrews, Glasgow and Galloway were summoned.[18] The summons to the first two of these marks a return to the practice of the 1240s,[19] but Galloway is an interesting addition.[20] There is no doubt that the current bishop there (Thomas de Dalton/Kirkcudbright) was a suffragan of York from the time when he had professed obedience at his consecration in 1294.[21] But as records of the York provincial council become available in 1286, 1290 and 1297 we can see that the bishop of Galloway was not then being summoned to attend, presumably because the business which was

[13] Hunter Marshall, loc. cit., 282–3.

[14] Cf. *APS*, i, 464–5; cf. ibid., 289–90 for lists of bishops at these two meetings. At Ayr arrangements were made for the future Bruce succession to the throne, which would be a suitable occasion for reviving the earlier declaration in favour of the family.

[15] See above p. 95.

[16] *CPL*, ii, 49; see J. Lecler, *Vienne* (Paris, 1964), 25.

[17] Ibid., 27–8.

[18] *Regestum Clementis V* (Rome, 1885–92), iii, 396, no. 3631; cf. CPL, ii, 49.

[19] See above p. 87.

[20] Cf. above p. 101.

[21] Watt, *Fasti*, 129–30; Watt, *Dictionary*, 308.

stirring the archbishops of York into metropolitan activity revolved around requests from the English king for subsidies from his clergy[22] – and there was no doubt that Galloway was in the kingdom of Scotland. And the papal chancery was continuing to treat Galloway along with the Scottish sees in matters to do with crusading or taxation.[23] It was perhaps this very anomaly which led to the summons of this particular bishop to Vienne. In the event the start of the council was on 4 April 1310 postponed until 1 October 1311,[24] and then it did meet, holding its three full sessions on 16 October 1311, 3 April and 6 May 1312, with commission meetings in between.

What attendance was there from Scotland? When the original summons was sent out in August 1308, Bishop William Lamberton of St. Andrews was just being released on onerous terms from an English gaol, where he had languished for nearly two years as a result of his support for Robert I.[25] He was now to be loyal to Edward II until at least November 1313, apparently spending much of his time in Scotland. It was Edward who on 24 July 1311 wrote to the pope asking that Lamberton be excused attendance at Vienne, and three times during 1312 this king was to write again asking that he be excused the penalties for non-attendance because he was so useful in Scotland.[26] Clearly he did not go to Vienne. Probably, however, Bishop Robert Wishart of Glasgow did so, though in unusual circumstances. He had been still in prison in England when summoned in August 1308, but was then released into papal custody while King Edward's charges against him were being investigated. He is likely to have been at the papal court for much of the period from late 1308 to early 1313 in some sense under supervision, even if he was never condemned by the pope, and so he may well have attended the council even if there is no specific proof that he did.[27] Bishop Kirkcudbright of Galloway certainly did not attend. He was from March 1306 a consistent enemy of Robert I, and forced as a

[22] *C&S*, II, ii, 978–82, 1093–6, 1185–6; cf. 944–5, 1113–15, 1162, n. 2.

[23] E.g. *CPL*, ii, 43, of August 1308.

[24] *Regestum Clementis V*, v, 397–9, no. 6293, where the bishop of St. Andrews is wrongly styled an archbishop; *CPL*, ii, 78.

[25] Watt, *Dictionary*, 322.

[26] Ibid., 323.

[27] Ibid., 589.

consequence to live for more than eight years outside Scotland. He chose to live in the north of England and take employment as a temporary suffragan bishop in both York and Durham dioceses, notably reversing recent trends by attending as bishop of Galloway at least three meetings of the provincial council of York in 1310, 1311 and 1314. In such circumstances he was hardly a fit representative of the Scottish church at Vienne, and it may have been a helpful response to his problems when Archbishop Greenfield in July 1311 appointed him as substitute bishop at York while he himself went to Vienne.[28]

Perhaps, therefore, out of the three bishops summoned from Scotland only Wishart attended the council; and though it is possible that some other Scottish bishops chose to go, none of the others then in office can be shown to have done so[29] – and with King Edward II campaigning in Scotland from September 1310 to July 1311 probably none of the bishops who supported Robert I would have been free to do so. But William de Sinclair had been at the papal court trying to obtain recognition as the elected bishop of Dunkeld. He was to be confirmed and consecrated in fact at Vienne on 8 May 1312 just after the council ended,[30] so that he may well have been admitted to its affairs as bishop-elect.[31] Two Scots at any rate therefore seem likely to have been at Vienne, so that there appears to be substance in the report that some 'prelates of Scotland' were among those who voted in the council early in December 1311 to allow the Templars' defence to be heard.[32]

In the circumstances of the select method of nomination to this general council there was no call as in 1273 for the Scottish

[28] Ibid., 309.

[29] The bishops of Brechin and Dunblane were at St. Andrews on 12 September 1311 (ibid., 304); the bishop of Argyll was under the protection of Edward II (J. Dowden, *The Bishops of Scotland* [Glasgow, 1912], 380); the bishop of Moray was at Inchture, Perthshire on 7 April 1312, as were the bishops of Aberdeen and Dunblane (*Scone Liber*, 97, no. 131). The whereabouts of the bishops of Sodor, Ross and Caithness are unknown.

[30] Watt, *Dictionary*, 496.

[31] Nine unnamed bishops-elect are said to have taken part (Lecler, *Vienne*, 54).

[32] S. Baluzius, *Vitae Paparum Avenionensium*, ed. G. Mollat, i (Paris, 1914), 42; *Archiv für Literatur- und Kirchen-Geschichte des Mittelalters* [*ALKG*], iv [1888], 421.

bishops to meet over who was to go to it and who was to stay behind.[33] But the initial bull of summons of 12 August 1308 did follow the precedent of the bull of 1272 summoning the Second Council of Lyons[34] in demanding local enquiries into matters needing correction and reformation which should be brought to the notice of the council. In England a series of complaints (*gravamina*) for this purpose were prepared by the Canterbury provincial council of November–December 1309,[35] and the matter was raised in the York provincial council of May 1310.[36] There must have been some similar discussion in Scotland (perhaps at the meeting planned for 24 February 1310 at Dundee which may well have been abortive,[37] but it could have taken place at any time between late 1308 and summer 1311), for the product was a list of *gravamina* from the 'ecclesia regni Scocie' which did somehow reach Vienne. There they were enrolled with a similar list from Ireland on what was described as 'XVII rotulus'.[38] There may have been anything up to twenty-four articles of complaint on this list,[39] but we know of the content of only two (nos. 2 and 8) because they alone were selected from this *rotulus* by a commission of the council who were compiling a summary of similar items from a mass of more than thirty *rotuli* from many provinces for inclusion in a master-list under topic headings for the pope's consideration.[40] Under the topic of improper lay intrusion into church liberties, the two Scottish articles complain firstly about improper procedures over the trial of criminous clerks, and secondly about improper pressure on bishops and other prelates to give their approval to new incumbents nominated by army captains for benefices found to be vacant as a result of the ebb and flow of war, under threat of denunciation as traitors

[33] See above p. 96.

[34] *C&S*, II, ii, 1350–1; see above p. 95.

[35] Ibid., 1264–9.

[36] Ibid., 1278, 1284. This business was continued to the next meeting of the council, but was apparently not in fact dealt with at the meetings held in May and July 1311 (ibid., 1319–48).

[37] See above p. 105.

[38] *ALKG*, iv, 430.

[39] The surviving Irish items have numbers from no. 25 upwards, while the Scottish ones have lower numbers.

[40] *ALKG*, iv, 376, 383; cf. Lecler, *Vienne*, 60–1. Only about half of these summaries survive (ibid., 115).

to the head of state (*presides regni*). (Though it is not clear which side in Scotland is being complained about, we can have understanding here about the problems of prelates in Scotland at a time of civil war.) Somewhat feeble remedies were put forward for these problems,[41] but in the end the council was abruptly dispersed without any papal pronouncements in answer to the *gravamina*; and when reforming decrees were eventually issued by Pope John XXII in 1317, they touched only briefly on the problems of lay pressure which had been a matter of general concern at the council.[42]

Two other matters which were raised at Vienne may also have been of concern at meetings of the Scottish council that have not left any trace. There was the matter of the examination and condemnation of the Templar knights. In August 1308 the bulls summoning the council at Vienne ordered the hastening of enquiries into the activities of the Templars, and at the same time provincial councils were authorised to pronounce sentences on individual knights.[43] A commission of enquiry under Bishop Lamberton is known to have held one session for taking evidence in Scotland at Holyrood Abbey on 17 November 1309;[44] but it did not proceed further because of the dangers of war. No sentences are known to have been passed in Scotland as they were in England,[45] though since the Templar Order came to be dissolved in Scotland as elsewhere, it is at least inherently probable that the provincial council was involved in the process. And then there is the question of papal taxes. The novel tax called annates, payable from the revenues of benefices that happened to fall vacant within three years of 1 February 1306, had been levied in Scotland as well as England at a time when the kingdom of Scotland seemed to be as securely under the rule of Edward I as the kingdom of England and the 'provinces' (*partes*) of Ireland and Wales.[46] And William Testa the principal papal collector had

[41] *ALKG*, iv, 403, 407; cf. Lecler, *Vienne*, 118.

[42] Lecler, *Vienne*, 146, 148–9; cf. Tanner, *Decrees*, 363–4, no. 7; 388–91, nos. 33–6.

[43] *C&S*, II, ii, 1241.

[44] Watt, *Dictionary*, 322.

[45] *C&S*, II, ii, 1242, 1278, 1285–6, 1298, 1319, 1356.

[46] W. E. Lunt, 'The first levy of papal annates', *American Historical Review*, xviii (1912–13), 48–64, especially 63.

appointed John de Solerio as his assistant for Scotland.[47] Not surprisingly in the circumstances of the time in Scotland payments from there were reported at a very low level in accounts dated June 1308 and June x September 1310.[48] The level of this tax was a matter of complaint at Vienne, though whether it was the English, the Scots or the Irish who raised the matter is not known;[49] but no decision was reached.[50] The council did however order the levy of a tenth for six years for the Crusade, and letters for its collection were sent out on 1 December 1312. In England at any rate the duty of collector was on this occasion placed on the shoulders of each diocesan bishop; but in the end the money was collected for only one year (for the terms October 1313 and April 1314) because of the death of the pope.[51] It is not known what happened in Scotland regarding this levy.[52]

As King Robert came to secure the allegiance of most of Scotland (especially after the battle of Bannockburn in 1314), there was a period of political reconstruction which saw meetings of a number of national assemblies of a parliamentary type and including the leading clergy as members.[53] There was also the general gathering at St. Andrews on 5 July 1318 for the dedication of the cathedral church there at a ceremony remembered as a national thanksgiving for Bannockburn, when the king, seven bishops, fifteen abbots and 'nearly all' of the nobility of the kingdom were present.[54] But not until the 1320s is there evidence again of meetings of the provincial council. It is noteworthy that

[47] Ibid., 56–7. He took part in the enquiry at Holyrood Abbey in November 1309.

[48] W. E. Lunt, 'William Testa and the parliament of Carlisle', *EHR*, xli (1926), 353, 354; cf. 355–7.

[49] *ALKG*, iv, 412.

[50] Lecler, *Vienne*, 133.

[51] Lunt, *Financial Relations*, 396–9.

[52] The council also approved a scheme for the teaching of oriental languages for missionary purposes at various centres (Tanner, *Decrees*, 379–80, no. 24). The expense of this at Oxford was to be met by levies on the clergy of England, Scotland, Ireland and Wales; but the scheme was abortive (cf. R. Weiss, 'England and the decree of the Council of Vienne on the teaching of Greek, Arabic, Hebrew and Syriac', *Bibliothèque d'humanisme et renaissance*, xiv [1952], 1–9).

[53] Duncan, 'Early parliaments', 49 ff.

[54] *Chron. Bower*, vi, 413.

two of these meetings at any rate were held at the same time as parliaments held at the same place. The first was at Perth on 9 July 1321. We know of it only[55] by the chance survival of the record of a particularly elaborate conveyance of land in Aberdeenshire, when the seller of the land first took a public oath to keep her bargain 'in presencia universorum prelatorum in concilio apud Perth', and then formally resigned the land into the king's hands as he sat 'in pleno parliamento' at Perth at the same time.[56] Bishop Lamberton of St. Andrews appears to have presided over this council meeting, even if he is not specifically styled Conservator, and certainly he and four other bishops were among those whose seals were added the next day to a record of the transaction. Why this modest piece of business was conducted in so elaborate a manner is not clear: perhaps a legal plea of some kind lies behind it – for example the seller may have been trying to back out of an agreed bargain and so was liable to proceedings under canon law – though the way in which the result was publicised was more for the security of two parties concerned with a business deal than for any factor of public interest in it. But perhaps we can see here an example of how the council as well as parliament could serve a generally useful and perhaps popular side-purpose apart from their main functions. It remains possible, however, that we have here an example of both king and bishops for some unknown reason together exercising pressure on the lady who was selling this land. Certainly the buyer seems to have been a favoured supporter of the king, who acquired a good deal of property in the north-east of the country, had served the king in 1319 as a justiciar of some kind,[57] and was to become sheriff of Aberdeen by 1328.[58]

The second council of the 1320s that can be traced was held at Scone on 21–22 March 1325 just before a parliament held there on 28 March.[59] On 21 March four bishops and five abbots issued letters of *inspeximus* for Coupar Angus abbey concerning a papal

[55] But see above p. 103.

[56] *APS*, i, 478–9; *RMS*, i, 24–5, no. 84; *SES*, i, p. lxxii.

[57] Barrow, *Bruce*, 295; *RMS*, i, 460, appendix I, no. 67.

[58] *The Exchequer Rolls of Scotland* [*ER*], ed. J. Stuart and others (Edinburgh, 1878–1908), i, 107; cf. p. clxxxi.

[59] *APS*, i, 483; cf. a royal grant 'in full parliament' dated '26 March an. 20', i.e. 1325 (*RRS*, v, 532–3, no. 269; cf. 127–31 for dating).

privilege exempting Cistercians from paying certain teinds; this was done *in concilio Scoticano*, and it was further certified that this privilege had been exhibited before William de Sinclair bishop of Dunkeld and the clergy *in concilio provinciali*.[60] Bishop Sinclair was clearly presiding over this meeting, and that he was doing this as *Conservator tocius cleri Scoticani* becomes clear from the record of a different piece of business done in what is called the *concilium generale* on the following day, 22 March.[61] Here the Conservator was adding his seal to an explanation offered by John de Lindsay the new bishop of Glasgow to the effect that he was accepting for the time being the traditional regalian right to present to benefices in the gift of the bishop of Glasgow in a time of vacancy right up to the time when a new bishop swore fealty for his temporalities. At the same time he was not denying the novel competing papal claim to reserve for papal provision any benefices vacated by a newly appointed bishop. Lindsay was taking a 'middle way' very much with an eye to pressure exerted by the king. No doubt it had been a matter for anxious discussion in the provincial council, and presumably also the king's proctors to the council had been active in pushing for a declaration that was much more clearly in the king's favour than the pope's.[62] It was a test case in a novel area of strain as the pope was pressing ever more extensively his claims as universal patron. All the prelates at the council would have been concerned with the solution of this test case, which would then be the precedent applicable to similar cases throughout the kingdom of Scotland.[63] It is a not insignificant accident that it is on this occasion that for the first time we have preserved for certain the name of the Conservator who was in office, even if that office had already been in existence for a hundred years.

But before we review progress since 1225, there is one more piece of evidence to consider.[64] It is another form-letter in which

[60] *Coupar Angus Chrs.*, i, 225–8, nos. 105–6.,

[61] *Glasgow Registrum*, i, 230–1, no. 270; *SES*, i, p. lxxvi, n. 1. The Conservator's Christian name has been wrongly copied as 'Walter' in this Glasgow register.

[62] See above pp. 103–4.

[63] For a discussion of this topic see *SES*, i, pp. lxxiii–lxxvi, and Donaldson, *Church History*, 38.

[64] *Formulary E*, pp. 51–2, no. 114.

a king of Scotland is ordering his unnamed but presumably local officials to assist the agents of some bishop to collect a tax from certain tenants of an abbot and the master of a hospital by seizing their goods and chattels or imprisoning them if necessary. The main point of the letter presumably concerns these instructions for enforcement of a bishop's authority by the secular arm at his request when his spiritual penalties have proved ineffective. But what was this tax, and how and when was it levied? It was a tax on clerical temporalities, the proceeds of which were to be sent to the pope *pro statu regni nostri et cleri Scocie*: it had been ordained by the prelates and clergy of all the kingdom in the last *consilium Scoticanum* at Perth. This is our first hint that the council was a body that could initiate a tax, for this is not the language of agreeing to a mandatory tax ordered by a pope, such as those of 1215, 1245, 1274, 1291, 1306 and 1312 which we have considered. And so this text appears to derive from a situation similar to that which may be deduced from the absence of the clergy from the parliament of 15 July 1326, when the earls, barons, burgesses and freeholders had for the first time granted their king a tax of one-tenth of their revenues for his lifetime.[65] When such an experiment was being made, it is unlikely that the clergy were not also asked to make a contribution, and they may well have reacted in the same way as the contemporary English clergy did by preferring to respond to a request from the king for money in their own council. Perhaps they met a week before parliament as in 1325, though this time in a different place. It is likely enough also that this was the occasion when the king sent two doctors of civil law as his proctors to raise matters *pro nobis et statu regni statuque vestro et ecclesie Scoticane*.[66] We cannot, however, attach this document to the council that met in 1326, for in that case none of the levy that was then discussed was to go to Rome. But the prelates were involved in 1328 along with the other magnates in promising with their king to pay £20,000 to King Edward III of England as part of the Treaty of Edinburgh–Northampton of 17 March in that year as a 'contribution for peace'.[67] They

[65] *APS*, i, 475–6; cf. R. Nicholson, *Scotland: The Later Middle Ages* (Edinburgh, 1974), 114–15.

[66] See above p. 103.

[67] Stones, *Documents*, 168.

certainly paid their share on this occasion by dioceses,[68] unlike the laity who followed the method of collection by sheriffdoms agreed for the tenth of 1326;[69] and so they may well have met again in council at Perth in the early months of 1328 in advance of the parliament held at Edinburgh 28 February–12 March[70] to decide how their share was to be levied, and agreed there like the laity to follow the methods of 1326 (which would account for some similarity of wording between this text and that derived putatively from a 1326 council). Since by August 1329 some of this money had been diverted to the Roman court,[71] presumably as payment towards the £2,000 which was by October 1329 paid to the pope as part of a bargain concluded by the king's envoys there between early May and 28 July 1328 for papal recognition of Robert I,[72] it could well be that the tax authorised by the provincial council as the clergy's share towards all this money-raising 'for the benefit of our kingdom and the clergy of Scotland' was regarded as going to Rome.[73] Even if we cannot date the council meeting mentioned in the form-letter exactly, it was most probably held early in 1328 or (less likely) in the autumn of the same year.[74] Taxation of this kind was to remain very exceptional in Scotland, unlike England;[75] but when it was necessary, the *consilium Scoticanum* was by the time of the death of Robert I equipped with royal backing to take on the job of organising the share of the clergy as a whole.

If we pause at the death of Robert I in 1329 and consider the first hundred years of the Scottish provincial council, what can be identified as its general features? At the most our evidence for its activities arises from only some fifteen occasions when it can be shown or presumed to have met. But this should not be taken as

[68] *ER*, i, 181.

[69] Ibid., p. cvi.

[70] *APS*, i, 483–4.

[71] *ER*, i, 181–2.

[72] Ibid., pp. clxxxiii–iv; cf. p. 211; for dating see Watt, *Dictionary*, 37, s.v. 'James Ben', and 550, s.v. 'Walter de Twynham'.

[73] This follows the suggestion of Professor Duncan in *Formulary E*, p. 52.

[74] This latter alternative would allow for a meeting called to authorise the diversion of funds voted in the early part of the year for the 'contribution for peace' to help pay the sum now due to the pope.

[75] Nicholson, *Later Middle Ages*, 115.

an indication of the infrequency of its meetings; indeed the creation of the office of Conservator seems likely to have led to regular routine meetings in a way that metropolitans in other provinces were not impelled to organise. So casual are some of the references to the Scottish council that it may well have met annually for much of this first period as the Fourth Lateran Council intended. That council had called (in its canon no. 6) for the review of abuses and the punishment of wrong-doers within the general framework of the canon law. There is certainly no evidence that the procedure laid down in canon no. 30 for an annual review of church appointments by the 'prelates of churches' in each province was ever attempted, and it would have been singularly difficult to arrange in a council where no one bishop had permanent authority over the others. And we have no evidence that the agenda of council meetings included the regular reading out of the canonical rules. Yet regular contact was in fact maintained with developing central definitions of the canon law, both by the presence of some Scots at each General Council of 1215, 1245, 1274 and 1311–12, and by appointments to church offices in Scotland of bishops and cathedral clergy trained in the academic study of the canon law in continental universities right through the period.[76] When the Scottish council met, it comprised many members with legal expertise; and after 1239 there was no call for a legate to come to Scotland in the old way to force the local church to come up to date along international lines.

The council was therefore equipped to tackle 'censure of transgressions and the correction of *mores*'[77] by devising statutes on a considerable scale for general guidance throughout Scotland. No doubt there were preliminary enquiries behind most of these as envisaged in canon no. 6 of 1215, as there seem to have been on a wider scale in anticipation of the general councils of 1274 and 1311. It was all a process which helped to develop a corporate sense among council members on a national basis, and as the bishops took turns as Conservator they must have learned to take responsibility for action in defence of the church laws in which they jointly had an interest. This was certainly true when there

[76] These can be traced in Watt, *Fasti*, and Watt, *Dictionary*, *passim*.

[77] See above p. 44.

was some question of a threat to the privileges enjoyed by the church (as in 1242, 1250, 1325); but though we can see the council being asked to back up one of its number in 1280 in a case of excommunication, we have no other evidence (except perhaps from 1321) of how it proceeded (either collectively or through its Conservator) to 'impose due penalty on transgressors' as envisioned in canon no. 6 of 1215. If it did, however, take action against the Templars after the enquiry of 1309, it would have been a precedent of a kind for its future concern with heresy cases. What we have positively seen is the council as a forum for the resolution of disputes between ecclesiastics of two religious orders or two dioceses in 1230 and 1268, or between a bishop and an earl in 1238.

As papal taxation of the church developed during the period, it seems likely that such resistance as there was in Scotland to these new demands was marshalled in the council. This was clear in 1275, and probably earlier in 1266–9. At this latter time the king's support for conciliar resistance is notable, and it is a feature of the whole period that king and council worked together. There was a mechanism for ensuring this through the proctors whom the king sent to council meetings to protect the interests of the crown; but he could also back the council in person at a time of crisis as in 1242. The reverse side of this relationship was the political support which a council could be asked to give to Robert I in 1309 and perhaps 1314 x 1316. This relationship was much easier than in England because of the absence on the king's part of desire to make financial demands on the Scottish church. He would support their opposition to papal exactions because unlike the English king he had no hopes or intentions of profiting from the proceeds; and there was as yet no development in Scotland to match the temporarily successful experiments of Edward I in England from the 1290s in bringing both upper and lower clergy into his parliaments so as to tax all sections of the community together. It made for much easier relationships while the Scottish king was normally content to govern on the basis of a traditional income with little obvious desire to develop extraordinary taxation.[78] Of course the leading clergy are found advising and supporting their king when he assembled a large

[78] Cf. Duncan, *Scotland*, 388–9, 486, 523, 602–3.

council as in 1227 and 1276,[79] or developed meetings called at first *colloquia* and later parliaments.[80] But this did not lessen the quite separate need for them to continue meeting also in their own provincial council, as the parallel meetings of their council and parliament in the 1320s make clear. It is particularly interesting that when in 1326 and again in 1328 the king was pursuing policies which made national taxation necessary, the clergy seem to have met separately and made their own decision about the contribution they would make. The king was not expecting them to do anything else.[81] Thus at last was a move made which looked like developing the Scottish provincial council more in line with its English counterparts, who had greatly strengthened their solidarity as a result of frequent squabbles with their king over his demands for taxes and their counter-presentation of grievances at least from the 1280s onwards. But there seems to have been an important structural difference in the composition of councils in the two countries which was a consequence perhaps of the comparative lack of concern with money in the Scottish council. From as early as the 1250s the English councils had for some of their meetings at any rate added a representative element to their composition, drawn from the lower clergy.[82] In Scotland the sederunt at council meetings had widened from the bishops mentioned in 1225 to abbots and priors, deans and archdeacons, and sometimes expert clerks as well: but there is in this period no sign of a regular representative element, whether elected or selected.[83] Basically the Scottish council remained an assembly of major and minor prelates,[84] there by right of an office which implied jurisdiction; and it must have been because of its long freedom from royal demands for taxation that it held on to this custom for so long.

[79] *APS*, i, 406, 427.

[80] H. G. Richardson and G. Sayles, 'The Scottish parliaments of Edward I', *SHR*, xxv (1928), 300–17; Duncan, 'Early parliaments', 36–58.

[81] Cf. ibid., 51–2.

[82] Kemp, *Counsel and Consent*, 70–1; cf. 72.

[83] Cf. above p. 94.

[84] See definitions based on the Decretals of Gregory IX in *DDC*, vii, 176; cf. *APS*, i, 466, for a parliamentary definition of 1318, where a prelate is equated with others entitled to hold a court.

9

Provincial councils and the Three Estates 1329–1424

THE reconciliation of King Robert with the papacy just before his death was followed by a vigorous effort on the pope's part to put relationships between Avignon and Scotland on to a normal footing. Towards this end two papal nuncios, Bertrand Cariti and Raymund de Quercu, were on 25 April 1329 appointed collectors in Scotland for two new taxes on the clergy for the pope's benefit – annates for three years from all vacant benefices and a tenth for three years on clerical revenues.[1] As they set out later in the year these nuncios were given wider powers to deal with a number of other matters not connected with their prime task as collectors: for example, absolution might be given to those who had been excommunicated for supporting King Robert, dispensations might be given for irregular noble marriages, and confirmation might be given to recent gifts to religious houses that were presumably in some way open to question.[2] But they did not have legatine powers, and, though they can be traced in Scotland from April 1330 onwards,[3] there is no suggestion that they either held a council (which was presumably beyond their powers) or attended a meeting of the provincial council. Yet they did bring papal authority to bear within the kingdom once more.

[1] *CPL*, ii, 489–90.
[2] Ibid., 496, 493–4, 304, 310–11.
[3] Theiner, *Monumenta*, 253–8, nos. 502–4.

There is indeed no evidence of any meeting of the council for thirty years after 1329.[4] It may, of course, have met regularly, for in April 1343 and again in November 1345 it was apparently the usual thing for a bishop of Moray and then a bishop of Aberdeen to refer casually to the authority of the *concilium Scoticanum* for rules about the excommunication of offenders against the properties and liberties of the church, or about the need for every parish church to be served by a resident rector or vicar.[5] But during this time when its activities are unknown to us, there were very important developments in the ways in which the Scottish clergy were involved in parliament, which seem to have reflected changing ideas about at least one aspect of the competence of the provincial council. We find that when it was next found necessary to ask both laity and clergy to pay special taxes for the king's benefit, the clergy were not consulted separately through their council (as had apparently happened in 1326 and 1328). It happened twice in connection with the expenses of bringing King David II back to Scotland from France in June 1341. There seems to have been one 'contribution' agreed at a parliament at Dundee late in 1340 or early 1341, and another at the parliament held by David after his return at Scone in September 1341.[6] From the accounts of the money collected we find that the royal clerks regarded each of these 'contributions' as having been granted (*concessa*) in parliament, and as collected from the clergy, the community (meaning here the sheriffdoms) and the burghs.[7]

The change in practice is confirmed when next there had to be an unusual financial effort: this was in 1357 when money had to be found for the ransom of King David from his English captivity. The arrangements made in advance of the treaty regarding this that were finally agreed at Berwick on 3 October 1357 included the collection of a dossier of sealed instruments from various elements of the clergy, lay magnates and burghs in Scotland, testifying to their willingness to accept the treaty, including the liability to pay a ransom at the rate of 10,000 marks

[4] But an unnamed Conservator was active 1338 x 1350, probably 1341 x 1346 (see below p. 132, n. 74).

[5] *Moray Registrum*, 127, no. 114; *Aberdeen Registrum*, i, 77.

[6] For the latter contribution see *APS*, i, 512–13.

[7] *ER*, i, 501–3; cf. pp. clxv–vi.

a year for ten years.[8] In the case of the clergy each bishop and cathedral chapter, and at least some of the abbots and their convents, were probably required to produce a separate letter authorising proctors to commit them to their responsibilities (though only some of these letters still survive); and furthermore on 26 September 1357 at Edinburgh seven of the bishops sealed an instrument on behalf of themselves and their chapters authorising three other bishops to enter into commitments on their joint behalfs.[9] This is unlikely to have been the product of a provincial council meeting, for the king's lieutenant was holding a *plenum consilium* at Edinburgh at the time to co-ordinate all this documentation,[10] and the act published by the bishops is in line with those produced by the nobles and the burgesses.[11] And then, once the king had returned, he held his *plenum consilium* at Scone on 6 November 1357, where the 'three communities' (*tres communitates*, later usually called the 'Three Estates') make their first appearance in record as the assembly of clergy, nobles and burgesses who jointly ordered new assessments to be made so that all three groups might be taxed to raise the ransom.[12]

Thus do we have confirmation that the clergy, who had briefly under Robert I agreed to taxation in their separate council, by 1341 and 1357 were willing (and perhaps preferred) to be taxed through the king's assembly of Three Estates, whether meeting as a 'parliament', a 'full council', or a 'general council'.[13] One reason for this change is to be found almost certainly in the way in which the assembly of Three Estates, as developed after representatives of the burghs had from the late 1320s been associated with the bishops and abbots, earls, barons and freeholders in some parliaments,[14] came to include not just major and minor prelates

[8] *CDS*, iii, 299–304, nos. 1642–8, 1650–4.

[9] *APS*, i, 515–16. The bishops of Galloway and Sodor are conspicuously absent from these arrangements. Both bishops at this date were probably orientated more towards England than Scotland (see Dowden, *Bishops*, 361–2, 282–5).

[10] *APS*, i, 518.

[11] Ibid., 516–18.

[12] Ibid., 518–21, 491. See Nicholson, *Later Middle Ages*, 166.

[13] This last term (*consilium generale*) is found from 1365 onwards (*APS*, i, 495). Cf. above pp. 103, 105, 113 for earlier usage of this wording.

[14] Duncan, 'Early parliaments', 51–2.

as in the provincial council,[15] but also representatives of the lower clergy of the dioceses. They may have been there already by 1341 and 1357; but they are demonstrably there from the mid-1360s onwards, even if we know very little about how they were selected, or their numbers, or how often they came, or how long they stayed.[16] Representation for taxation purposes in Scotland therefore was achieved just in the Three Estates, and so there was no pressing need for the provincial council to develop into a partly representative body like the convocations of England.

This willingness of the clergy to participate in national taxation levied through the Estates has, however, to be considered in the context of their liability to papal taxation. Various exactions were now made for the pope's benefit on a continuous basis, and this was fruitful over the period 1345–89 when a succession of Scots (William de Deyn bishop of Aberdeen, William de Grenlaw archdeacon of St. Andrews, and John de Peblis bishop of Dunkeld)[17] held the office of Collector in Scotland. Now in addition we come upon a novelty for the Scottish church: as part of a plan to raise more money for his ransom, King David sent an embassy headed by two laymen to Avignon in August 1359 to ask the pope to order the Scottish clergy to pay a tenth of their revenues. Though this procedure had been common in England, no pope had ever before authorised a mandatory tax in Scotland for the king's benefit rather than his own. Pope Innocent VI authorised this tenth for three years, though on condition that this should be the clergy's only contribution to the ransom; and the envoys are said to have returned home triumphant (*hilares*).[18] It is likely that they were back for a meeting of the *concilium*

[15] See above p. 118.

[16] R. S. Rait, *The Parliaments of Scotland* (Glasgow, 1924), 172–4. An example from January 1399 (*APS*, i, 574) where Raitt thinks that a 'Church Council' may have sanctioned a contribution to be levied on the clergy before the actual imposition of taxation by parliament, does not have to be read in this way (cf. Nicholson, *Later Middle Ages*, 217–18).

[17] Watt, *Dictionary*, 149–50, 243–6, 440–3. Note that Grenlaw's accounts for part of his period of office survive (Vatican Archives, Collectorie, 14, fos. 158–93), and cover all the Scottish sees including Galloway, but not Sodor. See A. D. M. Barrell, 'William de Grenlaw, papal collector in Scotland and his account', *Innes Review*, xlii (1991), 1–18.

[18] *Chron. Fordun*, i, 378; cf. *Chron. Bower*, vii, 312, where this adjective has been changed to 'content' (*leti*). For dating see ibid., vii, 488.

Scoticanum that is known to have been held in the Dominican church at Aberdeen on 26 November 1359 (which we know about just because the occasion was taken to have an *inspeximus* made of a papal privilege from the twelfth century kept in the archives of Aberdeen cathedral).[19] There was probably no objection at the time, for the exchequer rolls show that the money collected for this tenth was accounted for diocese by diocese between May 1360 and December 1364, with some arrears a little later.[20] And since the clergy were not recorded as paying anything for the ransom earlier, while the sheriffdoms and burghs were paying three annual contributions,[21] it is clear that their willingness to pay with everyone else at the meeting of the estates in November 1357 had been converted into a desire to pay along the familiar lines of church taxation which it took two years to realise. Presumably the yield of this tax was calculated to be sufficiently more than the king would otherwise obtain from the clergy for it to be worth his while seeking papal permission to collect it.

But the arrangement seems to have gone sour when in May 1365 a new truce with England necessitated a resumption of payments to that country (which had lapsed in 1360), and the estates on the strength of this in May and July 1366 again ordered a tax to be levied on both church and lay property based on a new assessment all round.[22] This time the clergy did find themselves paying taxes directly to the king for several years along with the sheriffdoms and burghs.[23] There is some evidence that the estates took the view that general imposts on the country should now be divided among the clergy, nobles and burghs in the proportion of 6:10:4.[24] In these circumstances it seems to have been thought right to put aside the pope's caveat in 1359 to the effect that the clergy must not be asked to contribute more to the ransom than

[19] *Aberdeen Registrum*, i, 84–6; *SES*, i, p. lxxvi.

[20] *ER*, ii, 75–6, 109–11, 153, 163, 171–2; cf. 219–20, 256. Note that this tax was collected from the dioceses of Galloway and Sodor despite the absence of the bishops of these sees from the commitments of 1357 (see above p. 121, n. 9). There was a new bishop of Galloway by 1359 (Watt, *Fasti*, 130).

[21] E.g. *ER*, ii, 5, 34–44, 46–8, 73–5.

[22] Nicholson, *Later Middle Ages*, 165–8, 172, 174–6; the assessment in *APS*, i, 499–500 includes Galloway diocese, but not Sodor.

[23] E.g. *ER*, ii, 255–8, 287–8, 303–4, 342–3.

[24] *ER*, ii, p. lxx, n. 1.

their tenth for three years: they were now compelled to pay on their lands and temporalities like the barons and freeholders despite their protests.[25] In fact the money was with parliamentary agreement used for a number of different purposes rather than just for the ransom,[26] so that the clergy probably lost sympathy for protesting on a technicality. They really were now absorbed into a national consultation and taxation system which took no heed of their traditional privileged position (*nullo privilegio obstante*).[27] On the taxation side the burden was to be only an occasional rather than a regular one. Though the clergy and the other estates paid regularly in the last years of David II and then in 1373, they were apparently not taxed again until 1399,[28] and then not again until in 1424 money had to be raised in connection with the return of another king (James I) from captivity in England.[29] Direct taxation was not yet a regular feature of government in Scotland, though the Three Estates probably met most years in parliament or general council for discussion of, and action on, other types of business (even if records survive now only patchily). It was at a parliament towards the end of his reign that David II had yielded to pressure from the bishops, and with the consent of the Three Estates renounced the royal claim to bishops' possessions at their death, allowing them to dispose of them by testament.[30] That is where the king now offered palliatives to the Scottish bishops as a group.

What then of the provincial council? Evidence of its meetings is exiguous still. In 1369 a stray case regarding the instrusion with the backing of lay power of a man belonging to Durham diocese into the church of Yetholm in Glasgow diocese on the

[25] As noted by a contemporary chronicler (*Chron. Fordun*, i, 378). For some reason this passage was not in the 1440s copied into *Chron. Bower*, vii, 312; cf. 488.

[26] Nicholson, *Later Middle Ages*, 176.

[27] *Chron. Fordun*, i, 378.

[28] Nicholson, *Later Middle Ages*, 188, 217–18.

[29] Ibid., 282–3; E. W. M. Balfour-Melville, *James I, King of Scots* (London, 1936), 108–10; and see *Chron. Bower*, viii, 241, and *ER*, iv, pp. cxxx–cxxxiii.

[30] *RMS*, i, 129–30, no. 372; cf. Donaldson, *Church History*, 31–9, especially 38–9, for explanation that this was not the end of the matter. It was 'all the bishops of the kingdom of Scotland' who approached Pope Gregory XI for a confirmation of this royal act granted on 1 January 1372 (Theiner, *Monumenta*, 346, no. 694; cf. *Aberdeen Registrum*, ii, 122–4).

border with England reached the papal court, and the pope had occasion to comment that at a recent Scottish church council it had been decided that all those who intruded into benefices should be excommunicated.[31] It would appear that the council was meeting as usual for routine business. But it is surprising how little evidence survives for the activities of the council when faced by the Great Schism in the papacy of 1378. Following the election of Urban VI on 8 April and then of his rival Clement VII on 20 September, two popes contended for recognition throughout Christendom, and governments everywhere were for forty years to be necessarily involved in decisions on which pope to support, and on when and how to join the various international attempts that were made to reach solutions to the problem. Most kings assembled councils of their clergy to advise them more or less freely on which pope to acknowledge. The king of France decided for Clement VII as early as November 1378, and then again more formally in May 1399.[32] Scotland was the ally of France, and King Charles V soon sent an envoy to King Robert II to secure adherence to the same pope.[33] Already by February 1379 agents of John de Peblis, King Robert's chancellor, were at Clement's court (then still in Italy before it moved to Avignon) arranging for his second consecration as bishop of Dunkeld, and by July 1379 cash collected by Peblis in his other capacity as papal collector in Scotland was being paid into Clement's treasury (now at Avignon).[34] This implies recognition of Clement by Scotland in a very practical way, and it seems to have been politics which had led to this decision, for the belief in Scotland that Clement was a lineal descendant of St. Margaret (through her daughter who married a count of Boulogne before her death in 1115) can hardly have been the deciding factor.[35] But Clement did send two Scots, Thomas de Rossy, O.F.M., and Hugh de Dalmahoy, in July 1379

[31] This case is cited in A. D. M. Barrell, *The Papacy, Scotland and Northern England, 1342–1378* (Cambridge, 1995), 251.

[32] E. Delaruelle and others, *L'église au temps du Grand Schisme et de la crise conciliaire 1378–1449* (Paris, 1962–4), i, 22.

[33] N. Valois, *La France et le Grand Schisme d'Occident* (Paris, 1896–1902), i, 197.

[34] Watt, *Dictionary*, 442–3. Peblis had first been consecrated by authority of Urban VI before doubts had been raised about this pope's legitimacy.

[35] *Chron. Bower*, iii, 407; cf. 488.

from Avignon to Scotland with copies of various propagandist writings in favour of his right to be pope; and from a treatise composed by Rossy himself we learn that he preached on 2 February [1380] before the king at Dundee *coram maxima multitudine populi notabilis*.[36] Though such business would be of central concern to the provincial council, it is not possible to suggest that the language of this source provides evidence for a council meeting at this time. We just do not know how King Robert was advised on the policy which he adopted on the Schism.

As time passed some leading clergy in Scotland began to emerge with obvious motives for supporting the pro-Clementine line which Scotland took uninterruptedly until 1418. Bishop Walter de Wardlaw of Glasgow accepted appointment on 23 December 1383 as one of Clement's cardinals, whilst remaining in Scotland as a diocesan bishop, and also as the pope's legate *a latere* for Scotland and Ireland from 24 November 1384.[37] He was the first Scot ever to reach such eminence. He had known Pope Clement in the 1370s when both had lived at the papal court at Avignon, and seems to have been an early visitor (before September 1379) to the new pope's court.[38] Within a few years most of the Scottish sees had new bishops who owed their appointment to Clement VII, and so had every interest in keeping Scotland firmly loyal to him. There was Peblis at Dunkeld, and Thomas de Rossy himself arrived with a papal mandate that led to his possession of the see of Galloway (though only after the expulsion of the Urbanist appointee, who lived thereafter in England).[39] The see of Aberdeen had another Scot from Clement's curia imposed on it in October 1380,[40] while at the same time a Scottish visitor to that curia secured the see of Dunblane.[41] The sees of Caithness and Brechin sent new bishops to Avignon for confirmation in late 1381 and June 1383.[42] That made a total of seven bishops out of twelve who had by 1383 particular reason to keep the Scottish church

[36] Watt, *Dictionary*, 472, 141; *Copiale Prioratus Sanctiandree* [*St. Andrews Copiale*], ed. J. H. Baxter (Oxford, 1930), p. xxxvii.

[37] Watt, *Dictionary*, 571.

[38] Ibid., 574.

[39] Ibid., 472.

[40] Ibid., 552, s.v. 'Adam de Tyningham'.

[41] Ibid., 359, s.v. 'Dugal de Lorn'.

[42] Ibid., 379, s.v. 'Alexander Man'; 95, s.v. 'Stephen de Cellario'.

loyal to Clement. When the see of St. Andrews fell vacant on the death of the elderly Bishop Laundels on 23 September 1385,[43] Clement was quick to appoint Walter Trayl, a Scot who had been working as a high official in his curia, first as an auditor of the Sacred Apostolic Palace, and since 1383 as a referendary of the Chancery, and who was to make a notable contribution to the ecclesiastical scene in Scotland from 1386 onwards.[44] Argyll's next bishop went to Avignon for confirmation in April 1387;[45] the sees of Moray and Ross had bishops who continued in office without questioning Clementine authority until as late as 1397 and 1398 respectively.[46] Only in the see of Sodor (or The Isles) did the incumbent choose to be loyal to the English-supported Urban. He was in consequence deprived by Clement in July 1387, who replaced him by an Irish Franciscan called Michael, who was presumably glad to be translated from the Urbanist archdiocese of Cashel, where he would not have been welcome.[47] Michael did come to Scotland, and is found by 1409 at any rate active in the company of the Scottish lord of The Isles.[48] Thus was a Scottish episcopate united in their support of Pope Clement VII achieved, so much so that Scotland under their guidance (whether or not expressed in provincial councils) was to remain loyal to him and to his successor Benedict XIII, even though her ally France was to withdraw obedience from the latter from 1398 to 1403 and again from 1407. The Scottish church was sufficiently united to follow its own line.

Some lasting changes in the boundaries of the authority of this church can be observed about this time. The diocese of Galloway was moving away from its formal subjection to York. No bishop of Galloway after 1355 offered an oath of obedience to the metropolitan there: the bishops from 1359 were appointed by papal provision, with York just being informed of the decision.[49]

43 Watt, *Fasti*, 294.

44 Watt, *Dictionary*, 539–42.

45 Ibid., 157, s.v. 'John Dugaldi'.

46 Ibid., 67–70, s.v. 'Alexander Bur'; 315–16, s.v. 'Alexander de Kylwos'.

47 Watt, *Fasti*, 202; Dowden, *Bishops*, 287; *Calendar of Papal Letters to Scotland of Clement VII of Avignon 1378–1394* [*CPL Clement VII*], ed. C. Burns (SHS, 1976), 130.

48 *RMS*, ii, 479, no. 2264.

49 Theiner, *Monumenta*, 314–15, no. 638.

And the tie with York was permanently broken when Oswald, O.Cist., the Urbanist appointee was forced to spend the years 1381–1417 as a mere suffragan bishop in the dioceses of York and Durham, whilst a succession of Clementist bishops held the see in Scotland without any reference to York at all.[50] In 1430 King James I for his part ordered that the clergy of the church of *Candida Casa* (i.e. Galloway) were to be treated on the same basis as other clergy of the realm *sic quod clerus ubique infra regnum de cetero non in disparitate et differentia, sed uno jure unoque privilegio et libertate generali toti ordini clericorum indultis gauderet et uteretur.*[51]

Rather different was the development in Sodor. Already by 1331 there is evidence of the pretensions of the 'canons of Snizort and the clergy of Skye', who exceptionally claimed a right in the selection of a bishop in contrast to the more usual 'clergy of Man' who were the effective electors in 1349 and 1374.[52] Bishop Michael probably found a welcome in the northern part of this scattered diocese from 1387 onwards as the Clementist appointee, even if his rival retained the Isle of Man with the cathedral at Peel. Perhaps for a time *c.* 1421 Bishop Richard Payl, who had been based on Man since 1410, managed to extend his authority as far north as Iona; and when in April 1422 Pope Martin V provided a Scot to a diocese described as 'Sodor in Scotland', it was not effective.[53] But the pope tried again in June 1426 with a provision of Angus de Insulis to the see of 'Sodor or of The Isles' which was said to be immediately subject to Rome.[54] Though there followed litigation of some kind at Rome, which he had to settle in person in February 1428, this man was in possession when visiting Islay as early as June 1427: he referred to his cathedral at Snizort in 1433, and had clearly become by then a

[50] Watt, *Fasti*, 131; Dowden, *Bishops*, 364–8, 375–6; *CPL Clement VII*, 26, 70; *Calendar of Papal Letters to Scotland of Benedict XIII of Avignon 1394–1419* [*CPL Benedict XIII*], ed. F. McGurk (SHS, 1976), 151, 318. Even Pope Martin V in 1422 no longer informed York when he appointed a bishop of Galloway (*CPL*, vii, 287).

[51] *RMS*, ii, 35, no. 164. See below p. 135 for representation of a bishop of Galloway at a Scottish provincial council in 1420.

[52] Watt, *Fasti*, 202.

[53] Ibid., 203.

[54] *CPL*, vii, 478.

firmly established bishop of a separate Scottish diocese of The Isles, while at the same time a series of English bishops of Sodor was recognised on the Isle of Man.[55] When the next pope appointed a bishop to The Isles in 1441, he took care to inform the archbishop of Trondheim in Norway as metropolitan;[56] but in practice from the time of the Schism the Scottish see of The Isles must have been regarded almost as much a part of the Scottish church as the see of Galloway was.

A third diocese which began to move into the orbit of the Scottish church as a consequence of the Schism was Orkney. This was something new, and in fact during the Schism itself this part of the Norwegian kingdom under the archbishop of Trondheim as metropolitan remained Urbanist. But the earldom of Orkney (including also the Shetland Isles), though politically part of Norway, had already been in the hands of noble Scottish families since the mid-fourteenth century, and the bishops there enjoyed an annual income from the Scottish crown revenues in the burgh of Aberdeen from at least as early as 1328.[57] Then in 1384 Pope Clement VII took the chance of a vacancy in the see of Orkney to provide Robert de Sinclair who was presumably related to the ruling Earl Henry de Sinclair, and who was said to have been elected previously by the canons of Kirkwall.[58] He was consecrated, but never obtained possession of the see.[59] After an interval during which only Urbanist bishops of Orkney are known, the Avignonese Pope Benedict XIII made further appointments of Scots to this see in 1408, 1414 and 1415.[60] These were probably only partly effective, if at all; but just after the end of the Schism Thomas de Tulloch from Brechin diocese was provided to the see of Orkney by Pope Martin V, and he and his successor William Tulloch were to hold this see from 1418 to 1477.[61] There is no doubt that they did so as subjects of the king of Denmark and

[55] Watt, *Fasti*, 203, 207. There was as late as 1498 a hope in Scotland that the church at Peel on Man might one day be recovered as the cathedral of a united diocese once again (ibid., 207).

[56] *CPL*, ix, 225.

[57] *ER*, i, 60, 90, etc.

[58] *CPL Clement VII*, 101–2.

[59] Watt, *Fasti*, 251; Watt, *Dictionary*, 495–6.

[60] Watt, *Fasti*, 252.

[61] Ibid., 252–3.

Norway until these Northern Isles were transferred politically to Scotland in 1468–9; but as Scots by origin they were also familiar figures in Scotland, while the see of Orkney was being further prepared for absorption into the Scottish church.

But these developments were for the future when Walter Trayl came home from the court of Clement VII at Avignon early in 1386 to take up his appointment as bishop of St. Andrews. As an ex-auditor of the papal curia he brought with him home to Scotland a special faculty to hear and decide legal appeals to the Apostolic See from the courts of the Scottish bishops and other ordinaries as well as from decisions of delegate and sub-delegate judges.[62] He appointed a commissary on 8 January 1389 to help him in this work,[63] which must have given him as bishop of St. Andrews especial pre-eminence among his fellow-bishops now that Wardlaw the cardinal-legate was dead. He also strengthened the administration of justice within his own diocese by the establishment of a second official with his court in Lothian archdeaconry (i.e. the part of St. Andrews diocese south of the Firth of Forth).[64] It seems highly likely that the second collection of synodal statutes found in the Lambeth MS.[65] date from his episcopate (though all we know for certain is that they date from the fourteenth century).[66] They build on the earlier synodal statutes of 1242 to some extent; but more obviously their compiler has been considering quite a number of statutes derived from edicts of the provincial council, and has strengthened them by developing points of detail and laying down specific penalties for offences, e.g. no. 142 on the provision of parish manses (cf. no. 12); no. 143 on concubines (cf. no. 8); no. 144 on the need for letters dimissory (cf. no. 14); no. 148 on confessors for the clergy (cf. no.

[62] *CPL Clement VII*, 116.

[63] *Registrum Monasterii S. Marie de Cambuskenneth* (Grampian Club, 1872), 101–3, no. 77; cf. 95–6, no. 75 misdated.

[64] Watt, *Dictionary*, 541; Watt, *Fasti*, 325.

[65] *SES*, ii, 64–72, nos. 140–63.

[66] No. 161 ends with an incomplete date. The exemplar from which the whole Lambeth MS. was later copied may well have been written for Bishop Trayl, ending with his own statutes. This could be the explanation of the reference in two of Bishop Bernham's statutes of 1242 (nos. 130, 132) to 'officials' in the plural – the scribe would be bringing his texts up to date to match a similar plural usage in these new statutes (no. 140; cf. nos. 144, 159).

16); no. 150 on clerical dress (cf. no. 10); no. 153 on leasing property to laymen (cf. no. 17); no. 154 against the involvement of clergy in secular business (cf. no. 22); no. 157 against lay maintenance in church courts (cf. no. 55). It seems clear from these examples that the provincial legislation of the thirteenth century was still used as a framework by a vigorous bishop at the end of the fourteenth century (if it was Trayl who issued these statutes), but that various practical points needed to be added to make them more enforceable. Certainly these statutes envisage a very active diocesan bishop going round on visitation (nos. 142, 160), holding annual consistories for the clergy of each archdeaconry (nos. 140, 144, 159–60), and assisted by energetic officials.[67]

It is not surprising to find some evidence of the activities of the provincial council once Bishop Trayl was around. There must have been a meeting at which he was chosen as Conservator sometime before 18 July 1388, for he was in office on that date as *privilegiorum et jurium ecclesie Scoticane conservator* when William de Busby, O. S. B., a monk of Urquhart priory in Moray diocese, appealed in Elgin Cathedral on behalf of this priory and others against an act of Bishop Alexander Bur of Moray dated 11 July previously when investing one John Mason (a monk of Dunfermline) with the priorship of Urquhart. The grounds of the appeal were that this office was at the time still occupied by Prior Adam de Hadyngton and therefore not vacant. This act of appeal was witnessed by the skilled canon lawyer William de Spyny,[68]

[67] A single statute (no. 164) on the way in which dues are to be paid when a polluted local church has to be episcopally reconciled is found as a single item in the Ethie MS. (at fo. 14) in a different hand from the thirteenth-century code. It may well have been added in the fourteenth century (as suggested in *SES*, i, p. cxciii, n. 2) and be a St. Andrews synodal statute (as suggested in *SES*, i, p. clxxxv), but nothing definite is known about it.

Two synodal statutes of Moray diocese on teinds payable by wood-carters and millers are known from a 'general chapter held at Elgin 6 March 1370' (*Moray Registrum*, 167–8, nos. 151–2).

Some synodal statutes for Sodor were issued on 23 February 1351 (Cheney, 'Manx Synodal Statutes', vii, 86–9; viii, 60–3), and are notable for starting with a version of the same preamble as used by Bishop Bernham of St. Andrews in 1242. Some of them deal in more developed form with topics treated in the provincial statutes nos. 3, 4, 5, 6, 12, but with only a limited amount of the same wording. The last statute cites II Lyons c. 25 (Tanner, *Decrees*, 328–9).

[68] Watt, *Dictionary*, 503–6.

and seems to have been reasonably founded in law, for on 16 August 1388 Bishop Bur allowed it to go forward.[69] It is interesting that Bishop Trayl is being appealed to as Conservator rather than as the man who had been commissioned to settle appeals from the Scottish bishops to Rome, for it demonstrates the undeniable and presumably customary judicial side of the office of Conservator in a case which appears to have raised general issues of canon law (under what circumstances is a monastic prelacy correctly vacant?) rather than to have been based on some identifiable ruling of the provincial council. We do not know how Bishop Trayl dealt with the case.[70] He seems to have decided in favour of the appellant, for Prior Hadyngton remained in office. But then Busby fell out with Hadyngton and on 23 January 1391 secured a crown letter in unusual form addressed to Bishop Bur ordering him to replace Hadyngton as prior by Busby himself.[71] This move was the subject of a protest by the clergy who met in the king's next parliament in March 1391, when Bishop Trayl was himself present,[72] and the king ordered the cancellation of his earlier letter, the restoration of Prior Hadyngton, and the disciplining of Busby by Bishop Bur with the help of the local royal officers if need be.[73] It was clearly convenient for the clergy to have access to the king in parliament so that he might put right what had come to be admitted was a case where crown authority had been misapplied; and it may be noted here that, whoever was in office as Conservator in 1391, it was presumably the practice then as it had been from the mid-fourteenth century that when representatives of the clergy appeared in parliament, the Conservator of the time was normally regarded as their leader or even spokesman.[74]

[69] *Moray Registrum*, 350–1, nos. 267–8.

[70] The summaries of this case in *SES*, i, pp. li–lii, n. 6 and Nicholson, *Later Middle Ages*, 238 are both erroneous.

[71] *Moray Registrum*, 351–2, no. 269 (note the near-contemporary rubric: *Litera indiscreta in defectu notarii*).

[72] *APS*, i, 578.

[73] *Moray Registrum*, 352–3, no. 270 (where the rubric declares the royal act to be *juxta canonem Si De Prebendis*, which is perhaps a reference to Clem. 2:1 [*CIC*, ii, col. 1158]).

[74] *SES*, i, p. liii, n. 1. This document of 1356 refers to a parliament held 1338 x 1350 (presumably 1341 x 1346 while King David II was in Scotland) where a certain matter was raised *in presentia Conservatoris et cleri et ... procerum*.

We do not know whether Bishop Trayl's special faculty to decide first appeals on behalf of the pope was continued by Pope Benedict XIII after his accession to the Apostolic See in 1394;[75] but if it was, it may well have been his approaching death[76] which impelled a piece of emergency legislation in the parliament of 21 February 1401.[77] This was a particularly difficult time for the exercise of papal authority. The French lead in withdrawing obedience from Benedict in July 1398 was not followed in Scotland (for reasons unknown); but Scottish access to this pope was severely restricted, for he was besieged by French troops thereafter in his fortress-palace at Avignon until his escape in disguise in March 1403.[78] The Schism was by now having a very practical effect on the hierarchy of ecclesiastical justice in Scotland, especially if nobody resident in Scotland was to be able to act with papal authority. With the consent therefore of the clergy, parliament passed a rule affecting cases where the legitimacy of a sentence of excommunication was challenged by any of the king's lieges. He could appeal from the *judex* issuing the sentence to the *Conservator Cleri*, who was to act on the matter interestingly with his advisers (*cum suo consilio*). Thereafter a further appeal might be made *ad generalem cleri congregacionem* (which appears to mean the provincial council, though this precise name for it is not otherwise found), where, so long as the Schism lasted, the matter was to be finally determined. This was clearly meant to be just a temporary arrangement, by which a convenient and workable procedure was being approved in the context that appeals to the Roman Court were for the time being impracticable. But its more general implications are ambiguous.[79] Was it the normal canon law route of appeal from the episcopal courts of dioceses which were immediately subject to Rome to that see that was being temporarily replaced by an internal appeal

[75] Cf. *CPL Benedict XIII*, 60, 63.

[76] This took place 5 March x 1 July 1401 (Watt, *Dictionary*, 542).

[77] *APS*, i, 576. Trayl was present at this parliament (*SHS Misc.*, v, 46–7).

[78] Even *littere communes* for Scotland seem to have been unobtainable between November 1398 and October 1402 (cf. *CPL Benedict XIII*, 89–93, where only three papal acts for Scots are listed in this period as fully transacted, and even those may well have been back-dated from a later time).

[79] It is too simple to regard this as just 'secular interference in ecclesiastical matters' (Nicholson, *Later Middle Ages*, 238).

route which was not normally used in this way? Or, since the matter of appeal concerned disputed excommunications (and many provincial statutes laid down the general rules in this field), do we have illustrated here the normal procedure of appeal open to persons who considered that the provincial council's statutes were being misinterpreted, with just the temporary qualification that such matters had for the present to be regarded as 'determined' at council level (with no appeal thereafter)? We cannot be sure which way to interpret this text. There is no earlier evidence that the Conservator used a council to advise him in his judicial capacity,[80] nor that appeal normally lay from his decisions between council meetings to the full council when it met; but both points are likely enough, and we may well have here an illustration of how the judicial mechanism of the Conservator and the Provincial Council normally functioned.

One piece of tantalising evidence about the composition of the council appears to survive from the 1390s. It is a form-letter which had been originally sent out by an unnamed bishop of Moray as *conservator consilii Scoticani* summoning a meeting of the provincial council in the Dominican friary at Perth on a specific day in October (the Wednesday after the feast of St. Luke), but with no year mentioned.[81] It has been correctly argued[82] that this letter implies that there must have been one provincial council meeting at which a bishop of Moray was chosen as Conservator, as well as the one which he was now summoning. But the year-dates of these meetings cannot now be certainly identified. Joseph Robertson suggested that the second of these meetings should be dated 'about 1390' in the aftermath of the burning of Elgin Cathedral by the earl of Buchan (the Wolf of Badenoch) in June 1390,[83] for in his preamble the bishop refers to the burdens (*onera*) that had been placed at that time on churches in his part of the country (*in partibus nostris*). Such timing seems rather too tight: it is preferable to suggest only that the council was called sometime in the period 1390–7 during the last years of the episcopate of Bishop Alexander Bur,[84] or possibly during the early years of

[80] Cf. above p. 83.
[81] *Moray Registrum*, 375, no. 295.
[82] *SES*, i, p. lxxvii.
[83] See *Chron. Bower*, vii, 447.
[84] Watt, *Dictionary*, 70; cf. above p. 85.

his energetic successor William de Spyny (1397–1406).[85] Whatever the original dating, the main interest of this summons lies in its definition of who was to be called to the meeting. Each bishop is to bring with him the prelates of his diocese and 'suitable representatives of chapters, colleges and convents' (*capitulorum collegiorum et conventuum procuratoribus ydoneis*). This contrasts with the earlier evidence which gave no hint in Scotland of the kind of regular representative element which was characteristic of provincial councils in England and on the continent.[86] It seems that experiments with clerical representation in connection with financial grants in parliaments of the mid-fourteenth century[87] had led to an expansion of the categories of clergy who were being called to provincial councils beyond those summoned by right of office (the major and minor prelates) to representatives of clerical corporate bodies (cathedrals, collegiate churches and monasteries), but not to representatives of the parish clergy. By the 1390s this would appear to have been customary even on occasions when the agenda was not specifically concerned with finance.

We get some important complementary guidance on procedure at the council from the first record of one of its meetings that has survived. This recounts the proceedings of a meeting of the *Synodus Provincialis et Consilium Generale cleri regni Scotie* held in the Dominican church at Perth on 16 July 1420.[88] It provides a picture of the composition and procedure of the council after nearly two hundred years of its existence, which can be compared with the mere hints which have been discussed above. Six bishops were present (Dunblane, St. Andrews, Glasgow, Dunkeld, Aberdeen and Brechin) and four others sent proctors to represent them (Moray, Galloway, Caithness and the elect of Ross[89]). It is interesting to see the bishop of Galloway there among the others.[90]

[85] Ibid., 503–6, especially 506.

[86] See above pp. 79–80, 94, 118.

[87] See above pp. 121–2.

[88] *Brechin Registrum*, i, 38–40, no. 29; *SES*, ii, 77–8, no. 166; Patrick, *Statutes*, 80–2, no. 166.

[89] This was John Bulloch, who was apparently consecrated within the next month (cf. *Moray Registrum*, 475, no. 23), even though he was not recognised by Pope Martin V until 1 February 1423 (Watt, *Fasti*, 268).

[90] Cf. above pp. 127–8.

Bishop Finlay de Albany of Argyll may not yet have returned from his consecration at the papal court at Florence earlier in the year.[91] In the Isles it is probable that there was no bishop in office at this date who was acceptable to the Scottish crown.[92] Five monastic heads were present (St. Andrews, Cambuskenneth, Lindores, Coupar Angus and Newbattle), and another eight were represented by proctors (Dunfermline, Kelso, Melrose, Holyrood, Arbroath, Jedburgh, Dryburgh and Paisley).[93] The rest of the sederunt is described only in general terms: 'very many deans, archdeacons, priors of monasteries and the greater part of the clergy who are usually gathered for Council and General Synod'. The composition of the council seems not to have changed since the thirteenth and fourteenth centuries: it is is still mainly an assembly of major and minor prelates there by right of office, accompanied by some lower clergy who may well by this time have been representatives of corporate religious bodies.[94]

Then we can learn more about what was presumably the normal procedural place of the Conservator in the council. His title is given as *Conservator Previlegiorum*.[95] We do not know who was the bishop holding this office that summoned this meeting and presided over its opening devotions.[96] But Bishop William Stephenson of Dunblane[97] was elected next Conservator, apparently (if the notary's Latin is to be interpreted strictly) just by the bishops and the proctors for absent bishops.[98] We can see now that this election took place after the opening sermon, and that the new Conservator definitely presided over the business of the council from then on. This may have long been the custom, but it is not demonstrable until this date.[99] The business was begun

[91] Watt, *Dictionary*, 4–5.

[92] See above p. 128. In any case at least some of the business on the agenda for this meeting (episcopal rights of testamentary jurisdiction) did not concern the diocese of The Isles, where Norwegian customs were to be permitted until 1552 (*SES*, ii, 130, no. 243).

[93] These were all religious houses founded in the twelfth century, but they do not appear to be listed in any special order of precedence.

[94] Cf. above p. 135.

[95] Cf. above pp. 81, 113, 131 for variations of this title.

[96] See above pp. 81–2.

[97] Watt, *Dictionary*, 506–9, s.v. 'Stephani'.

[98] Cf. above p. 81.

[99] Cf. above pp. 82–3, 113.

with a reading out of statutes and privileges, which perhaps means nothing more than a consideration of the minutes of recent meetings.[100] Then the Conservator introduced the main business with which the surviving record (preserved as copied into a register kept at Brechin Cathedral) is concerned, namely a review of the traditional jurisdiction of bishops and other ordinaries in the administration of the personal estates of deceased persons, whether dying testate or intestate. The senior members of the clergy from each diocese were invited to offer evidence on this matter on oath, and then a collated report was drawn up defining long-standing practice, including a definition of how court charges should be levied. The impression given from the description of the procedure followed is that this definition emerged from the discussion; but there may have been a draft policy document available as a basis for the discussion from the start. The Conservator decreed that this definition of custom should be observed henceforth by both clergy and people, and the bishops present attached their seals to a notarial record *cum congregatione Synodi* (which seems to mean 'on behalf of the assembly of the Synod'). We are left with a clear picture of the functioning of the provincial council as it defined for the common benefit of all the constituent dioceses a matter on which perhaps there had been some local variations of practice, or at least on which there had been doubts of some kind. It was convenient to have this mechanism for achieving a common definition for the whole kingdom. But we are left with just one copy of a sealed notarial document because it happened to have been copied into a register at one diocesan centre. No register of the provincial council itself was kept (so far as we know), nor indeed was there any continuing secretariat as the office of Conservator was regularly changing hands. Perhaps there was a chest somewhere containing the sealed master-copies of *acta* of this kind and of such 'statutes' and 'privileges' as were required for reading out and for reference at council meetings: and perhaps it would have been kept in the Dominican church at Perth. But this is just speculation: there is

[100] Cf. above p. 82 for an interpretation of the thirteenth-century *Modus Procedendi*, which in the light of this evidence may perhaps be thought mistaken. But there is nothing here about a ceremony of excommunication in connection with the reading of statutes.

no evidence, and our knowledge of the activities of this particular council meeting is based on the survival of a single document which may not fairly represent the various ways in which the total range of business was done.

Some more general hints about the nature and purpose of the provincial council can be gleaned from a letter written by Prior James de Haldeston of St. Andrews a hundred years later on 3 June of some unstated year during his priorate, i.e. 1418 x 1443.[101] He was replying to an unnamed Conservator[102] who had apparently consulted him about summoning a *consilium cleri* and asked him to preach the opening sermon. Haldeston agrees to do so, and urges old-fashioned strictness[103] in making sure that the prelates and inferior clergy who come to such a council meeting should come this time with all speed and properly attired. There is emphasis on 'the accustomed place and time', which probably means Perth in the month of July if all the known meetings of the provincial council between 1408 and 1472 at any rate are taken into account. The purpose of such a meeting is defined in terms of 'protecting and restoring the privileges of the Scottish church, and also its complete reformation both in head and members, that is both of superior and inferior prelates and their subordinates'. Haldeston seems to be guiding and encouraging a Conservator who had sought his advice – and he kept a copy of the letter because he liked the way he had composed this reply. We have therefore here one man's views on how the provincial council should be run and why, even if we cannot pinpoint the year during which these views were expressed.

There is casual mention of a provincial council meeting in the Dominican church at Perth on 18 July 1408, just because an important formal resignation of lands in Aberdeenshire and elsewhere was made by the heiress Elizabeth de Gordon at a time when this council was meeting: presumably the aim was to achieve

[101] *St. Andrews Copiale*, 104–5, no. 57.

[102] Perhaps the phrase *conservabitis alme vestre professionis honorem* points to Bishop John Bulloch of Ross (1418–39 x 1440), who had been a fellow-canon with Haldeston in the Augustinian cathedral priory at St. Andrews (Watt, *Fasti*, 268; cf. Watt, *Dictionary*, 52, s.v. 'James Biset', para. 6).

[103] This is taking the phrase *sicut facere consueverant temporibus retroactis* in a general sense rather than suggesting a new start (cf. Baxter's comment in suggesting the date 1420 in *St. Andrews Copiale*, 445).

full publicity for her declared willingness for her husband Alexander de Seton to be granted two days later a joint-title to these lands along with her. We know of the presence of six bishops (St. Andrews, Aberdeen, Dunkeld, Moray, Dunblane and Ross) together with the prior of St. Andrews as witnesses in connection with these transactions; and the duke of Albany as governor of Scotland for the absent young king James I (who was then a prisoner in England) was holding a council of his own at Perth at the same time – and was no doubt master-minding this land transfer.[104] Albany was described by his contemporary the chronicler Wyntoun as a hater of Lollards and heretics,[105] and this reputation was most likely earned by the encouragement which he gave to the leaders of the clergy for the trial and condemnation of the Englishman James Resby for adherence to Wyclifite doctrines, since Resby then suffered death by burning under the aegis of the secular arm (being the first known heretic to suffer in this way in Scotland). This trial was conducted at Perth by the theologian Laurence de Lindores as Inquisitor[106] in a council of the clergy (*in concilio cleri*) and the year was '1408', i.e. sometime in the period 25 March 1408 x 24 March 1409.[107] It seems most likely that this trial was the main business of the provincial council which we know to have met on 18 July 1408; and we have here the first example of a new category of business for it.[108] It is hardly surprising that a heresy trial of such substance and on such unfamiliar ground was not something that a single bishop would wish to undertake on his own: the provincial council

[104] National Archives of Scotland, Calendar of Gordon Castle Writs (GD. 44, no. 4; original document is missing).; *RMS*, i, 383–4, no. 905. This was presumably a full list of the bishops who attended this provincial council meeting: new bishops of Brechin and Glasgow were probably both then abroad (Watt, *Dictionary*, 198, 332); the bishops of Argyll and The Isles were both associates of the lord of The Isles and may well have been keeping out of Albany's way at this time (cf. ibid., 287–8; Watt, *Fasti*, 202); the whereabouts of the bishops of Caithness and Galloway are unknown (Watt, *Dictionary*, 379–80; Dowden, *Bishops*, 366–7).

[105] *Chron. Wyntoun*, vi, 417.

[106] Cf. Watt, *Dictionary*, 343–5.

[107] *Chron. Bower*, viii, 67–73; cf. L. Moonan in *Innes Review*, xxvii (1976), 9, n. 15 for correct dating (but see *Glasgow Registrum*, ii, 316, where '1407' is suggested, probably in error).

[108] Cf. Patrick, *Statutes*, p. xlv (wrong dating).

backed by the governor was available to provide a forum for national backing. There may possibly have been another heresy trial leading to an execution in 1420 or 1422,[109] as was certainly held for Pavel Kavar, a Hussite visitor from Prague, in July 1433 at St. Andrews.[110] Laurence de Lindores again conducted the second of these trials at any rate; but whether they were again held at the time of meetings of the provincial council is not recorded. It is not until the very end of the fifteenth century that major heresy trials were to be mounted in Scotland again.[111]

By late 1408 Scotland was becoming more closely involved in the international diplomacy which introduced the conciliar epoch of the early decades of the fifteenth century. The see of St. Andrews was now in the hands of Henry de Wardlaw, Cardinal Wardlaw's nephew, a firm adherent like his uncle to the Clementine cause now so stubbornly represented by Benedict XIII, who had in September 1403 imposed Wardlaw on the see of St. Andrews while he was a follower of the papal court.[112] He became accepted in Scotland as the colleague for nearly twenty years of Bishop Gilbert de Grenlaw of Aberdeen, who in 1403 had been the local choice for the see of St. Andrews, and who remained very close to the duke of Albany as chancellor of Scotland for more than twenty-four years 1397–1421.[113] These two men must have done much to keep Scotland unswervingly loyal to Pope Benedict longer than was thought advantageous anywhere else in Europe: and Wardlaw enjoyed special powers as resident papal legate for Benedict in Scotland for at least the two years from June 1410 and perhaps longer.[114] The latter part of 1408 saw the return to Scotland of the two other newly appointed bishops who seem to have missed the provincial council meeting held in July – Bishop Walter Forrester of Brechin, who was also closely associated with Albany's government as clerk of the rolls and register *c.* 1403–*c.* 1425,[115] and Bishop William de Lawedre of Glasgow, who had been used by Albany as a diplomat, and

109 J. A. F. Thomson, *The Later Lollards* (Oxford, 1965), 203.
110 *Chron. Bower*, viii, 277.
111 Nicholson, *Later Middle Ages*, 561–2.
112 Watt, *Dictionary*, 566–7.
113 Ibid., 237–8.
114 Cf. *CPL Benedict XIII*, 224–6.
115 Watt, *Dictionary*, 198–9.

who had probably helped to secure Forrester's confirmation at Benedict's court.[116]

These four bishops would have been particularly involved in formulating the Scottish response to two summonses to general councils that were now received. Benedict sent his summons to the Scottish king and clergy in the usual form on 15 June 1408, requiring the presence of representatives at Perpignan (on the modern French–Spanish border, then in Benedict's native country of Aragon) for a council in November 1408.[117] The notice was short, but it would have been normal for the provincial council to meet and discuss who among the bishops should attend. We do not know whether it did; but in the event this council attracted only a limited attendance at its meetings between 15 November 1408 and 26 March 1409,[118] and no Scottish bishops are known to have attended. Instead Simon de Mandeville, archdeacon of Glasgow, who was employed in Benedict's court as an auditor, represented the king and kingdom of Scotland.[119] This was a measure of the very limited political pulling-power of Benedict at this time, though personal business affecting individual Scots continued to be processed through the papal chancery during the period of this council.[120] It was clearly not the case that Perpignan was inaccessible from Scotland because of travel restrictions through France, where the government had from May 1408 ceased to recognise the authority of Pope Benedict.[121]

But there was a complication coming from France to Scotland which may well have affected the issue. The cardinals who had deserted the Roman pope Gregory XII as well as Benedict XIII had in July 1408 summoned a general council on their own authority to Pisa in Italy to meet on 25 March 1409: it did meet and arranged for the election of a third rival pope (Alexander V) before it dispersed on 7 August 1409.[122] The ex-Benedictine cardinals asked King Charles VI of France to try to persuade the

[116] Ibid., 332.
[117] *CPL Benedict XIII*, 176–7.
[118] Delaruelle, *L'église*, i, 143.
[119] *ALKG*, vii, 671, 691; cf. Watt, *Dictionary*, 380–2, s.v. 'Mandeville'.
[120] *CPL Benedict XIII*, 192–8.
[121] Delaruelle, *L'église*, i, 140.
[122] Ibid., i, 147–8, 154. See reference in next note for date of this summons.

Scots to send representatives to this council;[123] and we have the instructions given on 27 October 1408 by the French government to Robert l'Heremite for negotiations with Albany and the prelates of Scotland on this matter.[124] Did the provincial council therefore meet, say in December 1408? We do not know; but certainly no Scots went to Pisa, and Scotland remained loyal to Benedict XIII.

In the years that followed a number of envoys arrived in Scotland from France, first to seek Scottish adhesion to the pope elected at Pisa (Alexander V) and his successor John XXIII elected in May 1410, and then once another general council had on 9 December 1413 been called by this latter pope to meet at Constance on 1 November 1414 to secure Scottish representation at it. This diplomatic offensive was complicated by the continuing imprisonment in England of the young king James I, with his uncle the duke of Albany ruling as governor in Scotland in his absence. Such matters in most countries called for the summoning of church councils to offer advice to the ruler; but can any trace be found in Scotland of the involvement of the provincial council? One embassy left Paris in January 1410, including envoys from the king of France and the University of Paris (one of whom was a Master Thomas and the other the abbot of Pontigny in France), and it was supplied with letters from the university to certain prelates of Scotland who were Paris graduates. It is not known how this embassy was received in Scotland, except that it did not achieve recognition for Alexander V.[125] It was to be claimed by the university in December 1412, however, that this embassy had secured the detachment from adherence to Benedict of one Scottish prelate who was a doctor of theology,[126] and at this date they were writing again to Albany, urging him to bring his country

[123] Valois, *La France*, iv, 19, n. 1.

[124] *St. Andrews Copiale*, 228–30, no. 5.

[125] *Auctarium Chartularii Universitatis Parisiensis* [*AUP*], ed. H. Denifle and E. Chatelain and others (Paris, 1894–1964), ii, 66–7, 107, 118, 123. Cf. *ER*, iv, 132 for payments made to a John dictus Ryver, an envoy of the French king, at Dundee May 1409 x July 1410. See Watt, *Dictionary*, 183, 364–5 for possible identifications of the 'Master Thomas' mentioned in the text.

[126] *Chartularium Universitatis Parisiensis* [*CUP*], ed. H. Denifle and E. Chatelain (Paris, 1889–97), iv, 249, no. 1964. This is likely to have been Bishop Michael of the Isles, who was probably hostile anyway to the policy of the bishops who supported Albany (see above pp. 127, 139, n. 104).

and clergy into the obedience of Pope John XXIII, the hope then being that the Scots would come to a council which that pope was trying to assemble at Rome.[127] Again the Scots refused to co-operate, however the matter was discussed.[128]

As the time for the Council of Constance approached, the University of Paris sent John of Austria and the Scottish Master John Gray to both James I in England and to Scotland to seek Scottish participation. They had presumably seen James by early August 1414 when they were given safe-conducts to travel north from England to Scotland with the bishop of Lodi as nuncio of Pope John XXIII in their company. They may have been back in Paris by November 1414, as they certainly were by April 1415.[129] The instructions for the embassy survive,[130] and it is for our purpose noteworthy that they were told to try to arrange for a meeting of the Three Estates in Scotland 'as is usually done in such matters', before whom they were to argue their case in detail. Failing that, they were to deal with the nobles and prelates individually as they could find them. There is no word of a provincial council: the embassy were to tackle laymen as well as clergy. They were provided also with various letters to take with them which survive in various versions – letters to King James,[131] to the king of England,[132] to the duke of Albany and the earls of Douglas and March.[133] There were also letters to three individual

[127] Ibid.; Paris, Archives Nationales [AN], MS. M. 65A, no. 7 (this was written at the same time as the letter to John XXIII cited in previous note); cf. J. Maitland Anderson, 'The beginnings of St. Andrews University 1410–1418', *SHR*, viii (1911), 347.

[128] Only a knight and a squire are known to have come to Scotland as envoys from the king of France in the period June 1412 x July 1413 (*ER*, iv, 189).

[129] *AUP*, ii, 193; *Rotuli Scotiae* (London, 1814–19), ii, 209, 211; *Foedera, Conventiones, Literae et Cuiuscunque Generis Acta Publica*, ed. T. Rymer, original edition (London, 1704–35), ix, 157; *Acta Concilii Constanciensis*, ed. H. Finke (Münster, 1896–1928), i, 349; cf. ii, 57 for bishop of Lodi (and see *St. Andrews Copiale*, 9).

[130] C. Jourdain, *Index Chronologicus Chartarum pertinentium ad historiam Universitatis Parisiensis* (Paris, 1862), 232–3, no. 1083, as collated with corrected readings offered by Chatelain on a copy in the Archives Nationales in Paris.

[131] *CUP*, iv, 285–6, no. 2018; *St. Andrews Copiale*, 244–6.

[132] AN, MS. M. 65B, no. 79 (1), unprinted.

[133] Ibid., no. 78 (1); *St. Andrews Copiale*, 243–4, 246.

clergy – Bishop Walter Forrester of Brechin (who is reminded in one version that he had known John of Austria at Paris,[134] and who had indeed himself been hostile there to Pope Benedict XIII at the time of the French Withdrawal of Obedience of 1398),[135] a bishop of The Isles (presumably the bishop who had been responsive to the earlier mission of 1410),[136] and a Master Alexander (probably Master Alexander de Foulertoun, who is likely to have been in the service of the imprisoned King James at this time).[137] These envoys took also letters of general address to the nobles and bishops of Scotland,[138] in which there is some suggestion that the earl of Douglas was expected to be on the envoys' side. But despite all this literary outburst, the mission failed. We do not even know whether they got to meet the Three Estates as they had hoped. Albany and his group of pro-Benedict bishops were not ready to be attracted away from their papal allegiance. And Benedict had, of course, recently in August 1413 granted foundation privileges to Bishop Wardlaw's new university at St. Andrews which had been received there as recently as February 1414.[139]

Once King Sigismund of Germany had persuaded the Spanish kings to abandon Benedict in the Capitulation of Narbonne on 13 December 1415, the news was sent to Scotland by the king of Aragon from nearby Perpignan on 21 December 1415.[140] It may also have reached Scotland through Bishop Thomas de Butil of Galloway, who had been active in Benedict's court certainly as late as September 1415 and who has been said to have been at Narbonne.[141] He was back in Scotland by 17 March 1416, when

[134] AN, MS. M. 65B, no. 77 (2); cf. *St. Andrews Copiale*, 246–7. See *AUP*, i, 704–6 for an illustration of this contact in 1395.

[135] Watt, *Dictionary*, 197–8.

[136] *St. Andrews Copiale*, 247; see above p. 142, n. 126.

[137] Ibid., 248, where the king is mentioned also (cf. Watt, *Dictionary*, 201–2.

[138] AN, MS. M. 65B, nos. 77(1), 78(2).

[139] Anderson, 'Beginnings', 337–41, 342; cf. 348; *CPL Benedict XIII*, 276–8; R. Swanson, 'The University of St. Andrews and the Great Schism, 1410–1419', *Journal of Ecclesiastical History*, xxvi (1975), 223–45.

[140] Finke, *Acta*, iii, 490.

[141] Watt, *Dictionary*, 72; but he is not mentioned in the record of the meeting there – indeed no Scottish representative is mentioned (H. von der Hardt, *Magnum Oecumenicum Constantiense Concilium* (Frankfurt and Leipzig, 1697–1700), ii, 540–55).

he was present with eight other bishops and six abbots in a general council of the Three Estates at Perth, when, probably as a reaction to this diplomatic revolution and the new pressures that were being exerted on Scotland to support the Council of Constance,[142] a special notarial copy was made of old letters issued by King Edward III of England in March 1328 recognising Scotland as an independent kingdom.[143] Soon afterwards the governor seems to have sent the Dominican Finlay de Albany (who had started his career in his service and was now his confessor) to Constance, whence he was sent back with a Robert de Prestoun with letters inviting Scottish representation at the council. This embassy superseded a decision of the council on 4 February 1416 that the bishop of Lodi should return to Scotland as their envoy.[144] They published their letters from Constance at St. Andrews *presente episcopo et cleri et populi multitudine* (which does not suggest a formal assembly), and were answered temporisingly by the Governor from his castle at Doune in Perthshire on 4 November 1416.[145] Sometime between 25 March 1416 and 24 March 1417 the new abbot of Pontigny appears to have visited Scotland also as an envoy of the council, and put his case before the governor and the Three Estates in general council at Perth.[146] He may have brought with him another hortatory letter addressed by the University of Paris, just *Ad Scotos* this time.[147]

In the end it took nearly a year after the election of Pope Martin V at Constance on 11 November 1417 for the formal decision to

[142] But not at the request of the Council of Constance (as wrongly stated in Watt, *Dictionary,* 72).

[143] *APS*, i, 587–9; *Glasgow Registrum*, ii, 307–12.

[144] Finke, *Acta*, ii, 57. This bishop was still at Constance in May and perhaps June 1416 (ibid., 60–1; L. R. Loomis, *The Council of Constance. The Unification of the Church*, ed. J. H. Mundy and K. M. Woody (New York, 1961), 63, n. 20, 282–3). It is possible that this source is erroneous in confusing this bishop (who is said to be a Dominican master of theology) with Finlay de Albany, later bishop of Argyll (who was a Dominican bachelor of theology).

[145] Watt, *Dictionary*, 4–5; *St. Andrews Copiale*, 261–3; cf. Anderson, 'Beginnings', 350. On their return to Constance these Scots envoys were before 30 March 1417 reported as fighting wonderfully for Benedict (Finke, *Acta*, iv, 68).

[146] *Chron. Bower*, viii, 87. It hardly seems likely that Bower is confusing this visit with the one in 1410. Cf. *St. Andrews Copiale*, 9, where the order of the various embassies to Scotland is clearly confused.

[147] AN, MS. M. 65B, no. 29, which is datable July 1415 x July 1417.

be made in Scotland to adhere to him. Finlay de Albany was appointed with Griffin Yonge (newly appointed to see of Ross) as envoys of Martin to Scotland on 1 March 1418.[148] Yonge at any rate was still at Troyes in France on 5 July.[149] But presumably one or both were present at the grand debate held before the governor and the Three Estates in general council at Perth on 2/3 October 1418. Before then there seems to have been an assembly (*cetus*) of the prelates of the kingdom at some date after the adhesion of the captive King James to Pope Martin was known,[150] say July 1418, to which the earl of Douglas sent a letter (probably composed by Prior James Haldeston of St. Andrews) urging adherence to the new pope.[151] This would appear to have been a provincial council, held probably before 9 August 1418, by which time it was known at St. Andrews that a meeting of the Estates in October had been arranged to deal with the matter.[152] The bishops were now apparently open to persuasion, and the earl of Douglas was taking a different line from that followed by the governor. At the Perth meeting Benedict's case was argued by an English friar Robert Harding, who was favoured by the governor: Martin's case received more effective support from the representatives of the University of St. Andrews, from a monk theologian John Fogo, and from Bishop William de Lawedre of Glasgow.[153] It is not quite clear whether the final decision was made then; but when envoys were sent to Martin at Florence to offer the obedience of the kingdom of Scotland in August 1419, it was done on behalf of the governor and the Three Estates.[154]

[148] *CPL*, vii, 6–7; Theiner, *Monumenta*, 370, no. 739.

[149] *St. Andrews Copiale*, 391.

[150] Cf. E. W. M. Balfour-Melville, *James I, King of Scots* (London, 1936), 72–3. The date was probably at least a month or two after 21 April 1418, when the earl of Douglas had a nuncio at Martin's court (*Calendar of Scottish Supplications to Rome 1418–22*, ed. E. R. Lindsay and A. I. Cameron [SHS, 1934], 8), since the earl had had a reply from this pope before this assembly met.

[151] *St. Andrews Copiale*, 18–20; cf. 27–8.

[152] *Acta Facultatis Artium Universitatis Sanctiandree 1413–1588* [*St. Andrews Acta*], ed. A. I. Dunlop (Edinburgh and London, 1964), 12.

[153] Ibid., 12–13; *Chron. Bower*, viii, 87–9; *St. Andrews Copiale*, 3–4, 9–10; cf. Anderson, 'Beginnings', 358–60.

[154] *Chron. Bower*, iii, 435; *St. Andrews Copiale*, 23–9; cf. *CPL Benedict XIII*, 376–86 for papal graces still being issued for Scots by Benedict between November 1418 and January 1419.

We are left with the clear impression that the problems raised by the Schism in Scotland were not regarded as suitable for just the provincial council to decide. And when the Councils of Perpignan, Pisa and Constance came along, it was not just a matter of selecting which prelates were to attend or of collecting material for the agenda as had been suitable business for the provincial council in the thirteenth and early-fourteenth centuries. More was now at stake, and no Scottish bishops went to these councils anyway. It was apparently mainly in general councils of the Three Estates that Scottish policy over the Schism and its councils in the early fifteenth century was hammered out. Perhaps this is related to the fact that for much of the relevant time the government was in the hands of a governor rather than of an active king in his own right. In practice Albany may have had to govern by discussion with the Three Estates, and this was appreciated by those at Paris and Constance who sent embassies to Scotland in these years (especially during the decade 1408–18). The provincial council may have continued meeting between 1408 and 1420, but apart from 1418 we do not know that it did, and it certainly did not grow in authority in any way that was derived from tackling the problems raised by the Schism.

It was known for the five years before 23 April 1423 that the next general council would open then at Pavia in Italy in terms of the decree *Frequens* of the Council of Constance, and in some countries at least (though not in France, England or Spain) preparatory local councils were held to prepare matters for the agenda.[155] There is no evidence that this happened in Scotland, though it is quite possible that the provincial council did meet to define the ways in which *in regno Scocie ecclesia Dei magna indigebat reformacione tam in spiritualibus quam in temporalibus* (especially as a result of interference by temporal lords with church rights and jurisdictions) – to quote the language of the official delegation that was rather late in the day sent to this general council.[156] But it was Murdoch the second duke of Albany who as governor with the Three Estates in the absence still of their imprisoned king appointed a delegation to take part in the

[155] Delaruelle, *L'église*, i, 223.

[156] W. Brandmüller, *Das Konzil von Pavia-Siena 1423–1424* (Münster, 1968–74), ii, 357.

council, which had in July 1423 moved to Siena. This delegation comprised two bishops, one abbot and 'many doctors' (all unnamed), who travelled to Flanders in the winter of 1423–4 *en route* for Siena; but when they heard that the council was likely to be dissolved soon – in fact on 19 February 1424 it decided on Basel as the meeting place of its successor ten years hence[157] – they sent two of their number on ahead in disguise,[158] who joined with Andrew de Hawyk (a Scot who was already a member of the council as student-rector of the University of Siena)[159] to present the credentials of the whole delegation and be admitted to the council on 26 February 1424.[160] These three stayed to take part in the last days of this council until *c.* 9 March 1424,[161] whilst the main delegation never got there. It was an abortive effort, but one which in line with the practice of 1408–18 was organised by the governor and the Three Estates rather than by the provincial council. The delegates indeed brought separate letters of appointment (*procuratorium et mandatum*) issued by the governor and the Three Estates,[162] even if they were clergy sent to take part in a general council of the church.

Meanwhile there had been the well-attended meeting of the provincial council at Perth on 16 July 1420[163] at what may well have been 'the accustomed place and time'.[164] What then are we to make of a reference to a 'general council' held in the Dominican church at Perth on 18 May 1420, when Prior James Haldeston of St. Andrews as papal collector in Scotland issued a general

[157] Ibid., ii, 310–13.

[158] Brandmüller suggests that this was because they had to travel through lands held by the hostile English and Burgundians (ibid., 358). The two who went forward seem to have been Nicholas de Atholl and William Croyser, though the latter may have already been in Italy (cf. Watt, *Dictionary*, 19, 133).

[159] Watt, *Dictionary*, 256–9.

[160] Brandmüller, *Pavia-Siena*, ii, 356–9. The three had their own notary with them, Alexander de Castiltarris of Glasgow diocese (ibid., ii, 400). Another Scot, Thomas Morow abbot of Paisley was very active in the Council, but as an envoy of King Charles VII of France (ibid., *ad indicem*).

[161] Ibid., ii, 392, 394–5, 397–400, 430–3. The only business in which they were involved was to support their fellow-Scot Abbot Morow in attacking the case for the English to have a separate Nation within the Council's constitution. This reflected the contemporary political situation.

[162] Ibid., ii, 357.

[163] See above p. 135.

[164] See above p. 138.

warning to 'all and sundry prelates and all other persons whatsoever, both lay and ecclesiastical in the kingdom' who owed payments to the pope that they must pay up within six months?[165] It has been argued that this is more likely to have been a clerical gathering than an assembly of the Three Estates;[166] and certainly papal collectors have previously been known to deal with the Scottish clergy through the provincial council.[167] But it seems improbable that the council met twice within two months; and in any case the collector's warning is directed at some laymen as well as clergy. It seems best therefore to regard this meeting as a hitherto unknown gathering of the Three Estates in their general council[168] rather than as a purely clerical assembly. The two bodies necessarily found it advantageous to work together, as happens to be illustrated by a case datable 1419 x 1424. Measures were then being taken to secure the priorship of Coldingham in Berwickshire for a monk of Dunfermline, which involved taking action against a certain William Drax who was supported by the monks of Durham Cathedral for the post. The Scottish governor took action against this 'intruder' by two related routes – a 'general council of the Three Estates' decreed the seizure of his temporal revenues, and 'a council of the clergy' ordered the sequestration of his spiritual revenues.[169] It is clear that the functions and powers of the latter body had not been subsumed by those of the former one. There was a place for both.

[165] *St. Andrews Copiale*, 97–8.

[166] Ibid., 440.

[167] E.g. in the late thirteenth century (see above pp. 89–93, 97–8; cf. pp. 89–100).

[168] Cf. A. A. M. Duncan, 'Councils General 1404–1423', *SHR*, xxxv (1956), 132–43.

[169] *Chron. Bower*, vi, 71.

10

Last years of the traditional arrangements 1424–1472

THE return of King James from eighteen years of captivity in England in April 1424 introduced a few years of intensive reconstruction led by an active government. Full parliaments were now held again frequently (as opposed to the general councils of the Three Estates which had met during the period of the Albany governorships), and between 1424 and 1431 at any rate there was a spate of new legislation on a wide variety of topics, with the king and his advisers taking the initiative.[1] It was part of James's framework of thinking in the parliament of March 1426 that everyone in Scotland should 'be governed under the king's laws and statutes of this realm only and under no particular laws nor special privileges nor by any laws of other countries or realms'.[2] One aspect of this approach was that parliament was regarded as omnicompetent, so that we find legislation confidently regulating the activities of the clergy, whether controlling their freedom to leave Scotland to visit the Roman Court and interfering with some aspects of their freedom to negotiate there for benefices in Scotland,[3] or ordering bishops to be active with the help of the secular arm in pursuing heretics, inspecting hospitals, and seeking out lepers.[4] But of course the clergy took part in the parliaments that approved these new laws, and like the other

[1] Nicholson, *Later Middle Ages*, 304–5.

[2] *APS*, ii, 9, c. 3.

[3] Nicholson, loc. cit., 294.

[4] *APS*, ii, 7, c. 3; 7, c. 2; 16, c. 8.

groups at parliaments they were at least formally consulted about matters which affected them. Yet the king was not wanting to work only through parliament. He saw a use also for additional bodies representing sectional interests, provided their activities were subordinate to his own in parliament. It has been argued, for example, that he encouraged the development of the traditional Court of the Four Burghs into a Parliament of the Four Burghs (in practice attended by commissioners from all the royal burghs south of the River Spey), which met annually in October for deliberative as well as judicial business, and which may well have helped with framing the legislation that was eventually passed by the Three Estates in Parliament on matters affecting merchants and burghs.[5]

The traditional provincial council of the clergy provided a parallel assembly for another subordinate interest group in the country, and there are interesting examples to show how the system worked. The parliament of March 1425 decreed that all bishops should order their clergy by letter to say special prayers for the king, queen and their children.[6] The matter was taken up again in the parliament of March 1426, when the clergy are recorded as agreeing to a more elaborate ordinance on the same subject, putting some teeth into it. Each bishop is now to order his clergy at his next synod to say a particular collect for the royal family whenever they say mass, under threat of a defined financial penalty and ecclesiastical censure. And it is further agreed that a general statute on this matter should be issued at the next general council of the clergy.[7] The regularity of meetings of synods and provincial council is taken for granted, and it may well be that the council did meet soon afterwards at Perth in July 1426 to follow this matter up. The pattern is more specifically demonstrated in the following year when parliament met rather unusually in July 1427 at Perth. Then, as part of a continuing review of judicial procedures in the various courts of the kingdom,[8] an act was passed on 11 July reforming the procedure in church courts in cases where a layman was the plaintiff against a clerical

[5] A. A. M. Duncan, *James I* (Glasgow, 1976), 11; cf. Nicholson, *Later Middle Ages*, 264–5.

[6] *APS*, ii, 8, c. 18; *SES*, i, p. lxxix.

[7] *APS*, ii, 10, c. 12; *SES*, i, p. lxxx; ii, 272. Cf. above pp. 148–9.

[8] Nicholson, *Later Middle Ages*, 309–12.

defendant *ad parcendum expensis et vexacionibus pauperum* and *ad abbreviandum lites pro expedicione.*[9] This time it is not the clergy in parliament who are said to have proposed this statute: it is much more likely that it was being imposed on the church by a masterful king and his advisers; and again to give it teeth the statute ends: *Et quod istud statuatur de presenti auctoritate consilii provincialis.* Here the provincial council is being ordered by a superior authority (according to the king's framework of thought) to give effect to a royal act by adding its own authority to it. And the meeting of the council is expected to follow at once.[10] It was July and the place was Perth. We may assume that the provincial council had been called at the usual time and place, and we do not learn of any objection on its part against doing what it was told. The church always enjoyed its 'liberty' at the discretion of the state.

The next general council of the church was formally opened at Basel on 25 July 1431 and held its first full session on 14 December of that year. It was already at loggerheads with Pope Eugenius IV, and we find that it was from the council rather than the pope that letters were sent on 19/20 December 1431 to Scotland asking for representatives to be sent. The king was asked to send *aliquos insignes viros . . . de omni statu vestro et regni vestri plene instructos.*[11] The bishops, abbots and other clergy (*personae ecclesiasticae*) of Scotland who *ad generalia concilia de iure et consuetudine venire tenentur* were ordered to set out in person within a month, or to send one or more persons as proxies *pleno cum mandato.*[12] No doubt this invitation and instruction were much discussed in Scotland, though there is no reference to any meeting of the provincial council at this stage. Two Scots did incorporate individually as members of the council towards the end of 1432 – Abbot Thomas Livingston of Dundrennan on 14 November and John Winchester canon of Moray who was in the

[9] *APS*, ii, 14, c. 5; *SES*, i, p. lxxxi.

[10] Cf. Balfour-Melville, *James I*, 152–3, which follows Hannay in *SHR*, xv (1918), 190–1 in straining the Latin here to mean that the council had already concurrently given its authority to this statute. See also discussion in *SES*, i, p. lxxxi, n. 2.

[11] *St. Andrews Copiale*, 85–7.

[12] Ibid., 88–9.

king's service on 15 December.[13] Then the pope added his own summons to the council (with which he was now reconciled) probably in February 1433,[14] and by 22 June 1433 the king was writing to Livingston to say that he would be sending his representatives soon.[15] He did in fact appoint a delegation of eight clergy (including Livingston) on 31 July 1433 to go *pro nobis et regno nostro*, consisting of two bishops, two abbots and four dignitaries,[16] and of these six (including Bishop John Cameron of Glasgow the chancellor of Scotland) did in fact travel to join Livingston at Basel in January/February 1434.[17] There is no word of them going in the name of the Three Estates as had been the case at Siena in 1424;[18] it was the king alone who had been summoned, and who presumably was alone responsible for this choice of a delegation.[19]

What about the response from the Scottish clergy who were summoned? This must surely have on occasion been a matter for discussion in the provincial council over the years during which the general council met, but the response does not appear to have been a communal one. The summons was to individuals and to corporations: it was as individuals and holders of offices such as bishoprics, monastic headships or cathedral dignities or canonries that most of the twenty-eight other Scots clergy were described when they were incorporated as members of the council at intervals over the period February 1434–February 1437.[20] Only one other bishop went in person in this period (Bishop Henry de Lychton of Aberdeen), and another (Bishop John de Crannach of Brechin) sent a proctor in January 1436. Only the abbot of

[13] J. H. Burns, *Scottish Churchmen and the Council of Basle* (Glasgow, 1962), 12–13; cf. *St. Andrews Copiale*, 431–2 (where a wrong year is given for Winchester).

[14] Burns, *Basle*, 14; Watt, *Dictionary*, 134, s.v. 'William Croyser'.

[15] *SES*, ii, 247; Patrick, *Statutes*, 218.

[16] *SES*, ii, 248, as corrected in R. K. Hannay, 'A letter to Scotland from the Council of Basel', *SHR*, xx (1923), 50, 54; cf. *St. Andrews Copiale*, 432.

[17] Burns, *Basle*, 16–20.

[18] See above pp. 147–8.

[19] In France King Charles VII was advised by a council of clergy early in 1432 before he decided to send a delegation, a leading member of which was John de Kirkmichael, the Scot who happened to be bishop of Orleans (Watt, *Dictionary*, 311–12).

[20] Burns, *Basle*, 20–54.

Holyrood from among the monastic heads went in person, while the prior of Paisley probably represented his abbot and the prior of Urquhart is likely to have represented the abbot of his mother-house at Dunfermline. Otherwise it was a question of four cathedral deans, four archdeacons, two other cathedral dignitaries, and ten canons of cathedral or collegiate churches.[21] One clerk (Robert de Essy) was distinguished in the council records as a Licentiate in Theology rather than as a benefice-holder, and it was presumably as a learned theologian from St. Andrews University that he was accepted as a council member, for this was allowed under the rules.[22] Apart from him, those who held benefices below the level of dean or archdeacon were presumably there as proctors for their chapters, even though this is nowhere stated in the record; and though we know very little about how long these lesser figures remained at Basel, it is probable that in the cases of the chapters of Moray, Ross and Aberdeen at any rate, a succession of such proctors served in turn. Such representation was not evenly spread through the various dioceses of Scotland, for none came from Argyll or The Isles, and the major diocese of St. Andrews lost out in not having a secular cathedral chapter to send a proctor.[23] Perhaps there was an overall plan behind all this involvement in the Council of Basel for which the provincial council was responsible, but it cannot be identified.

In the middle of the meetings of this council Scotland had the unfamiliar experience of a visit from a papal legate. This was Bishop Antony Altani of Urbino,[24] whom Pope Eugenius appointed to this mission in July 1436.[25] There had been controversy for nearly ten years over the king's policy towards churchmen and the church in Scotland, some of it aired in debates

[21] A master of the Bethlehemite hospital of St. Germains in East Lothian and a canon (O.S.A.) of Holyrood (Burns, *Basle*, 24–5) may have come to Basel mainly on business as litigants, but were accepted for a time as members under the rather elastic interpretation of the rules that was in force (cf. ibid., 32, 55). Other Scots clergy who seem to have visited Basel on personal business in the curia there appear not to have been incorporated as members (ibid., 41–2, 51–2, 57–9).

[22] Ibid., 32.

[23] Cf. ibid., 55.

[24] *St. Andrews Copiale*, 461; see biography in *Dictionnaire d'histoire et de géographie ecclésiastiques*, ii, 777–9.

[25] *CPL*, viii, 229, 288–90; *SES*, i, p. lxxxvi, n. 3.

at Basel. Technically it was the king who asked for this visit through his envoys Bishop Cameron and Abbot Paniter of Arbroath,[26] who in the previous year had arranged a loan of 1,000 ducats on the market at Bruges to pay for the expenses of a legatine visit. It is interesting that in the bull of appointment the pope described his responsibility for the spiritual welfare of Scotland not only as papal, but also in a special way as metropolitan (*specialiter jure metropolitico*), and the legate was given wide-ranging powers for the reformation of the Scottish church.[27] Had all gone well, he would no doubt have held a legatine council in Scotland to announce his reforming constitutions, and there would also have been need for the provincial council to discuss how the Scottish clergy were to be taxed to repay the loan raised for his expenses, the pope having agreed in advance that this might be done either by a levy of procurations or by a 'charitable subsidy' (either of which would have required consultation with the clergy concerned).[28] But of course this visit did not turn out as expected. The legate arrived in Scotland before Christmas 1436 and had a preliminary meeting at Perth with what was either a parliament or a general council of the Three Estates on 4 February.[29] The king was in some way formally reconciled with him in mid-February,[30] and then assassinated on 21 February. This led to the abandonment of the legate's mission before he had held a council in Scotland, though the pope does seem to have encouraged him to stay on.[31] It is not known how or if the loan for his expenses was ever repaid.

[26] William Croyser claimed the credit of persuading the pope to agree (Watt, *Dictionary*, 134). For Paniter see ibid., 437–9.

[27] *SES*, i, p. lxxxvi; *CPL*, viii, 229.

[28] Theiner, *Monumenta*, 375, no. 746; cf. above pp. 50, 90–4 for such levies in connection with thirteenth-century legatine visits (which were the most recent in Scottish experience).

[29] *Chron.Bower*, viii, 297; cf. *SES*, i, p. lxxxvii and *Liber Pluscardensis* [*Chron. Pluscarden*], ed. F. J. H. Skene (Edinburgh, 1877–80), i, 388–9. Cf. Nicholson, *Later Middle Ages*, 301–2.

[30] *Chron. Pluscarden*, i, 389–90.

[31] *St. Andrews Copiale*, 146–8; cf. 138–46; cf. undated papal letter in *SES*, i, pp. lxxxvii–lxxxviii, which was probably written on 5 May 1437 (*CPL*, viii, 230). He seems to have certainly left Scotland by October 1437 (*EHR*, lii [1937], 491, n. 6). See also discussion in A. I. Dunlop, *The Life and Times of James Kennedy Bishop of St. Andrews* (Edinburgh and London, 1950), 22–3.

On 18 September 1437 the pope instructed the Council of Basel to move to Ferrara in Italy, and whilst some of the members obeyed him, many remained behind in rebellion against his authority. He sent a nuncio who visited Scotland between December 1437 and April 1438,[32] and on 9 April 1438 summoned all the bishops and prelates of Scotland to attend his council at Ferrara.[33] The response was slow, though Bishop James Kennedy of Dunkeld and William Turnbull canon of Glasgow did appear at Florence (whither this council had moved from Ferrara in January 1439) in time for the famous session of the council on 6 July 1439 when the Union of the Eastern and Western Churches was proclaimed.[34] There had therefore been at least some support in Scotland (where Archibald earl of Douglas was lieutenant-general for the young James II until his death in June 1439) for Eugenius and his council and against the continuing council at Basel. But Scottish links with Basel had not been entirely broken: Abbot Livingston was now a leading figure there as that council moved towards its extremist phase in deposing Eugenius on 25 June 1439 and electing Felix V as an alternative pope on 5 November 1439.[35]

It was to prove attractive to rival political factions who were seeking to control the government of Scotland during the continuing royal minority to support the alternative popes, with drastic effect in the form of rivalry over church appointments within the country. The 'Little Schism'[36] had a much more divisive effect in Scotland than the Great Schism had had, for this time the country was split. In many cases there came to be two claimants for bishoprics and lesser benefices, whose hopes of securing possession depended on the ups and downs of the rival factions while the royal minority continued, and whose personal interest gave them continuing reason to support Eugenius on the one hand or Felix and the Council of Basel on the other, whatever the general merits of the case in the disputes between these two contending superior authorities. Felix in January 1440 wrote to the University of St. Andrews and to the Scottish government

[32] Burns, *Basle*, 59; Dunlop, *Kennedy*, 23, n. 1.

[33] *St. Andrews Copiale*, 165–9.

[34] Burns, *Basle*, 62.

[35] Ibid., 62–4.

[36] A phrase coined in Nicholson, *Later Middle Ages*, chapter 12.

seeking support,[37] and possibly it was Abbot Livingston in person who came to plead this pope's cause.[38] Sir Alexander Livingston of Callendar was currently a leading political figure in the government. No official declaration in favour of Felix and the Council of Basel is known to have been made; but the flow of individual Scots clergy to Basel as incorporated members of the council there was resumed between April 1440 and June 1441,[39] with others also accepting benefices from Felix in this period.[40]

A notable old member of the council who returned to it from the service of Eugenius between August 1440 and May 1441 was William Croyser.[41] He was a kinsman of James earl of Douglas who was in alliance in the minority government from November 1440 with Sir Alexander Livingston, and it may well have been Scottish politics which decided Croyser on his change of papal politics.[42] Certainly this earl of Douglas chose until his death in March 1443 to support the Basel cause in Scotland. This did not mean, however, that he had things all his own way. James Kennedy had now moved to the see of St. Andrews, and returned to Scotland in the Spring of 1441 to push the cause of Eugenius against Basel; and it is said to have been at a meeting of the Three Estates that he secured what was presumably then a majority declaration that 'no Scot may go to Basel, adhere to the council or obey it'.[43] There is no doubt that at some date the general council of the Three Estates enjoined obedience to Eugenius, for there was to be a reference to this on 4 November 1443;[44] but it does not appear to have been proven that this anti-Basel declaration was made as early as May 1441. For one thing, the Three Estates had met as recently as 3 April 1441,[45] and there is

[37] *St. Andrews Copiale*, 188–96.

[38] Cf. Burns, *Basle*, 68.

[39] Ibid., 65–77 (with comment p. 77). There had also been one new Scottish incorporation as early as April 1439 (ibid., 63).

[40] *St. Andrews Copiale*, 483.

[41] Watt, *Dictionary*, 135.

[42] Cf. Dunlop, *Kennedy*, 37.

[43] Hannay, 'Letter to Scotland', 54. But this source offers no evidence on the date of this declaration (cf. Dunlop, *Kennedy*, 44; Nicholson, *Later Middle Ages*, 335). Bishop Kennedy is first found in Scotland in government circles as witness to crown charters on 26 May 1441 (*RMS*, ii, 61, nos. 266–7).

[44] See below p. 159.

[45] *APS*, ii, 56–7.

no evidence that they met again as soon as May. And the fact that Bishop Kennedy came home from the Roman Court to join the Livingston – Douglas government for a time is hardly proof of so positive an attitude in any provincial council at this stage. At any rate the earl of Douglas was finding it convenient just at this time to further his family ambitions by arranging for Felix to promote one of his sons to the vacant see of Aberdeen.[46] This general council therefore may well have met considerably later. Indeed it may have met in association with a provincial council which met probably some time before 31 August, perhaps in July, 1442, at which four bishops recently appointed by Pope Eugenius secured a decision against all adherents of Basel, though the earl of Douglas so threatened them afterwards that 'certain prelates' fled by night and the rest of the business was put off for four months.[47]

It is reasonable to conclude that only a minority in Scotland were supporters of Douglas and his pro-Basel policy. On 27 October 1442 the council there again tried an approach to the magnates in charge of the minority government of Scotland.[48] This letter may well never have been delivered, for William Croyser who was to carry it to Scotland is next found in prison in Strasbourg.[49] Anyway James earl of Douglas died in March 1443, and without his support the minority support in Scotland for Basel rapidly dwindled. The consistent majority opinion was confirmed at a general council of the Three Estates on 4 November 1443, after time had been taken for due deliberation (rather like the meeting of October 1418 at the end of the Great Schism).[50] Reference was then made to the earlier pronouncements of both the general council and the provincial council which have already been discussed, and firm adherence to Eugenius was ordered, with

[46] *St. Andrews Copiale*, 313–14 of 30 May 1441; see also 311–13 and 315–21. The earl had temporary success in getting the government to grant the temporalities to his son (ibid., 322).

[47] Ibid., 322–4, 483–4; cf. Dunlop, *Kennedy*, 44.

[48] Hannay, 'Letter to Scotland', 54–6. The reference to a crown edict against adherents of the Council of Basel would appear to relate to a recent event. If this edict had the support of the Three Estates behind it (as is likely during the minority), then the general council thought by some to have been held in May 1441 is more likely to have been held in the Summer of 1442.

[49] Watt, *Dictionary*, 135; cf. Burns, *Basle*, 79–80; Dunlop, *Kennedy*, 45.

[50] *APS*, ii, 33; cf. *St. Andrews Copiale*, 330–2.

an instruction that no one was to change this decision without an ordinance of the king and the kingdom. This was effective, and little more is heard of the pretensions of the handful of clergy who had nailed their colours to the Basel mast until that council was finally wound up in 1449. There had never been official support from the government in Scotland for Basel once it had denounced Eugenius IV; but conditions during the minority of James II had made it impossible for several years to enforce a single policy. Both the provincial council and the general council of the Three Estates could play their parts in suggesting a line to be followed; but the Schism continued as it did because these bodies did not have the power which only a king in full manhood had to take a line and enforce it. At least conciliarist ideas clearly did have a long run in Scotland whilst the country's allegiance was so uncertain.[51]

The first 'Conservator of the Privileges of the Scottish Church' to be known by name since 1420 appears in office on 28 June 1445. This was Bishop John de Crannach of Brechin,[52] who with John de Scheves official of St. Andrews (as clerk of the rolls and register) issued a formal transumpt of two old papal bulls at Edinburgh at the time of a parliament.[53] The circumstances are intriguing, if not demonstrably clear. It was the bishop of Moray who on behalf of the prelates and clergy of all Scotland asked for this publicity to be given to these documents. The two were quite different in subject: one was a bull of March 1375 against the Scottish royal custom of seizing a dead bishop's goods, and the other was the helpful response of Martin V in May 1426 when King James I had wished proceedings to be started against a traitor bishop. Both were matters that were presumably of interest to the current parliament, a large delegation from which (including Bishop James Bruce of Dunkeld the chancellor of Scotland) was listed as witnesses of the occasion. Presumably there had been uncertainty about the factual content of the old bulls, and they were copied to clarify the position. It is not surprising that the clergy in parliament as a whole would be interested in obtaining

[51] Burns, *Basle*, 85–6.

[52] Watt, *Dictionary*, 118–22

[53] *Brechin Registrum*, i, 98–104; D. Wilkins, *Concilia Magnae Britanniae et Hiberniae* (London, 1737), iii, 544–7; cf. *APS*, ii, 59 for Scheves on duty at this parliament as clerk of the rolls and register.

a clear picture of old (but neglected) guidelines on the rights of bishops to dispose of their goods freely by testament, and in fact this was to be formally guaranteed them in some consolidated legislation passed at the parliament of 24 January 1450.[54] But to rake up the old bull about a traitor bishop appears to be more partisan. It has been usefully pointed out that three bishops who together had been particularly stalwart supporters of Pope Eugenius (Kennedy of St. Andrews, Lindsay of Aberdeen, and Tulloch of Ross) are not mentioned in connection with this business;[55] and it looks rather as if pressure was being put on the Conservator (who had been closely associated with the same side in ecclesiastical politics) to dig up this old precedent – it was the bishop of Moray who was in a sense usurping the Conservator's function in speaking for the clergy as a whole. The incident smells, indeed, of partisan politics: it seems likely that Bishop Kennedy was temporarily the object of excited speculation on what could happen if a pope was co-operative in responding to a royal request for the removal of a bishop who was politically for the time being on the wrong side.[56] A Conservator of Privileges could sometimes be made to act as no doubt befitted his office, but this was hardly helpful for preserving the liberties of churchmen. If only Bishop Kennedy had not been quite so involved in the politics of the minority government in the first place!

We know of two meetings of the provincial council which took up the matter of the crown's claim to exercise episcopal rights of patronage during vacancies of sees, which had long ago in 1325[57] been a matter of definition at a council meeting, and which had as a part of the general parliamentary settlement of 24 January 1450 been defined once more in the crown's favour in return for privileges which the crown was then granting to the church.[58] At the 1457 council (presumably in July) at Perth a definition of this

[54] *APS*, ii, 37–8, 61–2; *RMS*, ii, 71, no. 307. See discussion in Donaldson, *Church History*, 31–9, chapter 4, 'The rights of the crown in episcopal vacancies'.

[55] Burns, *Basle*, 83, n. 195. They were not at parliament either (*APS*, ii, 59).

[56] Nicholson, *Later Middle Ages*, 342–3; for another interpretation see Dunlop, *Kennedy*, 63–4, 307–9.

[57] See above p. 113.

[58] Cf. Donaldson, *Church History*, 38–9

regalian right was agreed, which expressly excluded any cases where a general or specific [papal] reservation of the right to appoint applied. When the council assembled for its 1459 meeting at Perth, definitely in July, the king sent one of his knights (Sir Patrick le Graham) and one of his clerks (Master Archibald Whitelaw) to ask for a formal record of what had apparently been an informal (perhaps even unwritten) definition in 1457.[59] Bishop Thomas Spens of Aberdeen, who had probably just become Conservator on the first day of the council,[60] therefore took evidence from the clergy who had been at the council meeting in 1457 and duly recorded this earlier definition of what was described as 'ancient royal custom' on 19 July, the last day of the meeting.[61] The witness-list is not long on this occasion, but significantly it includes Bishop George Schoriswood of Brechin who was then chancellor of Scotland as the only senior prelate mentioned along with four lesser clerics.[62] The division between church and state was never a clear one when a royal chancellor could attend a provincial council meeting in this way as of right. And the government was to make use of this declaration in framing its very positive anti-papal definition of this matter in the parliament of 19 October 1462.[63] It was probably normal for the provincial council to subserve the secular organs of government in this way.[64]

Another normal aspect of the provincial council which was for the first time specifically stated in 1465 is that it met by ancient and approved custom and by papal authority as a general body each year at Perth on 17 July and the following days.[65] This *obiter*

[59] Cf. above pp. 103–4.

[60] He had moved from the see of Galloway only early in March 1459 (Watt, *Fasti*, 3).

[61] *APS*, ii, 83–4; *SES*, ii, 79–80, no. 167; Patrick, *Statutes*, 82–3. Cf. above pp. 136–8 for parallel procedure used in 1420.

[62] It has been pointed out that the king himself was in Perth during this council (Dunlop, *Kennedy*, 190, no. 2).

[63] *APS*, ii, 83–84; *SES*, ii, 282–3.

[64] Cf. above pp. 151–3.

[65] *SES*, i, pp. ccxlv–ccxlvii; cf. p. cviii, n. 3, and A. H. Dunbar, *Scottish Kings* (Edinburgh, 1906), 350 for date (associated with St. Kenelm); *Arbroath Liber*, ii, 144–5, no. 162; cf. Patrick, *Statutes*, 235. Cf. the contemporary canon law rule which recommended that bishops meet in council every three years (T. Winning, 'Church councils in sixteenth-century Scotland', *Innes Review*, x [1959], 311–37, especially 312). See also below p. 171.

dictum is found in a notarial record of an agreement made on the following day (18 July) in front of the Perth Town House between the bishop of Dunblane and the abbot of Arbroath regarding certain teinds in Abernethy parish in Perthshire: this is an example of business done at the time of a council rather than as part of its proceedings, as was doubtless often convenient when prelates were gathered together. But what can we learn about the council from this evidence? It is called a *concilium cleri*, which was the same phrase that was used in 1459 (though then they had looked back on the 1457 assembly as a *consilium generale cleri*). It is specifically stated that this body met annually at Perth, and this must surely represent current experience of at least a few decades. The provincial council of the fifteenth century at any rate can be traced as a much more regular instrument of church administration in Scotland than can so certainly be traced in the thirteenth and fourteenth centuries: but the argument here throughout the whole period from 1225 is that its regular annual meetings should be assumed unless there is evidence to the contrary. We are brought back to the evidence of 1418 x 1443 about 'the accustomed place and time' of its meetings.[66] In this 1465 evidence the date '17 July and the following days' may be read in the Latin as part of what was 'ancient and approved custom' about the time of meeting, or it may be read as a variable for just this one year. Probably the old rule of the 1240s that participants should expect to come for three days was still customary.[67] But was there by now a fixed starting date? We can consider such evidence as we have for dated council meetings from 1408 onwards;[68] in this year some business was done on Wednesday 18 July; in 1420 the meeting opened on Tuesday 16 July; in 1459 Thursday 19 July was the 'last day' of the meeting; in 1465 the council opened on Wednesday 17 July, and was still in session on the following day; in 1470 the council did some business on Tuesday 17 July. We may conclude that in the fifteenth century the council was accustomed over a long period to meeting in mid-week about the same date in mid-July, but that there was no fixed rule

[66] See above p. 138.

[67] *SES*, ii, 9. no. 1 (see above p. 83). These statutes were still being copied at the beginning of the sixteenth century (see above p. 63).

[68] Cf. the formulary copy of a summons in the 1390s to a council meeting in October of an unspecified year (see above pp. 134–5).

about starting on a particular week-day or a particular fixed date. Presumably this was each year a matter for the out-going Conservator to decide when issuing his summons.[69]

The last known assembly under the 1225 arrangements was held in the Dominican church at Perth on 17 July 1470, when Bishop Patrick Graham of St. Andrews presided as Conservator of the Privileges of the Scottish Church.[70] The scribe at this council was the notary Duncan Yalulok,[71] and he chose to denote this assembly by the older name of *concilium generale cleri Scoticani*.[72] Presumably it was he who was responsible for writing up the decisions of the council in the record known as 'the Provincialis Buk' which is mentioned in the by-going in the following year,[73] Only one bishop is mentioned apart from the Conservator: this was Bishop Thomas Lauder of Dunkeld, who had perhaps been in office as the previous Conservator and as such had summoned the council and started it off. Otherwise the sederunt was said to comprise 'other minor prelates, abbots and priors, and various clerics', and among this last group it is interesting to notice no less than three episcopal officials from St. Andrews, Dunkeld and Dunblane dioceses. The occasion was a domestic one for the University of St. Andrews, where the rector and masters had been resisting an attempt by the provost and canons of St. Salvator's College to put into effect a papal privilege of 25 February 1469 entitling them to grant their own degrees.[74] The matter was now resolved in favour of the university at large. But it was apparently a matter of the interpretation of conflicting papal privileges which the bishop of St. Andrews (who was also chancellor of the university) could not, or would not, resolve himself. The provincial council was there as a forum for hearing the parties in a

[69] See above pp. 81–2.

[70] St. Andrews, University Muniments, MS. Registrum Evidentiarum et Privilegiorum Universitatis Sanctiandree, fos. 70v-72v; cf. J. Herkless and R. K. Hannay, *The Archbishops of St. Andrews* (Edinburgh, 1907–15), i, 36–7 for a summary of this text.

[71] The name of the council's scribe in 1459 (Donald Rede) is the earliest known (*APS*, ii, 84). For Yalulok see *St. Andrews Acta*, p. clii.

[72] See above p. 163 for similar usage in 1459.

[73] *APS*, ii, 99, no. 4; cf. 233; *SES*, i, p. lxviii. This record is mentioned as containing a version of the current 'Bagimond' valuation of ecclesiastical benefices.

[74] For the background to this dispute see *St. Andrews Acta*, pp. xxviii–xxxi.

judicial manner and providing authoritative guidance leading to an agreement which the parties would at least temporarily accept. It is interesting that it is this judicial side of the council's business, that had been emphasised from the start in its thirteenth-century terms of reference,[75] which happens to be illustrated here just before its demise as a consequence of the erection of the bishopric of St. Andrews into a metropolitan see on 17 August 1472.[76]

[75] See above pp. 44–6.
[76] Theiner, *Monumenta*, 465–8, no. 852.

11

Epilogue

THE elevation of the see of St. Andrews as the metropolitan see for all the dioceses of the kingdom of Scotland has been described reasonably enough as 'on the face of it . . . a carefully thought out and sensible solution to the many frustrations then facing both the Scottish church and the crown'.[1] The diocese of Galloway was now formally transferred from the English province of York,[2] as was the diocese of Orkney from the Norwegian province of Trondheim following the pawning of Orkney and Shetland to the Scottish crown as recently as 1468–9.[3] This definition of a new ecclesiastical province coterminous with the kingdom of Scotland was expressed in standard terms that were customary throughout the Western church, and must have had much to commend it. The provision of a new level of appellate authority above the diocese that was now to be available within Scotland, which would eliminate time-consuming and costly dependence on appeals to Rome, was certainly advantageous. But this fundamental reform affecting the parity of the Scottish bishops with their long-standing custom of working with each other as equals in a provincial council was blighted from the start, because it was arranged at Rome by Bishop Graham on his own without any mandate from his fellow-bishops in Scotland,[4] and

[1] L. J. Macfarlane, 'The primacy of the Scottish church 1472–1521', *Innes Review*, xx (1969), 111–29, especially 112.

[2] See above pp. 24, 29, 101, 127–8, 135.

[3] B. E. Crawford, 'The pawning of Orkney and Shetland. A reconsideration of the events of 1460–9', *SHR*, xlviii (1969), 35–53.

[4] Cf. above p. 44 for the way the provincial council had been authorised with general support in 1225.

without the support of King James III. This was unacceptable all round from the first; and though the holding of provincial councils by a metropolitan archbishop on his own authority should have been a simpler procedure than what had been customary in Scotland for 250 years, one consequence of the way Graham had proceeded was that no provincial council of any kind was to meet in Scotland for more than sixty years.[5] And by 1536 when councils began to be assembled once more quite frequently,[6] the church as a whole was having to face up to the unprecedented challenges of the Reformation, which was to provide a new context within which to judge the character and effectiveness of the Scottish provincial council as a forerunner of the General Assembly of the reformed kirk of 1560 onwards rather than as a reorganised mechanism of the medieval church. This is why the story here after 1472 is best regarded as an 'epilogue' that marks the end of a distinct period of Scottish church history rather than as a bridge to new developments that were unimaginable at the time. To adopt a famous comment on the disappearance of the parliament of Scotland in 1707 into the new parliament of Great Britain: 'Now there's ane end of ane old song.'[7]

How did things go so wrong? Graham remained overseas until at least September 1473, by which time financial pressure was being put on him by the king;[8] and by February 1474 he was losing the support of Pope Sixtus IV who had created his archbishopric, when Thomas Spens bishop of Aberdeen was by papal authority granted personal exemption from Graham's authority.[9] Thus began an unhappy pattern of challenge to the position of the archbishop as defined by standard canon law, which others were to continue and develop. Graham appears to have had a mental breakdown under the strain, so that after a formal papal enquiry he was deposed from his see in January 1478, with a

[5] *SES*, i, p. cix.

[6] Ibid., i, p. cxxxiv ff.; see below pp. 171–2.

[7] *The Oxford Dictionary of Quotations*, 2nd edition (London, 1953), 370, no. 4: comment of the earl of Seafield as he signed the Act of Union 1706.

[8] Macfarlane, 'Primacy', 114.

[9] Theiner, *Monumenta*, 473–4, no. 858. A similar exemption was to be granted again on 6 July 1490 for a later bishop of Aberdeen, William Elphinsone (*CPL*, xv, 184–5, no. 377).

royal nominee, William Scheves, being appointed in his stead in the following month.[10] This settlement marks the king's acceptance of the archbishopric, and on 27 March 1487 this was confirmed by James III when he gave his support to a further papal grant to Scheves of the powers of primate and *legatus natus*, as had long been accepted in England for the archbishop of Canterbury.[11] Even with these extra powers, however, there is no sign that Scheves ever tried to instruct his fellow-bishops to attend a provincial council. Probably most of them were not responsive to his leadership, for even before the assassination of his sponsor the king on 11 June 1488, two other bishops had persuaded the pope (now Innocent VIII) to grant them personal exemption from the archbishop's authority – Andrew Stewart (the king's uncle) bishop of Moray on 10 April 1488 and Robert Blacader bishop of Glasgow on 25 May 1488.[12]

The latter was soon to benefit in his personal rivalry with Scheves from the political revolution that followed the king's death, for he now had the support of the government of the young King James IV in conducting a campaign at the Roman court against the interests of the archbishop with the aim of securing the elevation of his see of Glasgow also to the status of a metropolitan see. This was successful when Pope Innocent constituted Glasgow as a second Scottish archbishopric on 9 January 1492, with the bishops of Galloway, Argyll, Dunblane and Dunkeld as suffragans.[13] Protests by Scheves were stifled when in June 1493 parliament forced the two archbishops to accept this division of the church in Scotland into two small provinces on a permanent basis.[14] Scheves did at least prevent the archbishop of Glasgow from obtaining the status of primate and *legatus natus*, which remained the privilege of St. Andrews alone. This theoretically empowered the St. Andrews archbishop to call a provincial council for the whole kingdom; but this did not happen, for Blacader and his two immediate successors (James Beaton 1508–23 and Gavin

[10] Watt, *Fasti*, 295; Theiner, *Monumenta*, 479–81, no. 863; *CPL*, xiii, 277; cf. 68–9.

[11] *CPL*, xiv, 152.

[12] *The Apostolic Camera and Scottish Benefices 1418–88*, ed. A. I. Cameron (Oxford, 1934), 223; *CPL*, xiv, 220–1.

[13] Theiner, *Monumenta*, 505–6, no. 889; Macfarlane, 'Primacy', 118.

[14] *APS*, ii, 232–3.

Dunbar 1524–47) secured exemptions for their whole province from this superior authority of St. Andrews.[15] In practice the archbishops of St. Andrews could proceed only with the willing co-operation of the archbishops of Glasgow, and this was lacking for long enough. As late as 21 September 1531 Glasgow's exempt status was receiving papal confirmation.[16]

There was a further fluidity in the structure devised in 1492 when the diocese of Dunblane was on 28 January 1500 transferred back from the province of Glasgow to that of St. Andrews,[17] as was the diocese of Dunkeld sometime on or before 25 May 1515.[18] Glasgow was left with only Galloway and Argyll as its suffragan sees. St. Andrews for its part suffered when the see of Moray was again granted exemption from its metropolitan authority, this time under Bishop James Hepburn from *c.* 1516.[19] At least on negative evidence it appears that relationships between the Scottish bishops were not sufficiently stable in this period for provincial councils for the whole kingdom to be held, or even for separate councils to be held in either province. This did not, however, prevent the various bishops of the country continuing to hold diocesan synods along customary lines. Archbishop Scheves, for example, was active in this way in his own diocese of St. Andrews.[20] It is not certain whether synods were held in this diocese during the years 1497–1513 when the see was held by two royal minors in succession; but Archbishop Andrew Forman (1514–21) certainly arranged for annual synods to be attended by the clergy of the two archdeaconries at St. Andrews Cathedral and Holyrood Abbey respectively;[21] and a collection of twenty-seven statutes which he devised sometime during his episcopate for promulgation at such synods is known.[22] Synods can be traced in other dioceses too.[23]

[15] Dowden, *Bishops*, 344.

[16] Ibid., 345.

[17] *CPL*, xvii, part i, 211, no. 333.

[18] Dowden, *Bishops*, 333–4.

[19] *St. Andrews Formulare 1514–1546*, ed. G. Donaldson and C. Macrae (Stair Society, 1942–4), i, 168–9, no. 159.

[20] Patrick, *Statutes*, pp. cix–cxi; cf. ibid., 228–30.

[21] Ibid., 260, 279; cf. 230–3.

[22] *SES*, i, pp. clxxxvi, cclxx–cclxxxv; Patrick, *Statutes*, 260–78.

[23] Dunkeld *c.* 1517 (*St. Andrews Formulare*, i, 107–8, no. 96); Aberdeen 1540 (*SES*, i, p. cxci; *Aberdeen Registrum*, ii, 323).

Of course the bishops, some abbots and other senior clergy met on occasion in parliament, and it may well be that they took the chance of such meetings to transact ecclesiastical business of common concern without being constituted a formal provincial council.[24] The fact remains that for some sixty-five years after the council meeting in July 1470 there is no trace of any other general council for the whole kingdom or for one of its ecclesiastical provinces being called until 12 June 1535. Then at a parliament when Archbishop James Beaton of St. Andrews happened to be absent, but with the notable support of Archbishop Gavin Dunbar of Glasgow as royal chancellor, the Three Estates required Beaton under threat of going over his head to the pope to call a 'general provincial council of the realm' to meet on 1 March 1536 at Blackfriars in Edinburgh.[25] Beaton concurred and issued the necessary instructions (now known only in undated form) for such an assembly, reviving as he did so the traditional canonical definition of the purpose of such meetings:

> Since from the decrees and ordinances of the holy fathers so piously and so beneficially issued, it seemed good that there should be held, and there are commanded to be held, yearly or oftener, and with full attendances in every province councils-general of the bishops, as well as for the peculiar culture of the field of the Lord, which roots up the briars, thorns and thistles of heresy, error and schism, corrects manners and misconduct, reforms the deformed and restores the vine of the Lord to the fruits of richest fertility, as for the settling of the quarrels and controversies that are wont to arise between the various orders of the church: the non-observance of which councils spreads abroad and encourages the [evils] mentioned.[26]

[24] Cf. the clerical sederunt at a parliament at Edinburgh in 1531 (*APS*, ii, 332) with the notarial record of some business transacted there by seven bishops in the same year (J. Durkan, 'Chaplains in later medieval Scotland', *Records of the Scottish Church History Society*, xx [1979], 97).

[25] *APS*, ii, 342, no. 4.

[26] Patrick, *Statutes*, 238; *SES*, i, pp. ccxlvii–viii, appendix XVI; cf. appendix XVII. This knowledge that annual councils had once been the rule was not derived from recent experience; but the information would have been found in manuscripts containing the rules followed in earlier periods such as the Lambeth MS. 167 dating from the early sixteenth century (see above p. 56, n. 6). Annual meetings had been the rule in the thirteenth-century statutes (cf. above p. 81).

The business on this occasion was said to include 'troublesome matters touching the orthodox faith and the commonweal of the kingdom'.[27] It appears that in the event there was agreement under the latter heading to support a royal request for a tax on the clerical incomes of some sixty-two prelates in aid of the king's new College of Justice, but there was no agreement on some reforms of the clergy's own finances that were suggested.[28] Thus this experiment of reviving an old mechanism for consulting the Scots clergy as a whole was only partly efficient in achieving the ends which its sponsors had in mind. But the pressures for general reform of the church which were felt by the 1530s all over Western Europe were to ensure that this experiment was repeated in Scotland some eleven times between 1543 and 1559 as part of the build-up to the break with Rome in 1560.[29] Evidently the mechanism which had served Scotland well 1225–1472 was not in itself going to be adequate in up-dated form as an archbishop-primate's council to cope with the unprecedented challenges of the sixteenth-century Reformation. But that is another story.

[27] Patrick, *Statutes*, 239.

[28] *SES*, i, pp. cxxxvi–vii.

[29] Ibid., i, pp. cxlii–clxiii; see Winning, 'Church councils', 311–37 for a detailed discussion of these councils. It has been argued that they belong to a different, more modern period of the history of the Scottish church (J. Dowden, *The Medieval Church in Scotland* [Glasgow, 1910], 226), and that is the view taken here.

Index of Persons and Places

References are to the Scottish counties as defined between the 1890s and 1970s